ROUTLEDGE LIBRARY EDITIONS:
INDUSTRIAL ECONOMICS

Volume 15

THE IRC – AN EXPERIMENT IN INDUSTRIAL INTERVENTION

THE IRC – AN EXPERIMENT IN INDUSTRIAL INTERVENTION

A History of the Industrial Reorganisation Corporation

DOUGLAS HAGUE AND
GEOFFREY WILKINSON

Routledge
Taylor & Francis Group
LONDON AND NEW YORK

First published in 1983 by George Allen & Unwin (Publishers) Ltd

This edition first published in 2018
by Routledge
2 Park Square, Milton Park, Abingdon, Oxon OX14 4RN

and by Routledge
711 Third Avenue, New York, NY 10017

Routledge is an imprint of the Taylor & Francis Group, an informa business

British Library Cataloguing in Publication Data
A catalogue record for this book is available from the British Library

ISBN: 978-1-138-30830-5 (Set)
ISBN: 978-1-351-21102-4 (Set) (ebk)
ISBN: 978-0-8153-6909-7 (Volume 15) (hbk)
ISBN: 978-1-351-25316-1 (Volume 15) (ebk)

The IRC – An Experiment in Industrial Intervention

A History of the Industrial Reorganisation Corporation

DOUGLAS HAGUE and
GEOFFREY WILKINSON

London
GEORGE ALLEN & UNWIN
Boston Sydney

**George Allen & Unwin (Publishers) Ltd,
40 Museum Street, London WC1A 1LU, UK**

George Allen & Unwin (Publishers) Ltd,
Park Lane, Hemel Hempstead, Herts HP2 4TE, UK

Allen & Unwin Inc.,
9 Winchester Terrace, Winchester, Mass 01890, USA

George Allen & Unwin Australia Pty Ltd,
8 Napier Street, North Sydney, NSW 2060, Australia

First published in 1983

British Library Cataloguing in Publication Data

Hague, Douglas
The IRC—an experiment in industrial intervention.
1. Industrial Reorganisation Corporation—History
I. Title II. Wilkinson, Geoffrey
338.6'2 HD 3616.G73
ISBN 0-04-338105-7

Library of Congress Cataloging in Publication Data

Hague, Douglas Chalmers.
The IRC, an experiment in industrial intervention.
Bibliography: p.
1. Industrial Reorganisation Corporation. 2. Consolidation and merger of corporations—Great Britain—Case Studies. I. Wilkinson, Geoffrey. II. Title. III. Title: I.R.C., an experiment in industrial intervention.
HD2845.H33 1983 354.41'0082 82–25535
ISBN 0-04-338105-7

Set in 10 on 11 point Times by Alan Sutton Publishing Ltd, Gloucester
and printed in Great Britain
by Biddles Ltd, Guildford, Surrey

Contents

Preface

The Industrial Reorganisation Corporation had a short but active and controversial life. It was set up by the Wilson Government in 1966 and abolished by the Heath Administration in April 1971. It took almost a year to get under way and was effectively neutralised in the summer of 1970 when the Conservative Party was returned to power. In the three years up to June 1970, however, the IRC was scarcely out of the headlines, at least on the business pages, and often on the front pages of the National Press.

One of the final acts of the IRC was to commission a history to be written recording its objectives, its method of operation and the results of its activities. This book is an indirect result of that commission. Its publication has been delayed partly because the original author withdrew from the project. Also the idea of producing an 'official blessed' document has been abandoned because of difficulties relating to the confidentiality of the IRC papers now in the keeping of the Department of Industry. Nevertheless, we have been able to produce a book which we think gives a genuine flavour of the way the IRC worked. In this, we are indebted to Sir Joseph Lockwood, Sir Michael Clapham and especially to Sir Charles Villiers for their support and advice. All three were IRC Board members, with Sir Joseph Lockwood as Chairman from 1969 to 1971 and Sir Charles Villiers as Managing Director from 1968 to 1971. Together, they formed the 'IRC Committee' which has kept a helpful and watching eye on the book from the original commission to this publication. Without their support and encouragement, it would never have been completed. The authors, of course, are responsible for the opinions expressed in the book and for the interpretation of events.

In producing this history, we have had two overriding objectives. The first, and the more straightforward, is to bring together as much of the material relating to the IRC's activities as can practically be published. So we have reproduced some of the press statements released by the IRC explaining its involvement in key mergers. We have reprinted the IRC White Paper and have surveyed other material which influenced the establishment of the Corporation. We have also included extracts from the IRC's Annual Reports and Accounts which summarise all the projects in which it was involved and which give brief details of each of its financial commitments.

The second and more important objective has been to give as precise and detailed an account as possible of how the IRC actually operated. It was a most unusual public corporation. It undertook a very large amount of work with a tiny staff – only about ten executives and never more than about thirty people in total. Even more importantly it made decisions on major issues very quickly, and much more quickly than is normal at the interface between government and industry.

The heart of our book is therefore a series of case studies covering ten of the IRC's most important areas of involvement. In these we have given a full account of how the IRC's involvement came about, how it analysed the problems posed, how it reached a view on the most desirable course of action, and how it set about achieving the results it desired. We have then traced the subsequent history of the companies involved up to the end of the 1970s.

To put these case studies into context, we have included three chapters at the beginning of the book setting out the origins, structure and powers of the IRC and outlining its major activities. We have also included, at the end of the book, a brief review of the results of the IRC's work and lessons that might be drawn from it.

The individual case studies stand by themselves and, although the book can be read in order from cover to cover, there is no reason why the reader should not turn directly to the chapter on Rolls-Royce or GEC, AEI and English Electric, or the motor industry, or whatever is of most interest. What we do wish to emphasize is that the objectives of the IRC, and the way it saw its role, changed significantly during even its short lifetime. It started very clearly as a government 'merger broker' and the case studies in Part 2 of the book reflect this. As time went on, it saw a much wider role and to some extent began to doubt the validity of its original remit. This wider role was never fully worked out, but the beginnings of it are seen in the case studies in Part 3 of the book and are considered further in our concluding comments in Part 4. In the first three chapters we show how the IRC became involved, not only in major investment decisions, but also in the overall financing of companies and increasingly in top management selection and appointments.

It is doubtful that anyone would now argue that the government should recreate a public corporation with a specific remit as a merger broker. The case for and against a public 'merchant bank' or 'development bank' is much more interesting. Fashions on government intervention in industry come and go, but the fact of intervention in some form or other continues. Whether or not an IRC-type body, with a very different remit, could provide a more coherent and systematic vehicle than *ad hoc* intervention is an important question. We would not claim to have provided a definitive answer to it but we hope that we have given the reader enough material to form a view, not only on the IRC as it was, but also on the IRC as it might have become.

Autumn 1982

D. H.
G. C. G. W.

Acknowledgements

The authors gratefully acknowledge the permission of Professor W. G. McClelland and Williams & Glyn's Bank plc for the use of extracts from the article. 'The IRC – an experimental prod', published in the Three Banks Review. The authors are also grateful to Her Majesty's Stationery Office for permission to use quotations and extracts from the IRC Annual Report and Accounts and the other White Papers and Acts of Parliament included in the list of works cited on page 307, and to Cambridge University Press for permission to reproduce the diagram on page 6, which is taken from 'The Evolution of Giant Firms in Britain' by S. J. Prais.

Acknowledgements

[illegible]

The IRC –
An Experiment in Industrial Intervention

A History of the Industrial Reorganisation Corporation

PART ONE

THE IRC

1

The Origins of the IRC

'IRC – sheer wanton murder': this was the reaction of the industrial editor of the *Sunday Times*, Nicholas Faith, not to the activities of the Labour Government's Industrial Reorganisation Corporation, but to the decision of the Tory Government, in 1970, to abolish it (*Sunday Times*, 1 November 1970). The decision was announced in the House of Commons in Anthony Barber's first budget speech on 27 October 1970 and it brought to an end four years of government-sponsored attempts to 'rationalise' Britain's industrial structure. The biggest budget headlines were reserved for 'sixpence off income tax' but the IRC had become sufficiently well known for its demise to make the front page of that night's evening papers (e.g. *Evening Standard*, 27 October 1970).

Barber claimed that he would be saving an anticipated expenditure of £40 million per year. This was in sharp contrast to the attitude of Labour Prime Minister Harold Wilson when, almost four years before, on 7 November 1966, he had invited the members of the newly constituted IRC Board to an informal dinner at 10 Downing Street. Then, Wilson had been most concerned to discuss whether or not £150 million was likely to be sufficient as the initial financial allocation for the IRC's activities.

To understand the origins of the IRC we have to look back to those early years of the Wilson government. In addition to the ill-fated 'National Plan' there was a general commitment to the 'white hot technological revolution' and to any necessary government intervention to achieve it (see White Paper Cmnd 2764, 1965, for a statement of the National Plan). More specifically there was a willingness to use every means available to improve the competitiveness of British industry. This was certainly one factor behind the creation of the IRC. A second was the merger fever of the 1960s, then approaching its height. It was felt that too many of the mergers that took place were motivated by either mainly financial or defensive considerations and contributed little, or even negatively, to industrial regeneration. So, on the one hand, it was thought that some opportunities for industrial restructuring were not being taken, either because of sluggish management or because the benefits were too long term. On the other, it was feared that the increasing number of mergers that were taking place often failed to achieve, and sometimes made more difficult, restructuring that was desirable on industrial grounds. The Monopolies Commission had powers to investigate mergers but it was argued that a more positive approach was also required. In this chapter we shall look briefly at these factors and at the ideas of some of the people who were most concerned with the creation of the British government's first merger broker.

INTERVENTION – DIRECT OR INDIRECT

Government intervention in industry dates back as far as the Industrial Revolution and some would argue even further:

> Centuries ago the economy began to evolve from a "natural economy" in which money did not exist to a "money economy" in which it did. Once that happened then *de facto* governments began to interfere with the prevailing market conditions by levying taxes and regulating trading conditions (Young and Lowe, 1974, p. 11).

Certainly in a modern mixed economy like that of the UK almost everything that government does has a direct or indirect impact on industry. It is not the intention here to trace the historical development and growth of government policy towards industry (this is discussed in Young and Lowe, 1974, Chs 1–3, and more extensively in Skuse, 1972). It does appear, however, that in the early 1960s there was a clear change of emphasis towards more direct and specific government intervention in private industrial decision making (see, for example, Young and Lowe, 1974, p. 13). The close controls, established during the Second World War, had been followed by very active policies of the 1945 Labour government. These included not only the major nationalisation measures, but an extensive system of controls over the private sector. The 1951 Tory administration reversed many of these policies. It denationalised the steel industry and reverted to more indirect influences on industrial decision making, attempting merely to determine the climate within which business decisions were made through overall fiscal and monetary policies. In the early 1960s, however, growing concern over the UK's relatively poor performance in terms of the growth of industrial output and productivity was reflected in the establishment of a series of government agencies, all of which are still in existence. The first was the National Economic Development Council (NEDC), established in 1962. This was designed as a forum in which the government, businessmen and the trade unions could discuss economic and industrial planning. Its creation reflected the Tories' conversion to the idea that such a forum was needed and that the government had a part to play in it. The NEDC was reinforced in 1964 when a series of 'little Neddies' (Economic Development Councils) was set up, each covering a specific industry. In 1964 the Tories also set up a series of Industrial Training Boards and extended the powers of the National Research and Development Corporation (NRDC).

Much of the groundwork for the 1964 Labour government's National Plan had, therefore, been carried out during the last two years of the Conservative administration (see Brittan, 1971). This had been done, not on the basis of any clearly defined ideology, but in an attempt to provide a practical response to the seemingly intractable problems of improving industrial performance. The National Plan was an extension of this process. In the event, it did not work; the attempt to improve economic performance through indicative planning did not lead to faster, sustained economic growth. Perhaps there was a fatal flaw. An important precondition, if firms were to be encouraged to undertake the investment necessary to increase productivity and sustain expansion, was higher aggregate demand. However, given the performance of UK industry, such an expansion of aggregate demand was likely to increase imports, reduce exports (which could be sold more profitably at home) and produce an unsustainable deficit on the balance of payments. The remedy used was deflation, and hence the negation of the original plans.

At the same time, there was a growing tendency to operate more selectively. Between 1964 and 1967 the number of EDCs was increased from five to twenty-three (Bailey, 1968, see his Appendix 111 for a complete list of EDCs) but many of these were seen, and used, largely as talking shops which had little real impact on the decision making of individual firms. The government therefore decided to take specific action to deal with what it saw as major problem areas. It set in motion the renationalisation of the steel industry and appointed a Shipbuilding Inquiry Committee which was to result in the establishment of the Shipbuilding Industry Board (see Ch. 13). In December 1966, it set up the Industrial Reorganisation Corporation to 'promote or assist the reorganisation or development' of industry in the UK (Cmnd 2889, 1966).

MERGER FEVER

In the introduction to this chapter we indicated why mergers came to be regarded as a fruitful area for positive government intervention. Unfortunately, reliable figures on the number and size of mergers are hard to come by, especially before the mid-1960s. A reasonably consistent set of data on mergers is, however, available back to 1963. For the period before that, there are only concentration ratios (i.e. ratios showing the proportion of output accounted for by a given number of the largest firms in an industry). Figure 1.1 is reproduced from S. J. Prais's major study on the growth of concentration in UK manufacturing industry 'The Evolution of Giant Firms in Britain' (CUP, 1976).

Prais's data shows that, after a period of relative stability from the beginning of the century up to 1950, the share of the largest hundred enterprises in manufacturing output in the UK grew rapidly during the 1950s and 1960s. Estimates vary as to how much of this growth was accounted for by mergers as against the organic growth of existing firms, but a reasonable guess is about half. So, despite the lack of precise figures, it is clear that, by the early 1960s, merger activity had increased significantly and seemed likely to grow still

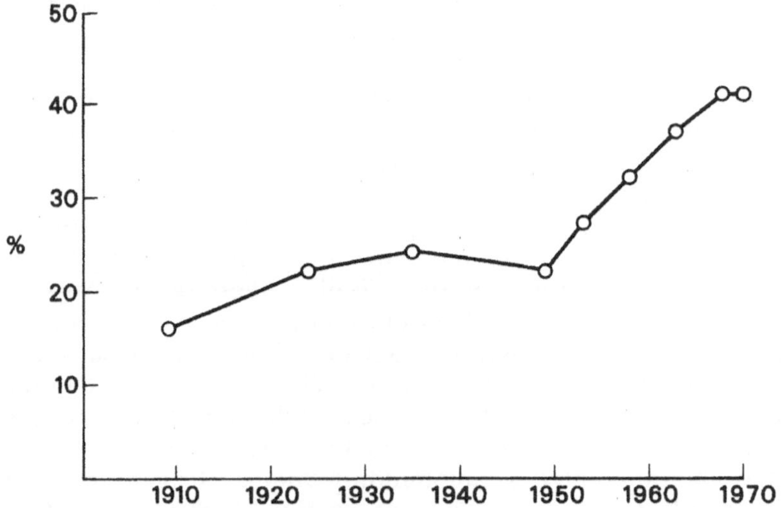

Figure 1.1 Growth of concentration. Share of the hundred largest enterprises in manufacturing net output, United Kingdom, 1909–70.

Table 1.1 *Merger activity, industrial and commercial companies 1963–77*

Year	*Number of Mergers*	*Consideration for acquired company*	
		Current prices (£ million)	*Index* *
1963	888	352	100
1964	940	505	134
1965	1000	517	146
1966	807	500	140
1967	763	822	216
1968	946	1946	362
1969÷	907	935	176
1969÷	846	1069	201
1970	793	1122	238
1971	884	911	164
1972	1210	2532	357
1973	1205	1304	213
1974	504	508	141
1975	315	291	64
1976	353	427	79
1977	482	812	117

Source: Business monitor M7.
* Consideration in current prices deflated by the FT Actuaries 500 Ordinary Share Index.
÷ Based on company accounts prior to 1970, and on the financial press and other sources since 1969.

further. Indeed there was something of a boom in mergers in 1964 and 1965. The number of mergers among industrial and commercial companies (a wider definition than Prais's) rose from 888 in 1963 to 940 in 1964 and 1000 in 1965, dropping back to 807 in 1966. A better measure of the 'volume' of merger activity is given by an index included in the government's consultative document *A Review of Monopolies and Mergers Policy* (Cmnd 7198, 1978; see Annex D, Appendix 1, p. 107). This takes the value of the assets acquired in mergers and 'deflates' it by the FT 500 Share Index to give a 'constant price' index of the value of merger acquisitions. This index is set out in the right-hand column of Table 1.1 It shows a 46 per cent increase in the 'volume' of mergers betwen 1963 and 1965, followed by a slight fall in 1966. The feeling that merger activity was likely to rise again was borne out, with the index rising to over 200 in 1967 and over 350 in 1968. The importance of merger activity in the 1960s, in terms both of its volume and of its impact on industrial concentration and structure, is clear. One of the main objectives in creating the IRC was to establish a body which would attempt to move at least some of this activity further in the direction of improving industrial performance. The IRC was conceived in and, at least until 1968, carried along by a wave of 'merger fever'. This is undoubtedly a key to an understanding of its behaviour.

AN INDUSTRIALIST'S IDEAS

In the two previous sections we have considered the general background against which the IRC was established. Before we go on to look at how it operated and what it did we shall, in the remainder of this chapter, examine some of the more specific arguments from which the concept of an IRC emerged.

As is often the case with 'inventions', the idea for an IRC occurred more or less simultaneously in slightly different forms to several different groups of people. The Labour Party and some government departments were considering the case for an agency of this kind, but an early detailed statement of the argument for a body like the IRC came from a businessman, Mr B. R. Cant.

He was head of an old-established family business, Hamworthy Engineering, which by 1964 was part of the Powell Duffryn group. In that year he wrote a paper entitled 'Attrition or breakthrough? Some notes on Britain's industrial future'. This paper was sent to the Powell Duffryn Chairman, Sir Henry Wilson Smith, a former civil servant. Cant asked whether his chairman thought that Sir Eric Roll, Permanent Secretary of the Department of Economic Affairs (DEA), might be interested. Wilson Smith thought that he would and sent copies of the paper to Roll, and to Sir Maurice Dean, Permanent Secretary of the Ministry of Technology (Mintech).

Largely on the basis of the ideas in his paper, Cant was seconded to Mintech as an industrial adviser with particular responsibility for studying ways of improving the structure of British industry. In that position he played an important role in the establishment of the IRC and, when the Corporation was set up, he became a member of its Board.

Cant's ideas emerged from a considerable amount of pondering on Britain's industrial problems rather than from any particular political ideology. His view was that current criticisms of British industry gave too great a significance to deficiencies in the British attitude to management. While accepting that some criticism of this kind was justified, he felt that much of it obscured the situation in which the British manager worked. It was important to enquire why British manufacturing, especially of capital equipment, was carried out in firms that were so small that they dissipated their selling effort and were not technologically strong enough to develop advanced products and to take advantage of automated processes. Because most of the critics were not themselves managers, Cant felt that they did not recognise sufficiently the achievements and efforts of British management in stemming the unfavourable tide.

Cant argued that Britain's past industrial supremacy had been rooted in British mercantile supremacy. Over a long period, merchant houses and companies had developed which were able to work successfully in alien surroundings and in conflict, often violent, with European traders. This led, by the late eighteenth century, to interlocking understandings about spheres of influence in terms of geography and/or products, so that by the end of the Napoleonic period these British merchant houses were in an unassailable position.

The practices thus established, for dealing with primary products, were extended to manufacturers of machinery. Well into the twentieth century, some merchant houses specialised in selling certain types of machinery in certain countries. Where two merchants were selling in the same area, they might specialise so as to limit the challenge to each other. Such arrangements led, according to Cant, to great strength of community and to a rapid build-up of trading volume. At the same time, he believed that the arrangements enabled a determined man to found a successful engineering firm with small resources, because of his links with export agents from different parts of the world. There was design specialisation in each company, to meet requirements in those countries where it had the best agents.

Cant therefore argued that, even in the free trade era, British firms had a four-tier protection. First, there was the ascendancy of British shipping and merchants. Second, there was the predominance of British investment in local development. Third, there was the working out of relatively separate fields of interest by British merchants. Fourth, there was design specialisation to meet local requirements.

What of Britain's competitors? In the USA Cant believed that a combination of rapidly increasing home demand, abundant natural resources and good internal communications led to an accelerating fall in the number of manufacturers. Because it was not necessary to develop export markets in order to obtain raw materials, there was no pressure to design the particular varieties of product that such markets demanded. This led to an increase in the size of firm and to a level of productivity not achieved elsewhere in the world, and this was true both of component manufacturers and final producers. The US economy was largely built on massive sales volume and limited product variety.

In Germany, largely as a result of strategic planning before and during the First and Second World Wars, massive industrial combinations had been formed with relatively little overlap between them. The result was an ingrained industrial philosophy of concentrating manufacturing activities in order to obtain high volume and to minimise conflicts in design, development and production. This was combined with a virtual re-equipment of German industry after 1945.

In France, a large number of substantial family businesses had traditionally satisfied the bulk of the country's demand for manufactured goods, perhaps because the British blockade of Napoleon's Europe had coincided with the beginning of the Industrial Revolution. While it might be going too far to argue that there was a maximum avoidance of conflict between the members of this industrial aristocracy, Cant believed that there were fewer conflicting interests than in the UK. With the development of the EEC the French were establishing formidable combinations, many with German companies, providing for a rationalisation of production between France and Germany and steadily increasing expenditure on development work and on the best production techniques.

Cant argued that Japan's main advantage in the early 1960s was cheap labour, but that its dependence on this should not be exaggerated. Japan also had a philosophy which drew on the best features of American and German experience. In the first half of the twentieth century, a determination to dominate Asia had led Japan to establish massive, vertically integrated manufacturing groups. With the USA assisting in the post-war revival of Japanese industry, Japan could combine a minimum of overlap in industrial effort with the American approach of getting the benefits of huge volumes of output. Both government and industry had adjusted themselves to make the best use of the resources available for exporting.

Turning back to the UK, Cant accepted that external factors like rising nationalism and changing international alignments had made the situation more difficult. But he claimed that the structures developed in the UK were unlike those elsewhere and had become singularly inappropriate for meeting international competition.

The UK, Cant believed, had relied on diversification – the formation of groups manufacturing diverse, or even unrelated, products – a development that he found easy to understand in the light of the analysis summarised above. Diversification fitted the historical pattern. Few companies had to sacrifice much of their independence, and the result was the development of competing groups, each containing a number of relatively small production units, and each competing with small units in other groups. Cant's view was that no other highly developed industrial society had evolved such a capacity for the mutual attrition of its constituent units or such a related incapacity to take full advantage of production volume to install automated processes and to allocate sufficient funds to sophisticated development projects aimed at world markets.

What was the solution? First, the UK must distinguish the need for competition at home from the need to concentrate on manufacturing facilities sufficiently large to compete effectively in world markets. The UK needed to accept that competition on an international scale would be the really effective spur to efficiency, rather than pressure from bodies like the Restrictive Practices Court or the Monopolies Commission. Cant therefore argued for bigger production units in Britain, for a realignment of the UK's overseas connections, and for more reciprocal manufacturing agreements with American and Continental firms. The initiative for such a change would not come, at least not quickly enough, from the companies themselves. The UK needed an organisation to act as a catalyst. Cant argued that because there were many sectional interests to be bridged, the State must unavoidably play a part. It would be necessary to provide revolving fund finance on a substantial scale to trigger off the realignments, once they had been agreed upon. What was needed, in Cant's view, was a quasi-governmental body with access to public money, but with a high degree of independence, that could identify the need for industrial restructuring and the best means of bringing it about.

This preliminary paper has been discussed at length because Cant played an important part in the creation and the development of the IRC. Whether or not his diagnosis was correct is another matter. Concentration in UK manufacturing industry had been increasing rapidly since 1950 and there was little systematic evidence to suggest that the size either of plants or of firms was generally smaller in the UK than in Europe, or even in the USA. Indeed, some evidence that has since become available suggests the reverse (e.g. Prais, 1976, Ch. 6). There were, however, important industries where Cant's arguments certainly did have merit and these were the sectors to which the IRC gave priority.

THE EMERGENCE OF THE 'CORPORATION'

By the middle of 1965 a clear proposal was emerging in Mintech for the formation of the National Corporation for Company Reconstruction and Development (NATCORD). It was seen as a corporation with 51 per cent of its shares held by the government and 49 per cent by a wide range of private interests. Its main objective would be to secure industrial concentration, subject to the normal checks of the free market economy and to the monopolies legislation. A subsidiary objective would be to take large interests in companies which might otherwise become the subsidiaries of foreign firms.

NATCORD was to achieve its objectives by persuasion, by providing loans and other financial incentives to key companies, or by buying controlling but temporary interests in these firms. NATCORD was intended throughout to draw a substantial part of its funds from the private sector and was expected ultimately to dispense with government financing, having established its own credit worthiness.

Much of the groundwork in developing the original concept into a workable proposal was done by permanent officials in the Ministry of Technology. In the summer of 1965 the NATCORD proposals were discussed with the DEA and with a select group of industrialists. The DEA was interested but, to prosper, the idea now needed powerful support from outside Mintech. That support came from Dr Thomas Balogh, a special adviser on economics recruited by Harold Wilson. Balogh had strong, though more socialist, views on the potential for NATCORD. He saw its responsibilities expanding far beyond the merger field and argued that it could become a vehicle for starting enterprises capable of bringing about national growth, efficiency and exports, even though they might initially incur losses.

Balogh's view was that the efficiency of large German and American companies was rooted in the creation of the powerful German chemical and steel trusts and of the US trusts, several of which were organised by J. P. Morgan. Balogh was proposing that the State should beat the capitalists at their own game. He observed that J. P. Morgan gained enormous profits from the creation of his trusts and wanted the British government to do the same. The UK needed a powerful corporation which would take over whole industries, injecting new capital, carrying through restructuring and bringing about re-equipment with modern machinery. Initial subsidies could be provided by outright grants or by converting current losses into capital losses. The State should take the profits arising from its initiative, though ultimately State participation in such holding companies would be a minority interest.

A Fabian Society pamphlet (Posner and Pryke, 1965) showed that some Labour Party theorists were thinking along similar, though even more left-wing lines. It suggested that a suitable corporation could provide machinery for establishing and controlling new public enterprises and could be used as a State holding company through which the government could act directly to speed up economic progress. It could effectively be used to achieve the aims of nationalistion without expensive and time-consuming nationalisation itself. In this way, the corporation could select and supervise new areas of public enterprise. It could pool the financial, administrative and technical expertise of firms in which it had an interest and it could reallocate investment funds between different public sector enterprises. Existing government shareholdings in companies like BP, Short Brothers and Fairfields could be vested in the holding company, which could also initiate joint enterprises with the private sector and offer shares to the public.

During the autumn of 1965 it became clear that the more limited view of the corporation's remit would prevail. (The more radical views later re-emerged, but were again largely defeated, in the debate on the establishment of the National Enterprise Board.) About the same time a new name was suggested and the proposed new corporation became the Industrial Reorganisation Finance Corporation. Its objectives were to be to make an immediate short-term impact, to increase exports and to improve the balance of payments. In the long term, the aim was to reorganise industry into larger, more efficient units and to facilitate the development of advanced technologies. Already the concept of a corporation staffed by men with industrial experience was favoured. While it was anticipated that it would build on the work of the DEA, Mintech, the Board of Trade and the EDCs it was also to try to discover for itself what industry wanted.

THE FINAL FORM OF THE IRC

By this time, it had been agreed that the corporation should have a wide degree of independence within broad policy objectives laid down by the government. On specific projects, it would be able to act on its own initiative, at the request of industry, in response to suggestions made by the EDCs, or at the invitation of government departments. One idea was that the corporation should select and support 'catalyst' firms. These would be private businesses thought to be well managed and which might take the initiative, with the corporation's help, in reorganising certain sectors of industry.

Another proposal was that the corporation should have a special division to handle exceptionally risky, or deliberately subsidised projects which could not be expected to break even, but this was rejected.

During the autumn, the aims of the corporation were refined and modified. Rationalisation was chosen as its major objective and this was seen to include (a) mergers of two companies of comparable size; (b) the formation of groups through leading companies taking over smaller ones; (c) a re-grouping of the subsidiaries of existing groups in order to provide a more rational use of resources; (d) the rearrangement of production facilities to obtain longer runs, to improve production methods and, through greater use of sub-contracting, to reduce variety.

Some of the groups created in this way could be expected to make their own moves towards increased efficiency, especially through the introduction of labour-saving machinery. To help the others to do the same, the corporation should have its own experts, and employ outside consultants, to achieve desirable improvements. The corporation was expected always to give priority to schemes which appeared to offer early returns in terms of increased exports or import substitution.

The intention was that the corporation would achieve its objectives both by persuasion and by the use of very substantial funds, initially between £100 million and £200 million. In most cases, this money would be used to provide loans to companies involved in mergers. Cash could also be advanced in the form of equity capital but it was thought that the corporation should sell any shares it acquired as soon as possible, provided only that it could at least recoup its investment. More often, it was hoped it would make a profit. Some argued that, in addition, the corporation should have compulsory powers in reserve, to use if the market was manipulated against it and to reinforce its strengths. In the event, compulsory powers were never granted. The counter-argument, which prevailed, was that compulsory powers would create the impression that the new corporation was a vehicle for back-door nationalisation.

Although most of the preparatory work for the proposed new corporation had been done in Mintech, as the idea was developed strong support for it came from Mr George Brown, Secretary of State at the DEA. Since it was clear that the idea's chances would be much greater if George Brown were permitted to take the scheme under his wing, Mintech officials were prepared to see their brainchild adopted by the DEA. However, they made strong and successful efforts to retain a considerable influence, as was shown almost immediately when, in December 1965, Mintech provided the suggestion for the first chairman of the corporation. The name, for which there was overwhelming support, was that of Sir Frank Kearton, Chairman of Courtaulds. He had earned his reputation by successfully fighting off the ICI takeover bid for his company in 1962 and then by building Courtaulds into a much larger and more profitable company.

In January 1966, when the White Paper on the corporation was published, 'finance' had been dropped from its title (Cmnd 2889, 1966). There was a strong feeling that the new body should not be presented as just another financial institution. Great efforts were made both in the White Paper and in public pronouncements to give the Industrial Reorganisation Corporation an image that would be widely accepted in business.

The arguments for establishing the IRC were summarised in paragraphs 2–5 of the White Paper:

> 2. The need for more concentration and rationalisation to promote the greater efficiency and international competitiveness of British industry which was emphasised in the National Plan [Cmd 2764, 1965, Ch. 1, para. 37], is now widely recognised. With the co-operation of financial institutions, many industries have already substantially altered their structure and organisation through mergers, acquisitions and regroupings. This process has been accelerating in recent years and may be expected to continue. Nevertheless, the pace and scale of change do not yet match the needs of the national economy.
>
> 3. Many of the production units in this country are small by comparison with the most successful companies in international trade, whose operations are often based on a much larger market. In some sectors the typical company in Britain is too small to achieve long production runs; to take advantage of economies of scale; to undertake effective research and development; to support specialist departments for design and marketing; to install the most modern equipment or to attract the best qualified management. Moreover, large groups may often have been built up haphazardly or solely to achieve wide diversification and may not therefore be organised to secure full efficiency in current conditions. Size and efficiency do not, of course, always go together – there are efficient small companies and inefficient large ones. What is needed is to create a structure which will enable us to make the most effective use, in the years ahead, of our resources of skill, management and capital.
>
> 4. There is no evidence that we can rely on market forces alone to produce the necessary structural changes at the pace required. Some of the industries most in need of rationalisation have an in-built tendency to stay as they are. Either there are a few large firms which are tempted to live and let live; or there are a number of small ones, none of which alone is strong enough to achieve the scale of operations needed for international competition. Moreover, some mergers simply lead to a con-

> centration of ownership without securing a more effective deployment of the assets of the merged companies and result in loosely-knit groups of comparatively small production units ranging over a wide variety of manufacturing activities.
>
> 5. Although there is now a large number of institutions which can provide specialist services to meet the financial and other needs of industry, there is no organisation whose special function is to search for opportunities to promote rationalisation schemes which could yield substantial benefits to the national economy. Merchant banks and issuing houses carry through a great many mergers every year, but they can in general only act at their clients' request. Desirable regroupings fail to take place through lack of initiative and sponsorship, or because, when opportunities arise, there is no one ready to grasp them. The Government consider that this gap in the institutional framework needs to be filled and they propose to set up a new statutory body for the purpose, to be called the Industrial Reorganisation Corporation. The necessary legislation will be introduced as soon as possible.

The White Paper went on to emphasize that

> 6. The Corporation will seek the fullest co-operation from industry and existing financial institutions, and schemes which it initiates will, whenever possible, be put into effect either through the normal machinery of the market or in close collaboration with the market. It will be able to acquire a stake in the ownership of new groupings or enterprises it helps to create or to expand. It will not, however, act as a general holding company and will be able to dispose of its investments when the profits of rationalisation have been assured and it can do so to advantage. The faster it turns over its capital, the greater will be its capacity to promote the objects for which it is being set up.

From this and other sections of the White Paper it was clear that the left-wing concept of the Corporation, as a body to extend public ownership and to 'beat the capitalists' at their own game, had been largely defeated.

But it was not simply the way in which the White Paper was written which ensured that the IRC would be a pragmatic organisation, seeking to promote industrial aims rather than to further political objectives. The choice of Kearton as Chairman and the composition of its Board, with its heavy weighting of industrialists (discussed in Ch. 2), did the same. Those members of the Labour government who would have wished it otherwise allowed their views to be overridden in the interest of achieving the possible.

APPENDIX 1.1

This appendix reproduces the original White Paper setting up the Industrial Reorganisation Corporation (Cmnd 2889, 1966) which was presented to Parliament by the First Secretary of State and the Secretary of State for Economic Affairs in January 1966.

INDUSTRIAL REORGANISATION CORPORATION

Our future prosperity depends on our ability to bring about a fundamental improvement in the balance of payments. If we are to succeed in this, new initiatives are required to enable British industry to meet more effectively the growing competition it will face in world markets. The new system of incentives recently announced by the Government will provide a powerful stimulus to modernisation and investment in key sectors of the economy, but further changes in the structure and organisation of industry are required to make this fully effective.

2 The need for more concentration and rationalisation to promote the greater efficiency and international competitiveness of British industry, which was emphasised in the National Plan [Cmnd 2764, 1965, Ch. 1, para. 37], is now widely recognised. With the co-operation of financial institutions, many industries have already substantially altered their structure and organisation through mergers, acquisitions and regroupings. This process has been accelerating in recent years and may be expected to continue. Nevertheless, the pace and scale of change do not yet match the needs of the national economy.

3 Many of the production units in this country are small by comparison with the most successful companies in international trade, whose operations are often based on a much larger market. In some sectors the typical company in Britain is too small to achieve long production runs; to take advantage of economies of scale; to undertake effective research and development; to support specialist departments for design and marketing; to install the most modern equipment or to attract the best qualified management. Moreover, large groups may often have been built up haphazardly or solely to achieve wide diversification and may not therefore be organised to secure full efficiency in current conditions. Size and efficiency do not, of course, always go together—there are efficient small companies and inefficient large ones. What is needed is to create a structure which will enable us to make the most effective use, in the years ahead, of our resources of skill, management and capital.

4 There is no evidence that we can rely on market forces alone to produce the necessary structural changes at the pace required. Some of the industries most in need of rationalisation have an in-built tendency to stay as they are. Either there are a few large firms which are tempted to live and let live; or there are a number of small ones, none

of which alone is strong enough to achieve the scale of operations needed for international competition. Moreover, some mergers simply lead to a concentration of ownership without securing a more effective deployment of the assets of the merged companies and result in loosely-knit groups of comparatively small production units ranging over a wide variety of manufacturing activities.

5 Although there is now a large number of institutions which can provide specialist services to meet the financial and other needs of industry, there is no organisation whose special function is to search for opportunities to promote rationalisation schemes which could yield substantial benefits to the national economy. Merchant banks and issuing houses carry through a great many mergers every year, but they can in general only act at their clients' request. Desirable regroupings fail to take place through lack of initiative and sponsorship, or because, when opportunities arise, there is no one ready to grasp them. The Government consider that this gap in the institutional framework needs to be filled and they propose to set up a new statutory body for the purpose, to be called the Industrial Reorganisation Corporation. The necessary legislation will be introduced as soon as possible.

6 The Corporation will seek the fullest co-operation from industry and existing financial institutions, and schemes which it initiates will, whenever possible, be put into effect either through the normal machinery of the market or in close collaboration with the market. It will be able to acquire a stake in the ownership of new groupings or enterprises it helps to create or to expand. It will not, however, act as a general holding company and will be able to dispose of its investments when the profits of rationalisation have been assured and it can do so to advantage. The faster it turns over its capital, the greater will be its capacity to promote the objects for which it is being set up.

7 The Corporation will give priority to schemes of rationalisation and modernisation which offer good prospects of early returns in terms of increased exports or reduced import requirements, and will have regard to the regional aspects of the Government's policies for economic development. It will not support ventures which have no prospect of achieving eventual viability.

8 In identifying the sectors where early action is needed, the Corporation will look for advice and suggestions from industry and the City, from Government departments and the Economic Development Committees. It will effect rationalisation and reorganisation by whatever method best suits the circumstances of the particular case. In many instances its role will be to act as catalyst, providing initiative and ideas, helping the companies concerned and their advisers to work out practical schemes and arranging for any necessary expert services to be made available. It will pay particular attention to the management needs of new groupings.

9 In order that the Corporation may be able to operate on an effective scale and to promote a number of schemes simultaneously, it

must have large financial resources at its disposal. It will need funds to help to put together new groupings on a sound economic basis. It may also need to provide capital for new projects or expansions of special importance to the economy. Some new groupings may initially have difficulty in raising finance, especially in the form of medium-term loans, and the Corporation will have to be in a position to make capital available for expansion of research, development and design facilities or for investment in new plant, especially cost-saving machinery of modern design. Most rationalisation schemes will of themselves remove the main impediments to the introduction of modern equipment, but in some instances the Corporation may need to take special steps to ensure that particular types of advanced machinery are installed. For this reason it will be empowered to hold physical assets, so that in appropriate cases it will be able to purchase machines and make them available to new groupings, by leasing them or by making other suitable arrangements. The Corporation will co-operate with the Ministry of Technology and with the National Research Development Corporation, which may be able to help it to make rationalisation more effective in industries which are passing through a period of rapid technological change. It will also co-operate with the Ministry of Public Building and Works in matters affecting the construction industry.

10 The terms on which it will be appropriate for the Corporation to make finance available will vary from case to case and it will need to be able both to make loans and to take up equity holdings. The Government propose that it should be given, in the first instance, the right to draw as needed up to £150 millions from the Exchequer. It would be required to make fixed interest payments on part of this; the remainder would take the form of Exchequer Dividend Capital, the dividend on which would be settled by reference to the profits available after the fixed-interest borrowing had been serviced and adequate provision made for reserves.

11 Many of the rationalisation schemes sponsored by the Corporation will result in mergers which come within the scope of the Monopolies and Mergers Act, 1965. As the Government made clear when the Act was introduced, it is no part of its purpose to hold back mergers which are desirable in the national interest. Arrangements will therefore be made, so that companies participating in the Corporation's schemes can be certain, before schemes are completed, that the resulting mergers will not be referred to the Monopolies Commission.

12 These proposals are an integral part of the Government's plans for modernising the economy and complement the new system of investment incentives recently announced. The Government consider that, in co-operation with industry and the City, the Corporation will be able to secure a lasting improvement in the structure and competitive strength of British industry.

2

The Structure and Powers of the IRC

The Industrial Reorganisation Corporation began its work in the summer of 1966, holding its first Board meeting in June. This was almost six months before its existence was legitimised when the Royal Assent was given to the Industrial Reorganisation Corporation Act of 1966, on 21 December.

The Act provided that the Corporation should consist of a Chairman and between seven and fourteen other members. Sir Frank Kearton, Mintech's first choice for Chairman, had accepted the position and the intention to appoint him had been announced when the IRC White Paper was published in January 1966. The Act provided that the Chairman was to be appointed by the Secretary of State at the DEA, George Brown, who was succeeded by Michael Stewart at the beginning of 1967. The other members were to be appointed by the Secretary of State in consultation with the Chairman. So Kearton had the opportunity, not merely to involve himself in the thinking on how the IRC would operate, but also to influence the selection of its Board.

THE IRC BOARD

Kearton and Brown decided that the Corporation should have a merchant banker as its full time Managing Director and Deputy Chairman. They chose Mr Ronald Grierson who was an executive director of S. G. Warburg. Eight part time Board members were appointed as follows: Mr J. P. Berkin, a managing director of the Royal Dutch Shell Group; Mr Bernard Boxall, a consultant to the engineering company Lindustries; Mr Leslie Cannon, General President of the Electrical Trades Union; Mr B. R. Cant, whose contribution to developing the concept of the IRC has been discussed in Chapter 1; Sir Joseph Lockwood, Chairman of EMI; Professor W. G. McClelland, Director of Manchester Business School; Sir Frank Schon, formerly Chairman and Managing Director of Marchon Products and a director of Albright & Wilson; Sir Donald Stokes, Managing Director of Leyland Motors; Sir Charles Wheeler, Chairman of AEI.

During the life of the Corporation, four members left, and Leslie Cannon sadly died in 1970. Two of those who left – Grierson and Charles Wheeler – resigned after the GEC bid for AEI in the autumn of 1967. Kearton and Berkin both left in December 1968 when their initial periods of office ended. Early in 1968, Charles Villiers, another merchant banker, this time from Schroder Wagg, became Managing Director, but the post of Deputy Chairman remained vacant until filled by Stokes on 1 January 1969. Lockwood became Chairman in succession to Kearton, also on 1 January 1969. In May 1969, three new members were appointed. They were Sir Maurice Bridgeman, Chairman of British Petroleum; Mr Michael Clapham, a deputy chairman of ICI; Lord Goodman, the public figure and solicitor whose clients included Harold Wilson.

The IRC Act provided that the members of the Corporation were to have 'wide experience of, and to have shown capacity in, industry, technology, commercial or financial matters, administration or the organisation of workers' (IRC Act 1966, Section 1 (4)), and it could certainly not be argued that the IRC Board fell in any way short of this requirement. This was an exceptionally strong and influential Board.

A schedule to the Act laid down provisions for any conflict of interest on the part of a member. Papers were witheld, and members excluded from discussions, on any matters where conflicts with their other interests could arise.

The Act put no limit on the number of the Corporation's employees but it was decided to operate with a small number of executives, working rather like those of a merchant bank. Out of a total staff of thirty, there were never more than ten executives at any one time, and only a total of about twenty executives was employed by the Corporation during the whole of its life. The Act made clear that the Corporation was neither a servant nor an agent of the Crown. Hence, it had neither the obligations nor the rights – in the form of immunities, privileges or exemption from tax – of the Crown.

THE IRC'S POWERS

The IRC's functions were set out in Section 2(1) of the Act as follows:

> The Corporation may, for the purpose of promoting industrial efficiency and profitability and assisting the economy of the United Kingdom or any part of the United Kingdom
>
> (a) promote or assist the reorganisation or development of any industry; or
>
> (b) if requested by the Secretary of State, establish or develop, or promote or assist the establishment or development of any industrial enterprise.

This was interpreted to mean that the IRC could act on its own initiative in situations involving mergers, i.e. 'the reorganisation or development of any industry'. But it was held to require a specific request from the Secretary of State before the Corporation could become involved with a single 'industrial enterprise'.

Almost all the IRC's activities were under Section 2(1)(a) of the Act. This section required the Corporation to determine which industries it would be most expedient to reorganise or develop, either to improve their own efficiency or profitability, or to help to develop the whole or a part of the British economy.

Having determined which industries it should assist, the IRC was given the power to do anything, whether in the UK or overseas, which would help it to carry out this task. This included (a) the acquisition, holding and disposal of shares; (b) the formation of bodies corporate; (c) the making of loans and the giving of guarantees with respect to loans made by others; (d) the acquisition and placing at the disposal of others of premises and plant, machinery and other equipment.

While Section 1(1)(b) of the Act restricted the powers of the Secretary of State over the IRC, Section 2(5) gave him general power. He was enabled, after consultation with the IRC, to give the Corporation general directives 'as to the exercise and performance by the Corporation of its functions', and such directives must then be put into effect. This power was never used.

The overall financing limits of the IRC were set by the Act at £150 million. Within these limits, the Corporation could obtain two types of finance. First, it could, on its own initiative, borrow funds temporarily, whether by overdraft or otherwise, from any source it chose. Second, and this was clearly intended to be the main source of funds, it could borrow longer-term money from the Secretary of State. He, in turn would obtain this, by Treasury loan, from the

Consolidated Fund. Payments of dividend and interest, and repayments of principal, on these longer-term loans were to be on terms set by the Secretary of State, subject to Treasury approval. The reason for these arrangements was that the IRC was financed only partly by ordinary loans at fixed interest rates. Its remaining funds took the form of Public Dividend Capital (PDC), which was to pay a variable rate of dividend to be agreed with the Secretary of State. Access to PDC gave the IRC scope for flexibility in the terms it could offer to clients, without putting at risk its ability to pay interest on its loans.

Not only were short- and long-term borrowings to be kept within the overall limit of £150 million. Any loans, for example those obtained by industrial firms, given guarantees by the IRC, would count against the limit. So would any loans which the IRC itself obtained from non-government sources, on which the Treasury gave guarantees. Within these general rules, for each accounting year the IRC had to determine how much, if anything, it proposed to pay to the Secretary of State by way of dividend, interest or repayment of principal. Subject to Treasury approval, the Secretary of State could then decide whether this, or some other amount, was actually to be paid. Indeed, the Secretary of State could go further and recommend what payments the IRC should make in future years. If he did this, the Corporation was then required to conduct its affairs with a view to putting itself in a position to be able to pay these amounts. Again, this power was never used.

The Act required the Corporation to produce annual accounts which were to 'conform to the best commercial standards', the form being laid down by the Secretary of State, with the agreement of the Treasury. Similarly, the Secretary of State was required to send to the Comptroller and Auditor General an account of the sums made available to, and to be repaid by, the IRC.

Within four months of the end of each accounting year, the Corporation was to report on its activities during that year. The report was to refer specifically to (a) any requests for action with respect to an industrial firm made by the Secretary of State under Section 2(1)(b); (b) any general directives given to the IRC under Section 2(5); (c) any recommendations made by the Secretary of State on future payments to be made by the Corporation; (d) a list of securities acquired and disposed of by the IRC during the year, together with a list of securities held at the end of the year, and the length of time for which they had been held; (e) all relevant information about the Corporation's projects, activities and its financial position. In addition, the Secretary of State could direct the Corporation to provide any information about these projects and activities and about its financial position. This power too was never formally used but the IRC Report and accounts always included a full review of its activities. The Act laid down that the annual report and Accounts, together with any statement made by the IRC's auditors, was to be laid before Parliament.

COMMENT

The main points which should be emphasised about the IRC's role and structure are these. First, the primary task of the Corporation was to investigate and, where appropriate, to attempt to develop or reorganise industries or sections of industries. In other words, it was to promote mergers. The criteria it was to apply in doing so were set out only in the most general terms, as were the means which the IRC could use to achieve its objectives. This gave the IRC the right to operate, without question, over a wide range of the economy. It also meant that the IRC was likely to find it difficult to decide quickly exactly how it could best approach this task.

Second, the inclusion of Section 2(1)(b) in the Act meant that it was envisaged, from the start, that the IRC's activities might go beyond mergers. It was because this section gave the IRC such wide potential powers, with no detailed guidance as to criteria and priorities, that action under it was constrained by the requirement for a 'request' from the Secretary of State.

Third, while it cannot have been clear at the time whether the overall financial limit of £150 million was adequate, there seems no doubt that additional funds would have been provided if necessary. The Prime Minister himself had indicated that more might be forthcoming if necessary at a dinner party for IRC Board members at Downing Street on 7 November 1966, before the IRC Act had received the Royal Assent. When its activities came to an end in 1970, the Corporation's actual total indebtedness was only £107 million; £64 million of National Loan Fund Borrowing, at various interest rates between 7½ and 9¾ per cent, and £43 million of Public Dividend Capital.

Fourth, just as the Act gave only the vaguest description of what the Corporation was to do, few inside or outside the government can have been clear about how it might operate. Although the Corporation was given discretion over the appointment of staff, Kearton and Grierson decided at the very beginning that it should be small and informal, with all its employees working on short-term contracts. As Grierson said in October 1967,

> I wasn't willing to set up a huge second Neddy with a lot of departments and a secretariat and accommodation for retired civil servants. I can't see the IRC becoming a career for anybody. It's an ideas job so it ought to be done intensively for a short while. [Quoted in Lejeune (1967). An outline of the experience and subsequent careers of the IRC executives is given in the postscript at the end of this book.]

That much was clear. Everything else remained to be worked out. A major role of this book will be to see how the working out process went. The book proceeds in three further stages. In Chapter 3 we give an outline of the IRC's activities over its whole life. Then in Chapters 4–13 we look in greater detail at a number of the IRC's interventions in particular industries. These chapters are divided into two sections, the first covering mergers and industrial restructuring and the second 'rescues'. In the concluding chapter, we attempt to evaluate the IRC's work.

We turn, first, to a brief description of the IRC's work.

3

The IRC at Work

The history of the IRC divides easily into three distinct periods. The first was from the middle of 1966 until October 1967, when Ronald Grierson was Managing Director. The second was a short, but critical, interregnum from November 1967 to February 1968, when the Chairman, Sir Frank Kearton, took over the day to day duties of the chief executive. From then until the Corporation was officially wound up in April 1971, Charles Villiers was Managing Director, first under Kearton and then under Sir Joseph Lockwood.

THE IRC UNDER RONALD GRIERSON

The outstanding characteristic of the first period was that virtually nothing appeared to be done. Part of the reason was that getting an organisation like the IRC working effectively took time. Inevitably, the early months were taken up with recruiting staff, discussing what kinds of things the Corporation could do, assimilating reports and starting investigations. Grierson undoubtedly made a major and lasting contribution in establishing the principle that the IRC would employ high-calibre executive staff, on short-term contracts, and then finding and appointing the first executive team.

Another reason for the initial lack of apparent activity, however, was Grierson's own view of how the IRC should tackle its job. He was careful to emphasize the negative aspects of the Corporation's role. In his first major public speech about the IRC, on 20 March 1967, he presented a long list of the things the IRC was *not* going to do:

> We are not in the business of drawing up blueprints for any particular industry . . . we shall not back any rationalisation project which merely results in the formation of a holding company without a real sorting out of operational responsibilities . . . we lean over backwards to avoid doing anything which could also be done by others . . . we are not marriage-

> brokers . . . we have no wish to own equity securities for the sake of owning them . . . we are not a state or public merchant bank . . . we do not regard the policing of foreign investment as an IRC role . . . we will never advocate bigness for its own sake (speech at a conference organised by the University of Strathclyde and the *Financial Times*, Glasgow, 20 March 1967).

In one sense, emphasizing the negative side of the IRC's role was justified. There were many who feared the IRC, and remarks like these were likely to allay fears. But there was more to it than that. The kernel of Grierson's approach is shown in another extract from the same speech:

> I am anxious to leave with you the thought of the IRC as essentially a very modest institution. Far from believing that we know the answer to any industry's problems, we start out from the premise that the only people from whom we can learn are the leaders of industry themselves – and by leaders I mean not just the big boys but the bright boys – and that any plan we might put before them has almost certainly occurred to them already.

These words reflected a conviction on the part of Grierson and many members of the IRC Board that nothing could be done without the co-operation of industry. There was a need to reassure businessmen that the IRC was not an instrument of the Labour Government which would be used to force them, for political reasons, to do things which they did not want to do.

Royal Assent to the Act establishing the IRC was not given until 21 December 1966, because of the disruption of the parliamentary timetable caused by the 1966 election, which returned the Labour Government to power with a secure majority. Nevertheless, work had started in the summer of 1966. The Board first met on 24 June at Kearton's Courtaulds office in Hanover Square. George Brown attended the meeting to give what amounted to a 'keynote address'. He told the Board that the industrial advisers at the DEA had prepared reports on various industries, including engineering, electrical machinery, chemical and process plant and machine tools. These would be made available to the IRC, as would EDC reports. There was also a suggestion, which was to recur at many of the early meetings, that the IRC should take the initiative in forming consortia for tendering for large engineering contracts abroad, rather in the way that the Italian body, Italconsult, did. It might enhance IRC prestige. (Though Grierson and a group of businessmen actually visited Italy, this proposal never came to anything.)

The Board also considered other problem areas of UK industry, including shipbuilding. It was decided that the IRC should not become involved, because the industry was the subject of a special inquiry chaired by Sir Ray Geddes (and was later the responsibility of the Shipbuilding Industry Board).

During the next few months, much time was spent in talking with industrialists to discover their plans and in responding to outside initiatives. Some of these came from the government. For example, there was a request to examine, with the Steel Nationalisation Organising Committee, whether there was any need for rationalising and restructuring that part of the steel industry which would be left in the private sector after nationalisation, and particularly special steels. There was also a request for assistance in providing financial help to International Computers and Tabulators. Other approaches were made by companies, mainly by those who wanted money.

As the information coming to it was sifted, the IRC was able to establish the guidelines on which it would work. Thus, in the computer case, the Board took the view that it should not provide financial assistance unless that assistance was tied to a plan for restructuring the industry. But it did not take a rigid attitude.

Working methods also began to evolve. The small executive (five had been appointed by the end of August) was composed of young and bright men with limited experience. The tactics were to back them with experienced men working part-time, as well as with the expertise of the Board. So Avison Wormald, former Managing Director of Fisons, was appointed a special adviser on steel. Sir George Middleton was appointed as a consultant to examine possible IRC initiatives in the promotion of heavy engineering exports. Reports were commissioned by professional consultants. Accountants Binder, Hamlyn were asked to report on wool textiles. Peat Marwick were asked to report on a request for £1.75 million of IRC finance for a four-company merger in the seed industry.

By the end of August, discussion within the IRC had led to agreement by the Board that the Corporation's activities should be all-embracing; that it should act as a catalyst in the merger field, and more generally as an entrepreneur. It should not be a party merely to financial analysis. It must equip itself with the power, in particular cases, to see that the necessary rationalisation took place. Putting these principles into effect, however, proved harder than agreeing on them.

As the autumn passed, discussions in the IRC Board remained nebulous. They dealt with diverse matters, like the use of the buying power of government or the nationalised industries to influence industrial companies. A good deal of time was being devoted to a field in which the IRC had already decided to interest itself, namely industrial investment. One proposal was that the IRC should assist Mintech in providing funds for machine tool companies (see Ch. 8). The response was interesting. The IRC was especially anxious that Mintech and itself should not set up rival schemes. It would prefer Mintech to channel enquiries through the IRC which would then, if necessary, seek to use the need for investment funds as a lever to force structural change on industry. The Board was also at pains to resist the appointment of a Bank of England director to the Board, fearing that he would be seen as a government nominee. Indeed, the IRC felt strong enough to resist the appointment of any additional Board members.

By November 1966 the IRC had moved into its permanent offices, two floors in a small modern building in Pall Mall. In the following month, the Corporation was plunged into the negotiations which produced its first public act following a request by the government to examine the situation of Rootes Motors, which was in severe financial difficulties. The Rootes case was thrust upon the IRC by the government, and it frustrated one of the decisions of the first Board meeting in June. This was that the first IRC project must be very carefully chosen to represent a significant reorganisation and to give the greatest prospect of success, in view of the public attention which was bound to be focused on it.

The main issue was that Rootes urgently needed £20 million. Chrysler would provide this, but only it it were allowed to extend its existing interest in Rootes to over 50 per cent. Because this would require government consent, Mintech was asked to work out an alternative solution. In the end, this was done by Chrysler and Rootes plus their financial advisers, in consultation with Grierson. Apart from accepting this role as 'fixer' the IRC, under heavy pressure from the government, made a commitment to take up to £3 million of Rootes' preferred ordinary and loan stock, with the right to appoint one director to the Rootes Board. The IRC Board agreed that the Corporation should participate along the lines worked out, and one of its members, Boxall, was appointed to Rootes Board. There was, nevertheless, regret over the political pressures which had led the IRC to make its first move in a situation where reorganistion was not the main objective. (Brief details of all the IRC projects are given in chronological order in Appendix A at the end of this book.)

The IRC had now made a start – not the kind of start it had sought, but a start nevertheless. It was also taking tentative steps in fields where it was later to be fully engaged.

In particular, as 1967 progressed, the IRC became increasingly involved in heavy electrical equipment, steelworks and process plant and machine tools, while talks were also going on between British Motor Holdings and Leyland Motors. But there was still uncertainty over exactly what the Corporation was to do, and how it was to do it. A discussion at a Board meeting held in mid-1967 concluded that a major problem was to find suitable leadership in order to bring about mergers. While industrial concentration should be allowed to develop naturally, the Board felt that the IRC should take every opportunity to put pressure on events. It might have to take a tough line if the subtle approach failed to produce results.

The Corporation also had worries about its own position. The government was talking of introducing legislation to enable Mintech to take initiatives which appeared very similar to those of the IRC and there were suggestions in the press that this was because the IRC had been inactive – which, of course, it had. At an IRC Board meeting late in July, Grierson indicated his unhappiness at the possibility of legislation which could be seen as creating a significant overlap between the responsibilities of the IRC and those of Mintech. He also saw the document as vague and its lack of precision as suggesting that the Government was not clear in its objectives. The Board considered writing to the DEA, but decided to wait until the Bill was published. If the considerations underlying it were political, the IRC should say nothing. It certainly should not act negatively or defensively.

At the end of June 1967, the IRC was able to announce the first merger in which it had played an active part and for which it had provided finance. This was an agreed deal in which English Electric acquired Elliott Automation to create one of the largest and best equipped European groups in the field of automation and industrial control systems. It was just the kind of arrangement that Grierson thought the IRC should support. There were no major differences between the parties, and the IRC was able to use its cash (£15 million in this case) to accelerate the process of rationalisation which had been under way for some time in the industry.

In the late summer the IRC was asked to advise the government on its financial dealings with Cunard, and work on a report on the telecommunications industry, also commissioned by the government, was nearing completion. Then, at the end of September, the IRC became involved, on its own initiative, in one of its most crucial projects. This was the General Electric Company – Associated Electrical Industries (GEC–AEI) merger. It was notable in three senses: first, because of the size of the deal; second, because the IRC did not remain neutral, but backed GEC; third, because following this involvment Grierson and Wheeler resigned from the

IRC Board. The full story is told in Chapter 4. The important point here is the new sense of cohesion and purpose which the GEC deal seemed to bring to the Corporation.

The IRC was backing the GEC bid despite the opposition of the AEI Board. Grierson said that while he could see nothing wrong in the IRC backing a scheme positively, he personally was totally opposed to the IRC publicly taking one side against the other or seeking to influence shareholders in the choice before them. If the general consensus of view on the Board was in favour of this course, then he would be unable to represent their views as the chief executive of the Corporation and would prefer to withdraw. He argued that the GEC–AEI merger raised a fundamental issue of principle. The question for Grierson was whether the IRC should support GEC rather than taking a position of strict neutrality, to which he was fundamentally committed. The IRC Board decided that in issues such as this it must back its judgment and take sides, publicly if necessary.

When Grierson resigned, the members of the Board expressed warm appreciation for his untiring efforts over the last eighteen months. It was largely due to Grierson that the Corporation had come to be recognised as an efficient operating unit, able to make a positive contribution to the development of a more efficient industry in Britain. In his retrospective look at the IRC, Young concludes that

> Grierson's most important contribution was more intangible. As the only full time Board Member, he appears to have helped, more than most, both to calm the fears of suspicious industrialists, and to persuade them that the IRC was there for their benefit. Indeed the IRC was able to move successfully into its active phase in part because of Grierson's skill in handling the passive stage of its development (Young and Lowe, 1974).

Without Grierson, the IRC would not have been what it was. Equally, until he left it, the Corporation was not likely to become what it did.

THE INTERREGNUM

The GEC case seems to have had three main effects. First, it removed a powerful influence for caution. Had the board taken the line urged on it by Grierson over GEC, it could scarcely have supported the Kent bid for Cambridge in 1968 with sufficient funds to ensure that Kent won (Ch. 5). And how could it then have reacted to stop the SKF bid for Ransome and Marles or, later, for Pollard (Ch. 6)? Second, the IRC Board members felt they had handled the GEC issue well and given the Corporation a standing it did not have before. Third, during the three month interregnum period, before the appointment of Villiers, Kearton himself took charge of the day to day operations of the IRC. This gave the Corporation a chief executive who was not only determined and used to getting results but who was prepared to seize opportunities and to be as controversial as necessary.

For these reasons, and because schemes that had been under consideration for some time were now coming to maturity, the IRC became much more active. IRC support for the merger between the private sector steelmakers, Dunford and Elliott and Hadfields, had been announced almost simultaneously with Grierson's resignation. This was followed, in November, by the publication of an IRC report on the paper and board industry and in December by IRC support for the acquisition by Nuclear Enterprises of the nucleonic instrument activities of Elliot Automation and EMI. January 1968 brought more deals. In the wool textile industry the IRC supported the merger between Coats Patons and West Riding Worsted and Woollen Mills. This was announced on 10 January and was followed three days later by news of IRC support for the takeover of Edwards High Vacuum International by the British Oxygen Company. Later in the month, the IRC supported the merger of two small engineering companies, W. H. Allen and Sons and Bellis and Morcom. None of these deals required IRC funds but on 1 February it was announced that the IRC had put up £1.5 million to finance a de-inking plant for the Reed Paper Group. This was a new departure for the Corporation, involving finance for a straightforward investment project, so a request had to be secured from the Secretary of State. Board members felt that this provision of finance was justified on the ground that it brought forward an investment that had direct balance of payments benefits by substituting de-inked paper for imported pulp.

By far the most important project during this period, however, was the merger between Leyland Motors and British Motor Holdings. IRC support, together with a commitment to provide finance of up to £25 million, was announced on 17 January and Kearton himself played a very important role in bringing the merger discussions to fruition. The full story is told in Chapter 7.

CHARLES VILLIERS TAKES OVER

Charles Villiers joined the IRC on 1 February 1968. The delay in making the appointment was caused partly by the suddenness of Grierson's resignation but also because of difficulties in agreeing the size of Villier's salary. Grierson, presumably because he wanted to retain as much independence as possible, had not drawn any salary as the IRC's Managing Director, and had been on secondment from Warburgs. The IRC Board felt that it was essential to replace him by another experienced and respected merchant banker and was quite happy to pay the rate for the job. However, this was put at £20 000 per annum (about £80 000 p.a. in 1981 money). It was significantly more than the Prime Minister and the Chairmen of nationalised industries received and, when agreed, it caused some consternation in the press and among politicians and led to questions in the House of Commons. Indeed, one MP, Roy Hughes, asked whether the government intended to refer the salary to the National Board for Prices and Incomes. The government declined to do this and the general reaction in the press was favourable. Villiers resigned from his bank, Schroder Wagg, and some journalists speculated that he might be taking a cut in salary (for example, *The Times*, 1 February 1968).

Villiers felt it was important that he should be seen to be fully committed to the IRC and he therefore resigned from, or put into abeyance, all his other interests. He soon made his presence felt in the organisation of the Corporation. He set up a more systematic planning system to identify priority areas for the IRC's attention and he initiated discussions with French and West German industrialists and administrators to explore possibilities for UK–European mergers. He also felt it important to establish the best possible relationship with the Tories and invited Edward Heath to lunch at the IRC and to meet Board members and executives. Heath told Kearton afterwards that he had thoroughly enjoyed the occasion and had found the discussion very stimulating.

The IRC organisation was also strengthened by the appointment of a full-time Secretary, a librarian and three numerate graduates in their early twenties. The latter were to act as 'assistant executives' and to undertake background research work as well as to assist executives in investigations, report writing, etc. The idea behind these appointments was to free the executives themselves for the increasing burden of discussion and negotiation that growing IRC activity was producing.

Meanwhile more of the projects worked on during Kearton's interregnum were coming to fruition. In February, Davy Ashmore announced that it had acquired The Brightside Foundry and Engineering Company and had agreed to buy two engineering subsidiaries from Tube Investments. The IRC had assisted with the negotiations and agreed to provide finance for further rationalisation if this proved necessary. Then, in March, Whessoe, another leading company in steelworks and process plant, announced that it had acquired the fabrication business of one of Davy Ashmore's subsidiaries with the help of a £3.5 million IRC loan. The details of these deals and the subsequent history of Whessoe and Davy Ashmore are covered in Chapters 9–11.

The IRC also played a major part in the merger between Broom and Wade and Holman, two leading UK companies in the compressed air business. But the first really major event of the Villiers era was the Rank, Kent and Cambridge battle. After several years of deliberation Rank decided to make a bid for the important independent scientific instrument company, Cambridge Instruments. The IRC had been studying the industry for some time and decided to support a counter-bid for Cambridge from another independent instrument maker, George Kent. The story of the ensuing battle, and the Corporation's use of government money to outbid Rank, which made this the most controversial of all its ventures, is told in Chapter 5.

The IRC was also active in the nuclear field. In April 1968, Mintech had asked it to sound out the commercial companies on their attitude to the establishment of a single design authority and to look at the structure of the industry. As views were canvassed, majority opinion among IRC Board members seemed to move in favour of the establishment of two design and construction groups. In June, Kearton told the IRC Board that when Tony Benn, the minister at Mintech responsible for the nuclear industry, had asked for his personal opinion on the industry, he had proposed the two-group arrangement, while emphasising that this was his own view. He had emphasised that the IRC was in no way committed to this, but the Minister had not taken the disclaimer too seriously. Following this discussion, Benn told Parliament that a single design authority would be feasible only if the government were prepared to nationalise the industry. The CEGB, AEA and the companies were all opposed to establishing a single design authority.

In July 1968, Benn formally invited the IRC to assist the nuclear industry in the creation of two design and construction organisations to be established in place of the commercial firms and the design teams working with the Atomic Energy Authority. In September 1968, it was announced that the IRC, Babcock and Wilcox, English Electric, Taylor Woodrow Construction and the Atomic Energy

Authority would set up British Nuclear Design and Construction (BNDC). The IRC took 26 per cent of the equity and nominated Alastair Morton, a member of the executive, to the Board. In January, it was announced that the IRC, Reyrolle-Parsons, Sir Robert McAlpine and Sons, Clarke Chapman, John Thompson, Head Wrightson, Strachan and Henshaw, Whessoe and the AEA would establish The Nuclear Power Group (TNP). The IRC took 10 per cent of the equity and nominated Berkin, its ex-Board member, to the Board of the new group. The total IRC investment in BNDC was £26 000 and in TNPG £150 000.

During the early summer of 1968, the IRC had also become increasingly involved with ball-bearings, where lengthy negotiations were to lead to the Corporation making its first bid for a company, Brown Bayley Limited, in order to put its ball-bearing subsidiary, Hoffmann, into an all British grouping. This did not come to fruition until almost a year later (Ch. 6).

In the meantime, the IRC took on a minor project for the government. This was an examination of the Army Kinema Corporation and the RAF Cinema Corporation, and it led to a merger between the two.

As in the previous year, the autumn of 1968 was dominated for the IRC by the electrical industry – this time by a GEC bid for English Electric (EE). The IRC again supported the merger, but did not clearly take GEC's side. Indeed, some IRC Board members expressed fears that English Electric managers might be subordinated to those of GEC and sought a 'real' merger. There were also suggestions that an IRC stake in GEC–EE might be needed to protect the public interest. An idea put forward to thwart the bid was a 'grand alliance' between EE, BICC, Plessey, Thorn and Reyrolle-Parsons. This idea was, however, regarded as absurd by the IRC executive. Board members saw it as a *folie de grandeur*. GEC's bid was made on 6 September, and succeeded. The story of this second GEC merger is also covered in Chapter 4.

Efforts continued in other industries. In the autumn of 1968, Villiers claimed that the IRC now knew more about the pump industry than almost any other but had so far been totally unsuccessful in promoting rationalisation. Perhaps it had been too anxious to be fair. It was essential, now, to push in the direction which seemed most likely to produce a result. The first move soon came. In November 1968, the Weir Group, to which the IRC had been giving general backing, made an offer for Harland Engineering, a counter-offer coming from Mather and Platt. Having studied both proposals, the IRC did not feel able to endorse one bid as clearly preferable in terms of the rationalisation and development of the pump industry and would not take sides. In fact, the Weir offer succeeded. About the same time, a merger between Sigmund Pulsometer Pumps and Plenty and Son was announced, the IRC welcoming it 'as another step forward in the rationalisation of the pump manufacturing industry' (see Appendix A, p. 269).

Towards the end of 1968, the IRC's continuing involvement in the pump industry led it into discussions with the Weir Group and Studebaker-Worthington Inc. Both firms had made bids for Worthington-Simpson, a British company in which Studebaker-Worthington had a minority interest. Weir and Studebaker-Worthington asked the IRC to decide which of them should make a bid for Worthington-Simpson if wider discussions they were holding broke down. Late in February 1969, the two firms agreed that they would establish a joint company to sell their products internationally and that Studebaker-Worthington would bid for Worthington-Simpson. The IRC was relieved of any obligation to arbitrate, but saw the agreement as 'of great benefit to the UK pump industry' (see Appendix A, p. 270).

PROCEDURES REVIEWED AND WORK CONTINUED

The IRC's second full year had been far busier, and in terms of deals completed far more successful, than its first. Moreover, a clear *modus operandi* had been developed. The executive team had been divided into two groups, one covering electrical engineering and the other mechanical engineering and miscellaneous industries. The dividing lines were not rigid and one of the electrical team also took on projects in the trawling and confectionary industries. But the loose structure meant that executives built up knowledge and experience of their sectors. Within each group, executives covered a range of industries and were expected to visit individual companies and analyse relevant financial and industrial statistics.

When it was decided that the IRC should take an initiative in a particular area, or once a particular situation had been brought to its attention, a standard approach was adopted. The appropriate executive took a major role in collecting information about the situation, analysing it and keeping other members of the executive informed of developments. At appropriate points, he was responsible for preparing a paper which either briefed Board members on the situation or sought their approval for particular actions. The individual executive was then responsible for seeing that the action was taken. In some projects, only one executive took this role; often the role changed hands once or twice during the life of a project.

When a project called for quick decision or action, more than one executive was often assigned to it. Moreover, a high proportion of the visits to firms were made by two or three executives. A member of the Board was sometimes associated with the individual or team working on the project, to keep the Board in close touch. And a major role was played in all projects by the Managing Director. He, and/or the Chairman, usually attended key meetings with representatives of firms or industries, while all important letters were written and telephone calls made by one or other of them.

These arrangements worked well. Relevant members of the executive were well informed about the actions of other executives, partly because of frequent meetings. Indeed, throughout the life of the IRC there was a daily early-morning meeting of the whole executive. In addition, all the major moves on any project were cleared with the Chairman or Managing Director, in the relatively small number of instances where one or other of them was not personally engaged.

Nevertheless, there were understandable tensions. There were suggestions, both in the City and in business, that the IRC executives might be very bright but that they were also very young and very brash. Such a reaction was inevitable. These young men were engaged in shaking the *status quo*, often in long-established businesses. Moreover, they were dealing exclusively in those areas of corporate policy usually reserved for the most senior managers. Doubtless they made some mistakes in the way they handled chairmen, chief executives and financial advisors.

Yet, as Professor McClelland puts it, 'Suggestions that the executive were too young and brash have been sufficiently refuted by the posts most of them have subsequently occupied' (McClelland, 1972, p. 37) (see the postscript at the end of this book). With hindsight it appears that the executives performed well, taking their lead, all the time, from the Chairman and the Managing Director.

There was also tension between the executives and the IRC Board. Board meetings, which were held at least once and usually twice a month, were at first very informal. All the executives attended and participated on almost equal terms with Board members. In November 1968, the Board decided that more care must be taken to prevent executives giving an appearance of overconfidence. It was agreed that Board members should be more closely associated with individual schemes and that a specific member would be designated to give overall guidance on each project. In addition, it was decided to end the practice whereby all IRC executives attended Board meetings. In the future, only those executives who had prepared papers, or who were explicitly invited, would attend. The seating in the boardroom was rearranged to reflect this more formal arrangement.

Work continued uninterrupted and the first few months of 1969 proved very busy ones. In January 1969, an IRC initiative and loans of £1 million each to the Reed Paper Group and the Bowater Paper Corporation enabled them to acquire jointly the Donside Paper Mill at Aberdeen. This purchase, together with a joint marketing agreement, was aimed at saving the mill from closure and at rationalising the manufacture and marketing of coated paper in the UK in line with regional policy and with the IRC report on the paper industry. During the course of this deal the IRC negotiated the first exemption under the new Restrictive Practices legislation. This permitted a restrictive practice (in this case the joint marketing arrangement) provided that its overall impact was beneficial. Also in January, the IRC made its bid for Brown Bayley. As explained in Chapter 6, this move was sparked off by the IRC's anxiety to establish a major British ball-bearing firm. The Swedish company, SKF, which was Europe's largest ball-bearing manufacturer, wanted to acquire the leading UK company, Ransome and Marles, and the IRC feared that the whole UK industry might become foreign owned. Instead, it wanted to merge Ransome and Marles with the two other largest UK producers, Pollard and Hoffman – a subsidiary of Brown Bayley. This objective was eventually achieved and, perhaps because the only real opposition came from a non-UK company, this radical action by the IRC caused less fuss than did its market intervention in the Rank–Kent battle.

Fortuitously, Brown Bayley's only other subsidiary was Brown Bayley Steels, with interests in the special steels industry which the IRC had also been studying for some time. Two-thirds of the UK's alloy steel capacity was owned by the British Steel Corporation and located in three larger and two smaller works. The private sector of the special steel industry was much more fragmented. Even the biggest private producer could make less than half as much steel as one of the bigger BSC plants. The IRC therefore took the view that economic operation and investment required bigger plants. The Corporation had already supported the merger between Dunford and Elliott, a leading re-roller, and Hadfields, which made alloy steel. So, besides giving it control of Hoffmann, the acquisition of Brown Bayley gave the IRC greater leverage in special steels, although it still took some time to make any further progress.

Late in February 1969, the IRC's efforts to rationalise crane production began to bear fruit, with a Clarke Chapman bid for the entire capital of Sir William Arrol Ltd. This was followed by an announcement that Clarke Chapman would take over the crane interests of Wellman Engineering. The IRC provided £2 million to enable Clarke Chapman to finance these moves. In September 1969 there was a further merger, this time between the Steel Group and Priestman Brothers, both of which had interests in cranes and in construction equipment. The IRC offered funds of up to £1.5 million.

For some time, the IRC had been trying to rationalise the mining machinery industry. There were about a dozen important independent firms in the industry and the available business had declined sharply following the significant reduction in the number of coal faces being worked by the National Coal Board (NCB). Mintech and the NCB felt that the UK suppliers would be considerably strengthened and more able to compete for export orders if they were rationalised into larger groups. The IRC was asked to assist in this process of rationalisation by considering the most appropriate structure for the industry and then persuading the firms to undertake the recommended mergers. The IRC decided that to form three groups, each with a comprehensive capability over the whole range of mining machinery, would be the best arrangement, but it was no easy task to bring this about. Several of the firms strongly resented the pressure put on them to sacrifice their independence. Mintech, however, fully supported the IRC's plans and, even more important, it was thought that the NCB might give preference, in placing its orders, to those companies who agreed to join the new groupings.

The IRC therefore entered into complicated negotiations simultaneously with eleven firms, whom it felt should make up the three groups. A merger between Dobson Hardwick and William Park, announced in March 1969, represented a major step towards the formation of the first of these groups. The merger of Fletcher and Stewart, Richard Sutcliffe and A. G. Wild, announced in May 1969, created another. In June, it appeared that the formation of the most important group was under way with the Dowty Group and Bonser Engineering agreeing to merge their mining activities. The final, and perhaps most important step, a merger of Dowty–Bonser with Anderson-Mavor, was announced in December 1969. This was later abandoned. Nevertheless, the IRC's intervention had a radical influence on the structure of the industry.

Operating somewhat outside its normal field, the IRC now took part in talks with the Ross Group and Associated Fisheries, which led the two companies to combine their trawler interests. As a result, British United Trawlers was established on 1 July 1969.

In the same month, for the first time, a company which the IRC had supported, and in which it had a financial interest, ran into serious trouble. This was Davy Ashmore, which came near to disaster because of a large loss on a contract undertaken by its subsidiary, Power Gas. The IRC's reaction to this is covered in Chapter 11. It succeeded in rescuing Davy Ashmore but this crisis effectively brought to an end the IRC's plans for further rationalisation in this area.

During the latter part of 1969, further developments came from the IRC's continuing effort to take advantage of the GEC–AEI–EE merger. On 17 July, BICC reported that it was to acquire the supertension cable and transmission line divisions of AEI and GEC, with the IRC offering a standby facility of up to £2.5 million. On the same day, Pirelli and Enfield-Standard announced that they would establish a joint company to rationalise the production of supertension cables. On 18 November, Joseph Lucas Industries announced that its aircraft equipment subsidiary, Rotax, had acquired from GEC the business of English Electric's special products group. The IRC, which had made a detailed study of the industry, hoped that this would make 'a significant contribution to the rationalisation of the UK effort in the aircraft equipment field' (see Appendix A, p. 288). The Corporation looked for results in exports and in R&D, lending Lucas £3 million in the hope of bringing about these developments. The IRC also encouraged a merger between Hawker Siddeley and Brook Motors early in 1970 with the intention of concentrating the UK production of electric motors into fewer units.

In September 1969 another new deminsion was added to the IRC's role when it was asked, by Mintech, to undertake a study of the forward financing needs of Rolls-Royce (RR) and to suggest ways of meeting any shortfall in its financing requirements. The results of the investigation and RR's subsequent history is set out in Chapter 12.

An even more surprising request came early in 1970 when Lockwood was asked by major institutional shareholders to join them when they confronted Vickers on its performance. Lockwood agreed only after consulting Vickers' chairman and a meeting took place in Janury 1970. Much to his surprise he reports that he was expected to act as the institutions' spokesman at the meeting. Desipite some acrimony, this eventually lead to Vickers' decision to split the jobs of chairman and chief executive and to bring in Sir Peter Matthews to fill the latter role (see Evans, 1978, pp. 159–164 and 252–253). Lockwood reported the meeting to the IRC Board which expressed its approval of this action by shareholders to improve management.

IRC METHODS AND INFLUENCE

The Vickers case illustrates how far the IRC had gained the confidence of many of the people who had initially seen it as another unwelcome branch of government. Although the IRC could and did use the fact that it had funds at its disposal to bring about industrial reorganisation, it achieved a good deal simply through advice, assistance and persuasion.

In his review of these factors, McClelland put most emphasis on what he calls 'sweet reason'. Where the IRC concluded that the rationalisation of a particular industry was desirable, or where it was trying to promote a particular course of action, it usually began its efforts by attempting to persuade key individuals of the merits of its case. As McClelland has said, it could usually be argued that the proposed reorganisation would be in the long-term interests of the shareholders of the firms concerned, as well as of the British economy in general, at least if fair terms could be agreed. Directors and senior managers did not always agree, not least because their prestige and status were often at stake. In these circumstances, using 'sweet reason' meant taking the opportunity 'to point out to them that the consequences of taking no action would be worse than those of taking the action indicated, or that the long-term balance of advantage would be different from the immediate balance of advantage' (McClelland, 1972, p. 32). Sometimes there was an appeal to patriotism; sometimes an appeal to a key individual to accept his responsibility as a 'leader' of his industry.

The IRC could do this the more easily because it could emphasize its role as a disinterested party and stress its primary concern with the national interest:

> This quality of disinterest on the part of the IRC quickly came to be recognised and the IRC offices in Pall Mall accepted as neutral ground. And as regards losing faith, reference to the IRC's good offices in a merger announcement meant that the management which was giving up its independence could if it felt like it claim, not that it had been worsted in a commercial struggle, but that it had nobly sacrificed its self-interest for the public good (McClelland, 1972, p. 32).

Because of this, relatively simple forms of assistance from the IRC were often surprisingly effective in bringing about agreement. Mediation between top executives was both necessary and effective. Thus, in the compressor industry, mediation, together with the assistance in devising appropriate financial agreements for the merger, were the key factors in bringing it about.

Where persuasion showed signs of failing, other measures had to be used. The offer of finance was one of these. Especially where reorganisation called for sums of money that were large relative to the size of the organisations concerned, the IRC's ability to provide finance, either by making loans or by purchasing some of a firm's equity, was the *sine qua non* of a merger. It has been suggested that the Corporation was simply 'bribing' firms to merge. In response, McClelland argues that because the IRC was much more closely involved in merger situations than even a merchant banker would normally be, it was able quite properly on occasions to advance money at less than commercial rates:

> These were not bribes to merge. They normally made it possible, either for the bidder to finance acceptable terms or for the merged company to incur capital expenditure that made possible the exploitation of the opportunities presented by the merger earlier than would otherwise have been the case. This is not to say that the prospect of such a loan did not increase the attractiveness of the merger to the parties concerned and thus act as an inducement to merge (McClelland, 1972, p. 33).

> IRC loans frequently provided for the deferment of interest for several years, which was convenient and appropriate, but on a d.c.f. basis over the whole period of the loan the rate of interest was never unduly low. In some cases there were options to convert into ordinary shares, so that the IRC, and through the IRC the taxpayer, would be able to share in the proceeds of success if it came (McClelland, 1972, p. 33).

If the offer of finance did not achieve what the IRC had in mind, it could use weapons that were more controversial. For example, it could acquire shares in the market, as it did to thwart the Rank takeover of Cambridge (Ch. 5). This was, however, the most criticised of all its actions and the IRC intervened significantly in the market in only one other case, its bid for Brown Bayley. For the reasons described above and in Chapter 6, this caused less controversy.

The IRC's actions over Kent–Cambridge and Brown Bayley were decisive, but these were only two out of well over fifty IRC cases. More subtle and ubiquitous, but often equally successful, were pressures applied in private. The most effective pressures came from Ministers, senior government officials and occasionally public sector customers, either in the form of appeals for help or of veiled threats.

McClelland also argues that the 'media' was important and that

> public support for an IRC view might have substantial influence on a reluctant management. Of course, this could easily rebound and had

therefore to be used with extreme care. But the fact that as time wore on it became known that the IRC view, if communicated to the press, might well be, at least, treated with great respect, undoubtedly gave IRC views added weight' (McClelland, 1972, p. 34).

In the end, of course, none of the IRC's attempts to bring abut mergers could have succeeded unless shareholders were convinced that merger terms were fair. With shareholders, the IRC could use three forms of influence. It could issue statements about its own views on the benefits of a merger; it could attempt to obtain favourable press comment on merger terms when these were announced; and it could influence the merger terms themselves, both by persuasion and by the provision of finance. It used one or more of these means, as appropriate, to gain acceptance for all the mergers it backed.

THE IRC'S LAST YEAR

Though no one knew it at the time, May 1970 saw the beginning of the last year of the IRC's activities. Its final transaction – a loan to Vantona/Hartley – was to be announced in April 1971.

It was an eventful year. In May 1970 agreement was finally reached on the first stage of the IRC's report on Rolls-Royce and the IRC announced that a loan of £10 million would be made to RR, under Section 2(1)(b) of the IRC Act, with a further £10 million to be made available during 1971, if certain conditions were met. On 11 November 1970, the government took direct responsibility for RR and announced that the IRC would not provide help beyond this initial £10 million.

There were four other major initiatives during this final year. The first resulted from the difficulties of Cammell Laird – the shipbuilding firm. By the end of 1969, it had become clear the company was in severe financial difficulties. With the Shipbuilding Industry Board unwilling to help, the IRC's solution, described in Chapter 13, was to separate Cammell Laird's shipbuilding activities from its remaining interests, with Cammell Laird and the government jointly acquiring the shipyard. The non-shipbuilding business remained an independent company. It was re-named The Laird Group, and put under the charge of a young member of the IRC executive – John Gardiner.

The first half of 1970 saw what meagre results there were from the IRC's lengthy attempts to reorganise the machine tool industry. In March 1970, the IRC agreed to make available up to £1.5 million to Marwin Holdings, to enable the company to continue to expand its production of numerically controlled machine tools. After prolonged efforts, the Corporation also arranged loans to Herbert/Ingersoll and to Kearney and Trecker. The loan to Herbert/Ingersoll was to finance expansion, but the firm became insolvent in June 1972. The loan of £0.3 million to Kearney and Trecker was matched by one from the Midland Bank Finance Corporation. The loans gave the IRC and the Midland Bank conversion rights amounting to 31 per cent of the equity of Kearney and Trecker – an interesting move, since Kearney and Trecker was the subsidiary of an American company.

More controversially, on 1 June the IRC announced that it had offered British Leyland, as a major user of machine tools, a scheme aimed at stimulating investment in the machine tool industry. Under it, the Corporation would provide a revolving facility of £10 million which British Leyland would use to purchase machine tools and to modernise and expand its production facilities. British Leyland had taken an initial £2.5 million of this facility on 1 June and three further instalments were foreseen. The British Leyland loan also led to abortive efforts to set up a more general IRC scheme to finance the purchase of machine tools. The IRC's activities in the machine tool industry are described in Chapter 8.

Between October 1970 and April 1971 the IRC made four loans to textile companies, following the government's request for the Corporation to consider applications for finance from medium and smaller-sized companies in the cotton and allied textile industry. The loans followed the IRC's study of the industry and the government's decision to bar any merger between the 'big five' textile companies. The four smaller firms receiving IRC aid were Harwood Cash, Perseverence Mill, Highams and Vantona/Hartley. The Corporation also agreed to provide up to £1.3 million to Spirella, to assist in restructuring part of the household textile industry. The IRC had earlier made a loan of £2 million to the Klinger Manufacturing Company and Qualitex Yarns and had provided £1 million to foster a merger between Hartley and Allied Mills.

The IRC had become much more than a merger broker. It was recognised, and used, as an independent body with industrial and financial expertise, with access to public funds and with a remit to pursue the 'national interest'. As such it was being used by the government to administer specific investment incentive schemes and to advise on major companies in trouble. It was also, on its own initiative, seeking to promote investment as well as rationalisation. However, all this was changed by the result of the 1970 election.

THE END OF THE IRC

As soon as the Conservative government took office in June 1970, discussions began on the IRC's future. Despite some initial encouragement, it soon became clear that the Corporation would be allowed only to carry out obligations already entered into. The reaction of the IRC Board members was to argue that they should seek private sector finance and should consider the possibility of a three-way link with the ICFC and FCI. During the summer of 1970, two meetings were held between officials of the IRC and of government departments, while Lord Sherfield took the initiative in trying to organise the three-way merger. The Conservative government's main objection was to the interventionist activities of the IRC, so the Corporation suggested how the IRC Act might be modified to meet that objection.

These efforts were not to prevail and, on 27 October 1970, in his budget speech, Tony Barber announced the end of the IRC. We started the book with one reaction to his announcement. Rather than attempting an assessment of the IRC's work at this stage, we shall first consider a number of the IRC's major projects in greater detail. This will provide the material from which some evaluation of the IRC's performance and contribution can be made.

PART TWO

MERGERS AND INDUSTRIAL RESTRUCTURING

4

GEC, AEI and EE

The electrical industry was given high priority by IRC from the beginning and the issues raised by its activities in this area make a good starting point for our detailed study of the IRC's work. This was the only industry where a group of executives was assigned to work full-time on rationalisation proposals and it provides the first example of a merger where the IRC decided to give public support to one side, the General Electric Company (GEC), in a contested bid. This raised new issues for the IRC Board, issues which cannot be separated from the desision of its first Managing Director to resign. The controversy raised by the IRC's support for the GEC takeover of Associated Electrical Industries (AEI) was soon followed by its equally controversial support for GEC in its battle with Plessey for the control of English Electric (EE). Both these cases illustrate how, when a bid was made, the IRC was able to reach a decision very rapidly because of its continuing study of the industry. They also illustrate the effectiveness of the IRC in ensuring that mergers it supported did take place and enable us to see in detail how it then tried to ensure that the merged firms carried out the rationalisation which had been envisaged.

EARLY MANOEUVRES

The IRC's first involvment with the electrical industry was in response to a request from the government to look at the scope for rationalisation among the producers of heavy transformers. This request was discussed by the IRC Board as early as its second meeting on 29 July 1966. Following massive investment up to the early 1960s and the subsequent cutback, there was chronic over-capacity among transformer producers. Grierson told the Board that the CEGB, which wished to see a reduction in the number of producers, had foregone competitive tenders on a bulk order for transformers in order to give the companies time to formulate rationalisation proposals. The case for there being a small number of more fully employed and more efficient suppliers, using the best of the existing facilities, was very strong. The merged businesses could expect to achieve the same market share as their constituent parts and thus to reap the benefits of rationalisation. The IRC was keen to be involved, but progress was slow because of the many conflicting interests. The Department of Economic Affairs raised the matter again in March 1967 and in May, after discussions with all the major transformer producers, the IRC put preliminary proposals to the four leading companies: AEI, EE, Ferranti and Hawker Siddeley.

While these negotiations were proceeding, the IRC had been considering and working on other possibilities for the industry, including some which were much more comprehensive and radical. The first deal that came to fruition was announced on 23 June. This was an agreed bid by EE for Elliott Automation, which created one of the largest and best equipped European groups in the field of automation and industrial control systems. The IRC supported the merger and advanced £15 million in the form of unsecured loan stock, which could later be converted into EE shares. This was an important and well-received deal (for favourable press comments see *Financial Times*, 23 June 1967 and *The Times*, 23 June 1967). Its completion owed much to the skill and ingenuity of Grierson, who himself conducted most of the negotiations with the chairmen of the two companies, both of whom he knew personally.

AEI – THE BIG BID

In September, a much more dramatic move was announced. Kearton called an IRC Board meeting for 27 September 1967 but asked two members, Lockwood (Chairman of EMI) and Wheeler (Chairman of AEI), not to attend. At the meeting he reported that on the previous afternoon Weinstock had told him that he intended to make a bid for AEI. GEC wanted no finance from the IRC but felt that the Corporation's moral support would be crucial. GEC had therefore proposed that, before their offer was announced, relevant ministries, the CEGB and the Post Office, should be told that the IRC supported GEC. Kearton made it clear that GEC fully realised that IRC support was conditional on both the merger and the merged businesses themselves being conducted in an 'industrial statesmanlike' manner.

Weinstock's intention came as no surprise to IRC. Indeed, in March Grierson had discussed with Weinstock a suggestion of the

IRC executive that the merger of GEC and AEI would both be desirable in its own right and would act as a catalyst for other necessary changes in the industry. This was not accepted IRC policy at that time, but it had made a clear impression on GEC's thinking. Weinstock was then considering a number of alternative moves and he had impressed Kearton and Grierson with his ideas on how the industry could and should be rationalised.

When the IRC Board was faced with the GEC–AEI merger as a definite proposal and not simply as one of a number of hypothetical realignments, it had to decide whether it had enough information to support GEC's proposals with the government and in public. It knew that AEI's reaction would be distinctly unenthusiastic but the IRC executives, who had undertaken a comprehensive survey of the industry, supported the move. The IRC Board decided that, at the very least, the merger would break the 'log jam' that was preventing the effective rationalisation of the industry. It therefore agreed to support the GEC bid and, if necessary, to provide finance, not for the bid itself but to assist subsequent rationalisation. AEI and GEC were immediately told of the IRC's decision.

Latham, Deputy Chairman of AEI, made it clear to the IRC that his company was completely against the GEC bid and would oppose it vigorously. He proposed alternative rationalisation measures and asked for support on these. One of AEI's proposals was the merger of its telecommunications business with Standard Telephone and Cables (STC), giving the US company management control; this was to become an important point in AEI's public defence against the GEC takeover.

As it happened, a sub-committee of the IRC Board had considered a report on the telecommunication industry produced for the government, at a meeting held at the end of September. This report had been submitted to the government on 2 October but AEI's suggestions were not in line with its proposals. When they met, on 23 October, to consider a reply to AEI the IRC Board members were therefore well informed on telecommunications and most of them had serious misgivings about any extension of STC's activities into the UK-owned sector. The Board agreed to write to AEI indicating that it approved rationalisation measures of the kind the company was putting forward, but expressing reservations about the STC proposal and seeking an assurance that, if such a deal were concluded, UK exports would not suffer. The Board also emphasised the benefits foreseen from a GEC–AEI merger and reaffirmed the IRC's support for it.

The Board met again the very next day. Grierson said he had called it together again so quickly because he wanted views on two important issues. The first was the effect of the reply to AEI on the IRC's position. While AEI had simply requested IRC support for particular rationalisation measures, the reply went beyond an answer on that single point, responding to some of the company's arguments and reaffirming IRC support for GEC. Grierson was worried that the tone of the IRC's reply might, in the full glare of publicity, contrast unfavourably with AEI's soberly worded approach. While Grierson was still fully in agreement with the IRC's reply to AEI, he thought it might be best to publish a separate press release. This would give the IRC's views on the AEI rationalisation measures, affirm its support for the GEC–AEI merger, and emphasise that it was for the AEI shareholders to decide what was in their own interests.

The second issue was a much graver one. Grierson was deeply concerned because the IRC Board was divided on the fundamental question of whether the Corporation should remain strictly neutral in the current struggle or come down firmly on one side or the other. He could see nothing wrong in the IRC backing a merger proposal positively, but he was totally opposed to supporting one party publicly or seeking to influence shareholders in accepting or rejecting a bid. If the IRC persisted in its present course, he would be unwilling to represent these views and would prefer to withdraw as Chief Executive.

Members discussed this at length. They agreed that the reply to AEI contained the Board's collective view and should stand. It was perhaps true that the tone of the letter that had been sent could have been improved but, unless the suggested press release contained any significant change of view or emphasis (which was not apparent), then the letter itself should be published. It would do more harm than good to prevent this, not least because the press knew that the letter had been sent. Moreover, the Board was certain that it was right for the IRC to form a judgment on industrial measures and, in this case, its collective view was in favour of the merger. This inevitably meant that they were behind GEC. It was the duty of members to express this view, although in doing so there was no intention of bringing influence to bear on shareholders. When this discussion ended, Grierson said he had reflected in depth on his position. Since the Board was against a position of strict neutrality, to which he was fundamentally committed, he wished to withdraw immediately as full-time Chief Executive of the Corporation.

On 28 October, the Board discussed a new letter from AEI but decided not to continue the correspondence. Grierson's resignation from the IRC was announced on the same day. He told the press that it had 'nothing whatever to do with the AEI situation. I can also authorise you to say that the Board of the IRC was and is absolutely united in its attitude to the bid' (*Sunday Telegraph*, 29 October 1967). Nor was his resignation connected with his opposition to proposals currently being mooted for the government to take equity stakes in industrial firms.

Not unnaturally, Wheeler also resigned from the IRC Board, sharply attacking the Corporation for backing GEC. As with the Leyland–BMH merger (Chapter 7), an IRC Board member was chairman of one of the companies concerned. Perhaps it is an indication of IRC's impartiality that, in this case, its support went to the opposition.

The merger battle continued. AEI emphasised the benefits of its proposed link with STC on telecommunications: 'We are excellent natural partners' (Sir Joseph Latham, quoted in *The Guardian*, 1 November 1967). GEC's response was to describe this as a 'sell out' to the Americans. If GEC won, this telecommunications operation would remain in British hands. Early in November, the IRC became worried that AEI might try to forestall GEC, by making an immediate deal with STC. The government told AEI that it would disapprove of any attempt to sign an AEI–STC agreement before the result of the GEC bid was known.

The AEI–GEC merger went through. At a meeting early in November, IRC Board members agreed that the matter had been well handled. AEI shareholders had accepted the merger, and the IRC's positive action had given it a standing it had not had before. Even so, the Board felt the need clearly to define its position. The bid did point to the dangers of contested situations. Clearly the IRC's support in these cases should be given only as a last resort, and after attempts to negotiate an agreed merger had failed. But provided that the IRC was satisfied on this point, and fully informed on the industrial arguments for and against it, it should not shrink from offering its support. The issue was not so much whether a contested situation existed, or whether IRC should back one company against another, as whether IRC regarded the move as a sensible initiative which could produce the desired results.

The GEC bid led to an adjournment debate in the House of Commons (see *HC Deb*, 23 November 1967, Cols 1604–1634). Several Labour MPs attacked both 'faceless managers' who had the power to take decisions on such massive mergers and Weinstock's willingness to accept the need for redundancies. For the government, Edmund Dell noted that the role of the IRC in the merger had 'received a magisterial accolade in a leader in *The Times*' (Col. 1624). He defended the need for rationalisation and rejected the idea that the merger was entirely unplanned. The 1965 National Plan had specifically mentioned the electrical industry as one where reorganisation might be needed to increase competitive efficiency. Where people were to be thrown out of jobs, the solution must be to ease the transitional unemployment rather than restrict the process of rationalisation. The IRC had not provided financial support for the merger, because GEC neither needed nor sought it. 'The IRC made no comment on the terms of the offer; it merely made a judgement – which, I believe, was influential – that the merger was of national benefit' (Col. 1633).

Dell told the House that while the Government welcomed the merger it had written to GEC asking the firm to allow for regional policies in considering any rationalisation measures after the merger. GEC had agreed to this:

> This merger between two great companies with interests in electrical, engineering, electronics and telecommunications covers many sectors of industrial activity. The full benefits of the merger will become apparent only over a period of time when the new company has decided its policies. We believe, however, that the rationalisation following the merger will strengthen the electronics industry and is likely to be of considerable benefit to other parts of the electrical engineering industry as well (Col. 1634).

AEI – TIDYING UP

Having supported the merger on the ground that it would permit rationalisaton, the IRC was now determined to do all it could to ensure that rationalisation was brought about. There was therefore a series of quarterly meetings between the IRC and GEC, usually represented by Weinstock.

The first meeting, in November 1967, revealed an immediate financial problem. GEC needed £20 million to finance the cash portion of the bid for AEI and £6 million of its money was tied up by a dispute with the South of Scotland Electricity Board over payments for the Hunterston power station. The money might be obtained from the banks, but a bridging loan from the IRC would be very acceptable. In the event, mediation by Kearton enabled GEC and the Electricity Board to settle their differences, and GEC's immediate cash problem was solved.

Apart from some consideration of rationalisation in the nuclear construction field, and on the issue of redundancies, most of the early discussions with GEC concentrated on turbogenerators. Negotiations between GEC and EE had revealed that EE wanted to expand in this field, taking over all GEC and AEI facilities for the production of rotary machinery. Weinstock was at first reluctant but the IRC Board later learned that GEC was prepared to sell the former AEI turbogenerator activities to EE. It was, however, unlikely that agreement would be reached on an exchange of equity, so that EE would have to find substantial funds for the purchase. One suggestion was that the IRC should provide cash by purchasing some £10 million of EE's debtors. Since the IRC was reluctant to do this, Weinstock estimated that the odds were 60:40 against this deal ever taking place. Indeed it never materialised, and the situation in the industry was completely changed by a surprise bid for EE from Plessey.

EE – ANOTHER TAKEOVER BATTLE

On 21 August 1968, Plessey gave the IRC a few hours' notice of the public anouncement of its bid for English Electric. The bid was an audacious gamble by a group whose activities, until a few years before, had been largely confined to electronic components. The very ambitiousness of the move gives an indication of the merger fever of the later 1960s but, from the outset, Plessey's bid sufered from severe handicaps, which were to prove fatal. First, EE was much larger in terms of both assets and employees. Despite its better current profitability, Plessey's bid was bound to lack credibility in the eyes of many observers. Second, and more important, this meant that Plessey could not improve significantly on its initial offer terms. Third, the potential benefits of the merger were limited largely to electronics. This sector was important but the IRC's overriding concern was with restructuring the heavy electrical industry, where Plessey had no interests. Finally, Plessey's bid met with instant and extreme hostility from some of the top management of EE and with little enthusiasm from the government departments or public corporations – such as Defence and Telecommunications – who were Plessey's main customers.

The bid did, however, succeed in bringing to a very rapid conclusion discussions which had only recently started between GEC, EE and the IRC and which had seemed likely to be much more protracted. In July, Weinstock had attended a meeting at the IRC's office in Pall Mall to consider a rearrangement of the nuclear power consortia. As that meeting broke up, he had asked to see Kearton and Villiers alone. He told them that a start had been made on combining GEC and AEI but that he could now see that the whole jigsaw could be put together much more sensibly if GEC also had the EE pieces to fit into it. This meant that the IRC was already seriously examining a possible GEC–EE merger before the announcement of Plessey's bid.

Within a few days, GEC confirmed to the IRC that it was preparing a counter-bid. The IRC already had a considerable understanding of the three companies, but with the merger an immediate issue it was now able to extract more detailed information from Plessey and EE, as well as to confirm and bring up to date its files on GEC. It was clear to each company that this was the kind of situation where the IRC would play a crucial role, and they willingly co-operated in supplying information and discussing issues. The IRC immediately held talks with Mintech and other interested government departments, as well as with the Post Office, the CEGB and all the other major companies in the electrical and electronics industry.

On the basis of its existing knowledge of the industry, plus the information and opinions elicited from these meetings, the IRC executives prepared a case for a Board meeting to be held on 6 September, sixteen days after the announcement of Plessey's bid.

At the Board meeting, the executive explained that Plessey had apologised to the IRC for not giving more time for their proposals to be considered. Plessey's financial advisors had told the IRC that news of the intended bid for EE had leaked out. So an immediate, and premature, announcement had become essential. The executive went on to review the IRC's earlier deliberations on desirable ways of reorganising the electrical and electronics industry but argued that the only practical consideration now was what should happen to EE. This could be considered under three hearings: (a) what was financially practicable; (b) what was sensible in the industry from the standpoint of the national interest; (c) what was practicable, given the abilities and views of the managements of the companies that were involved or could become involved.

Not least amongst the financial considerations was the fact that the £15 million IRC loan to EE could be recalled, at the Corporation's discretion and with a premium of 15 per cent, in the event of a takeover of EE. Nonetheless, the executive felt that Plessey's offer was an attractive one and that it could, if necessary, refinance the IRC loan. GEC had, however, greater financial resources than Plessey. Most other possible realignments with UK electrical companies could be ruled out on financial grounds, unless an agreed deal could be worked out with EE.

To help Board members to consider the industrial implications of the merger the executive set out the involvement and market shares of GEC–AEI, EE and Plessey, as well as of Thorn, Hawker

Siddeley, Reyrolle-Parsons and BICC, in each of the main sections of the industry (electronics, telecommunications, heavy electrical equipment, cables, domestic appliances etc). As we have said, Plessey's interests were almost exclusively in electronics and communications, whereas only about a third of EE's activities were in these areas. Plessey, however, had indicated to the IRC that, after a merger, a deal with Hawker Siddeley was a possibility. Hawker Siddeley had agreed that it might consider such a deal. So, to put Plessey's case in the best possible light, the IRC executive compared possible rationalisation after a GEC–EE deal with a realignment of EE with Plessey and Hawker Siddeley.

The IRC concluded that the arguments, in terms of industrial structure, were still in favour of GEC. The strongest possible UK combination must be achieved because international competition was very strong. It would be sufficient both to protect consumers' interests and to provide a spur for development. In electronics, there was greater scope for rationalisation between GEC and EE, especially in process control, automation and instruments. The combined group would be able to compete in the UK, and one could hope in export markets, with such international giants as IBM, Philips, Honeywell and IT&T. Plessey was strongest in radar and aerospace applications and in components, where the possibilities for growth were sufficient for it to expand without EE. On the electrical side, the balance was also thought to lie with GEC rather than Hawker Siddeley. In particular, the IRC and the CEGB had been trying to bring about a rationalisation of the turbogenerator facilities of EE and GEC. Advantages were also seen in the switchgear, transformer and domestic appliance fields.

The executive admitted that this kind of argument could not be clear cut and that the case should not be overstated. The range of products was very wide and problems of definition, together with the highly technical nature of the industry, made any assessment difficult. On balance, however, the executive argued that more rationalisation could be achieved more effectively and more quickly by GEC than by Plessey, with or without Hawker Siddeley.

This conclusion was clearly influenced by the IRC executive's view of the relative strengths of the managements of the groups. EE was a much respected company but its performance over the previous decade had been disappointing. Plessey's management was thought to be well organised but it was unproven in terms of its ability to give leadership and it was felt that this would be essential to the success of such an important merger.

The IRC executive therefore recommended that a merger between GEC and EE would be preferable to a Plessey–EE merger, to EE trying to remain independent, and to any other realistic alternative.

By the time the IRC Board met to discuss their position on the Plessey and EE bids, they knew what line EE was likely to take. Villiers was able to tell his board that EE would shortly announce that, after considering the alternatives, it had decided to begin discussions with GEC immediately. There had been a worrying moment the day before when the idea of a 'grand alliance' between BICC, Plessey, Thorn, Reyrolle-Parsons and EE had seemed to be gaining support but, after a meeting which the IRC executive had attended, EE had agreed to the announcement of talks with GEC.

Villiers also reported to the meeting that, although there was understandable hostility to a GEC–EE merger from the other companies in the industry, and of course from Plessey, the government and the major public sector customers were not against it. After a very lengthy discussion, members decided that a combination of the businesses of English Electric and the General Electric Company appeared to have greater merit in the national interest than any alternative solution mooted (including the acquisition of English Electric by Plessey). This was so provided that certain conditions were met:

(a) GEC and English Electric were merged in a way acceptable to IRC and recommended by the Boards of both companies.
(b) The IRC had a director on the Board of the merged enterprise.
(c) Firm undertakings were given by the Chairman and Managing Director of the merged enterprise (i) to co-operate with the IRC in effecting further rationalisation with other companies where appropriate, including rationalisation involving hiving-off of certain parts of the new enterprise, and (ii) to consult at an early date with the trade unions and government in advance of closures and the matters affecting the government's regional policy.

Accordingly, the IRC Board decided that it would support a merger between English Electric and GEC subject to the above qualifications, if the situation over the next few days showed this to be practicable. It was also decided that, in the event of a merger between GEC and English Electric, the IRC would give high priority to considering the rationalisation and development of the remainder of the industry.

The IRC Board went on to discuss what measures, if any, it should recommend to protect the public from abuse by this potential

UK monopolist whose creation it had decided to support. Members were also anxious that the best of EE's managers should be given suitable recognition in the new group. It was suggested that the IRC should take an equity stake in GEC–EE but Kearton said Weinstock would accept an IRC director on the GEC Board without this. In addition Lord Aldington, the GEC Chairman, would stand aside in favour of EE's Chairman, Lord Nelson. The IRC Board accepted that these arrangements were sufficient, together with assurances from GEC that it would confer with appropriate trade unions and government departments on any proposals which could significantly affect its employees.

Following the Board meeting, further discussions were held with the other major electrical companies, including Plessey, so that they could be told of the IRC's position before any public announcement was made. Their reaction was by no means uniformally favourable. They were naturally concerned about the competitive strength of the combined group. Some also suggested that EE was technically better than GEC in a number of fields, so that something would be lost if the merger went ahead.

Even more sensitive and crucial were discussions with the government. The IRC circulated a detailed explanaton of its decision to all the relevant departments as well as to Edward Heath, Leader of the Opposition, and his industry spokesman, Keith Joseph. A key meeting then took place at the Board of Trade. The proposed GEC–EE deal was a huge merger in a major industry and it had come as a complete surprise to the civil servants. It seems very likely that, given their attitude to competition, officials in the Board of Trade would have pressed strongly for a reference to the Monopolies Commission. However, a decision of this importance could be taken only by the President of the Board of Trade, then Anthony Crossland, and he summoned Villiers to come and state the IRC case. The IRC was strongly against a reference. In addition to the reasons it had spelt out in supporting the merger, the IRC argued that the delay and uncertainty caused by a Monopolies Commission investigation would be extremely harmful to both companies.

This view prevailed. Indeed, no IRC-backed merger was ever to be referred to the Monopolies Commission. Of course, it would hardly have been sensible for the work of one public body to have been negated by another but, given that Whitehall is less monolithic than it sometimes appears to outsiders, not impossible. The GEC–EE decision, with those that followed it, was also a reflection of the IRC's style of work. The fact that the IRC was very small, had virtually no hierarchy and was constantly looking to anticipate events meant that it could reach decisions, even on complex issues, very quickly. IRC decisions were often made, documented and presented while the wheels in government departments had scarcely begun to turn. And these wheels were designed not to produce decisions but only to recommend, or not to recommend, a reference to another body which itself would take several months to report. On organisation and timing, the Civil Service was no match for the IRC. In Whitehall, it pays to know before anyone else what one wants and to be able to give chapter and verse in support of one's case.

Having established that the government would not intervene, the IRC published a detailed statement supporting the GEC–EE merger on 13 September (included as Appendix 4.1 in this chapter). The EE Board recommended its shareholders to accept the GEC terms and the merger was concluded without further problems.

The IRC's work then proceeded on various fronts. It began to look at ways of strengthening competition with GEC–EE on particular activities; it attempted to make peace between GEC and Plessey; and it continued to look at possible rationalisation in other areas of the industry. Some of the results of this work were described in Chapter 3. In the remainder of this chapter we focus on the IRC's success in following up the mergers and ensuring that the benefits which had been envisaged were realised as fully as possible.

FOLLOW UP

The addition of EE to GEC–AEI made the IRC all the more determined to keep up pressure for effective rationalisation. It did not immediately take up its right to appoint a nominee to the Board of the new group but the quarterly meetings which had been arranged at chief executive level after the AEI merger assumed an even greater importance. These meetings, as well as less formal and more frequent personal contacts between the IRC executive and Weinstock, were a useful way for the IRC to keep in touch with GEC on a wide range of issues. Weinstock discussed his plans for the Scientific Apparatus Division of GEC (SAD) and this helped the IRC to formulate its policy over Kent and Cambridge (see Ch. 5). Weinstock also gave commitments not to dispose of GEC's holdings in the British Aircraft Corporation (BAC) or International Computers Limited (ICL) without IRC agreement. The main purpose of the meetings, however, was to discuss the rationalisation of the group's heavy electrical activities and the consequent financial and employment problems.

GEC made most of the running at the first meeting. It seemed that EE was in a worse financial position than had been anticipated, and Weinstock made no secret of the fact that, in addition to achieving savings in the company's continuing operations, he would have to sell off unwanted assets for cash. Nor was GEC's financial position helped by the fact that, in March 1969, it was due to repay £5 million, plus interest, out of the £15 million advanced by the IRC when EE acquired Elliot Automation. The IRC was sympathetic to GEC's cash flow problems and the repayment of the remaining £10 million was rescheduled.

This concession may well have contributed to IRC's success in meeting its main objectives at the next meeting. It was by then two years since the Elliot Automation–EE merger and eighteen months since the GEC bid for AEI. The IRC thought that it was time to arrange a substantial programme of follow-up visits to see what physical progress had been made. There was wide discussion at the meeting, covering all the points of concern to the Corporation. These included SAD, BAC and ICL; the parts of GEC where rationalisation might lead to substantial redundancies; the activities which were loss makers and which GEC was thinking of selling; and the areas where the IRC was actively looking at rationalisation proposals which might interest GEC. As a result of these discussions, Weinstock agreed to an IRC request that its executives should be allowed to visit any part of GEC. Indeed, he said that they could do this quite freely and without informing him in advance. His only proviso was that certain financial aspects of his businesses should be discussed only with his permission.

Despite the success of this meeting the IRC still felt it advisable to keep up pressure on GEC and in its second annual report, in June, GEC was publicly urged to take up 'the many opportunities' for further reorganisation. Interviewed by *The Times*, neither Villiers nor Lockwood would suggest for publication which parts of GEC should be sold, but they emphasised that these would be peripheral activities (*The Times*, 16 June 1969). *The Times* also revealed an interest in the question of IRC representation on the GEC Board, pointing out that the Corporation now had representatives on the boards of eight companies, but had not yet nominated anyone to GEC. The point was raised again in November 1969 in a parliamentary question from Norman Atkinson. Tony Benn, replying for the government, said that even where there was a government director on the board of a firm, he would deal with the company not through the director but directly with the chairman, 'which is the right way of dealing with the matter' (*HC Deb*, 10 November 1969, Col. 3106). Even so, the IRC took this opportunity to tell

Weinstock that it would take up its option to nominate a director, though it was prepared to wait for a reconstruction of the board, which was planned. No nominee was ever appointed.

The corollary of much of the necessary rationalisation was redundancies, and discussion of the problems that this was likely to produce dominated the quarterly meeting in July 1969. In power engineering, up to 2000 jobs were at risk, and it seemed likely that this would lead to major political and trade union problems. The government had already indicated its concern. GEC's position was that in this, as in other areas, the problems resulted largely from the failure of AEI and EE, before the mergers, to take difficult decisions. GEC also pointed out that, in some cases, the facilities that were being closed were in the more prosperous parts of the UK and that production of the products made there was to be concentrated in areas of high unemployment.

The IRC was concerned to ensure that redundancies were handled as constructively and humanely as possible. It encouraged companies to set up counselling courses, to provide information on alternative employment and to give the longest feasible notice of their intentions. But the IRC certainly did not see itself as in business to encourage unnecessarily high levels of manning, nor uneconomic duplication of activities, nor the operation of obsolescent facilities. Moreover the ultimate decision on redundancies had to be taken by the company concerned, not by the IRC.

THE RESULTS OF RATIONALISATION

By the summer of 1970 the IRC was keen to obtain an overall view of what had taken place in the two years since the merger and GEC was asked to make a presentation on the progress of its rationalisation measures. The managing directors of the main operating groups were asked to explain their problems in amalgamating elements from different companies, and their progress in raising productivity, the return on capital, exports, R & D and training effectiveness.

The presentation was made in late September 1970. Neither Lockwood nor Nelson was able to attend, but the latter reported to the IRC that he was very satisfied with the progress made. The presentation showed that, since the merger with AEI, the total workforce had been reduced by about 20 per cent, or 40 000. The aim was now to increase profitability with higher sales from the same, or fewer, people. The presentation lasted for six hours and left Villiers very enthusiastic. He told Weinstock that he was full of satisfaction, even excitement, at the way in which the concept embarked upon three years earlier was coming true.

Of course problems remain to this day, but one can rate the merging of GEC, AEI and EE as a success. Certainly, GEC has increased its profits – from £18 million on a turnover of £180 million in 1966–67 to £207 million on a turnover of £1752 million in 1975–76 and £416 million on a turnover of £3000 million in 1979–80, with exports accounting for over 25 per cent of this. GEC has a high technical and financial reputation and, with the period of large-scale redundancy over, as an employer. Profits have represented a return on sales of well over 10 per cent, and with the difficult economic and industrial scene in the UK, and intense competition for export business at a time of low growth throughout the world, high UK inflation and a strong pound, this has been an impressive performance.

COMMENTS

Its involvement with the heavy electrical industry faced the IRC with important policy issues. First, and most important, the Corporation had to decide whether to take sides in the contested GEC bid for AEI and, later, whether to back GEC against Plessey in the bid for EE. In retrospect, the IRC seems, on each occasion, to have backed the right side. At the very least, it would be impossible to argue that, up to 1980, the results of the enlargement of GEC have been unsatisfactory, though more difficult days may well lie ahead, with considerable and persistent over-capacity in the production of transformers and generators. Moreover, had these mergers not taken place, it is difficult to see how AEI or EE could have survived as independent companies. Apart from GEC, which had been transformed since Weinstock took charge, the major companies in the industry lacked clear structure and financial strength. Further, the heavy electrical industry, after the high investment by the CEGB in the early 1960s, was faced with an imperative need for a massive shake-out. There is room for many views on how this might have been done, but it is difficult to see how such major changes could have been achieved in such a relatively orderly way and with such little apparent long-term damage except through the creation of the present GEC. In Arnold Weinstock, the IRC found a man possessing almost the ideal qualities for implementing such restructuring. Two qualities above all were needed, and each of them Weinstock possessed to the full. First, he had the ability to identify, grasp and tackle problems – never pushing them away. Having identified rational solutions with intellectual clarity, he would push those solutions through, however unpalatable they might be. Second, he had the ability to delegate real authority to managers so that the massive tasks of reorganisation could be carried out.

No-one would claim that mistakes were not made, or that opportunities were not lost, but without these mergers the UK electrical industry would have had little chance of matching the capabilities, in technology and in selling in world markets, of groups like Siemens or General Electric of America. And when a final view comes to be taken on Weinstock and GEC, it is by comparison with such groups that the judgment will have to be made.

The second major issue faced by the IRC was how best to ensure that the group it had helped to form would not abuse its market position, and yet would carry through the rationalisation which the mergers made possible. At the time of the merger with EE, considerable weight was given to the assurances made by GEC, and to the IRC's right to put a representative on the GEC Board. The IRC never insisted on this right, though the option to do so existed up to the time the Corporation was disbanded. Instead, the IRC relied on the regular meetings with the GEC management, backed up by plant visits and by personal contacts with Weinstock which gave direct access to GEC's thinking. In this way, the IRC was kept informed on GEC's policies and on the progress of rationalisation. The extent to which the IRC was able to influence GEC is more open to doubt, but it is unlikely that an IRC director would have achieved as much as did the close understanding that developed between the managing directors of GEC and the IRC.

Weinstock emerged as Britain's most successful large-scale industrial manager in the 1970s, and the IRC must have been right to back him. The three companies now brought together in GEC had tried to merge at various times in the past and the IRC was clearly justified in acting as a catalyst. It was also right in continuing to monitor the results in various ways until it was wound up. What remains to be seen is how the GEC Board and shareholders perform once Weinstock's remarkable abilities are no longer available to them. Unless another industrial leader is found to continue the job, some of the benefits which Weinstock has achieved from the merger may be lost. If they are, one must remember that businesses rarely experience continuous progress. Even if GEC without Weinstock is less successful than at present, this provides no reason for regretting what has been achieved during the last decade. Weinstock's bid brought success and the IRC can claim the credit for having seen that he was the right man to back.

Finally we may note the debate within the IRC on whether or not it should have taken sides publicly in a controversial and contested merger. From the time of the AEI bid onwards, the IRC did take sides on almost every occasion when it was involved. Its Board members felt that their business careers fitted them to decide correctly on such issues where they were well informed. The IRC collectively took the view that, where it had access to the necessary information, it had a responsibility both to make a judgement on what was to be done and to act on this. After the GEC–AEI merger, the IRC was not always successful, but its activities were always well researched. The Civil Service, the CBI, the TUC and much of industry and the City came to welcome the intervention of the IRC in difficult industrial situations, where money was needed, management changes required, or where log-jams existed and, as in the electrical industry, an outside body was needed to break them up. The GEC mergers were a turning point both in the IRC's activities and for its public image.

APPENDIX 4.1

This appendix comprises the full text of the IRC's statement on the GEC–EE merger which was issued on 13 September 1968.

IRC STATEMENT ON THE MERGER OF THE ENGLISH ELECTRIC COMPANY AND THE GENERAL ELECTRIC COMPANY, 13TH SEPTEMBER, 1968

At its Board Meeting on 6th September, 1968, the IRC after considering full and objective studies of all feasible alternatives decided to support the proposed merger of The English Electric Company and The General Electric Company, subject to certain assurances which have been given and to which reference is made in the last paragraph of this statement. At the same Board Meeting, the IRC also decided to defer announcing its support for this merger until HM Government had had time to consider whether it should be referred to the Monopolies Commission. The IRC also wished to have further discussions with certain of the companies concerned as well as with Government Departments, and these have now been held.

IRC believes that the proposed merger is a further major step in promoting the efficiency, profitability and potential of the electrical and electronics industry in the UK and strengthening its competitive position in world markets. The facts and reasoning underlying IRC's support are as follows:

From its formation in December, 1966, IRC has given high priority to the range of industries concerned primarily with the twin technologies of electrical engineering and electronics. These industries employ a large proportion of the UK's scarce resources of scientists, engineers and technicians and are engaged in many activities which have a direct and fundamental effect on the country's economic growth and its balance of payments. Even a slight improvement in their productivity is therefore worth much effort to achieve; and there was every reason to suppose that the changes in industrial structure which IRC was set up to bring about would effect more than a slight improvement. IRC, therefore, with the help and co-operation of the Ministry of Technology, set out to gain as much experience as possible of these industries in the belief that this was essential if opportunities for reorganisation were to be properly assessed. IRC was fortunate in being invited almost immediately by the Government to undertake a survey of the telecommunications industry and its relations with the Post Office. This survey, which was carried out with full co-operation from the industry, covered the whole field of telecommunications equipment and thus afforded IRC an insight into the complexities and structure of a large part of the electrical/electronics industry. Simultaneously with this survey, IRC was investigating the whole heavy electrical engineering field where the rundown in the Generating Board's orders foreshadowed severe problems of excess capacity, to meet which rationalisation was urgently needed. Surveys were also undertaken at this time into other parts of the industry, in particular domestic appliances, scientific instruments, industrial process control and automation, and data processing computers.

By the middle of 1967, IRC had helped to bring about one important structural move – the merging of Elliott-Automation into English Electric – and was actively considering a number of others. By the end of the year, GEC with IRC support had combined its business with that of Associated Electrical Industries – a move which was intended to have and has already had profound effects on the structure and balance of the whole industry. In the following months, IRC participated in a number of smaller but significant operations in the scientific instruments field, and widened its experience of the electrical/electronics industry in a number of other sectors, including motor control gear, numerical control of machine tools, satellite ground stations, electronic valves, lamps and lighting and microelectronics.

In all this IRC has followed a policy of learning as much as possible about the companies, visiting different subsidiaries and talking with all levels of management in order to form a view of the relative significance of the companies in the areas in which they compete. It has also studied relevant reports of Economic Development Committees, the Prices and Incomes Board and the Monopolies Commission, and has had the benefit of working closely with the Department of Economic Affairs, the Ministry of Technology and the Board of Trade. By the time of the announcement of The Plessey Company's bid for English Electric on 21st August, IRC had therefore acquired over twenty-one months an understanding of large areas of the electrical/electronics industry.

The Plessey bid involved IRC for three reasons. First – and most important – it was immediately apparent to IRC that the bid raised some fundamental questions about the desirable structure for the whole electrical/electronics industry. In view of the duties entrusted to it by Parliament, IRC therefore had a clear responsibility to form a view. Secondly, IRC was an interested party financially since the terms of the £15 million loan made by IRC to English Electric at the time of the Elliott-Automation merger allowed IRC to demand repayment of this loan at a substantial premium in the event of English Electric becoming a subsidiary of another company. Finally, Plessey informed IRC before making the bid and Plessey, English Electric and GEC independently sought IRC's views.

Following the announcement of the Plessey bid, discussions took place at once with the Ministry of Technology and the other Government Departments primarily concerned. Both Plessey and English Electric were invited to give IRC detailed information in confidence to enable it to assess the rationalisation and development opportunities afforded by the proposed merger. The same information was subsequently requested from GEC, which had made its interest in a merger with English Electric plain to IRC well before the Plessey bid. All three companies co-operated fully. IRC also had a number of meetings with their top managements and in addition invited the views of the top managements of all the other major companies with substantial activities in the electrical/electronics sector and sufficient financial or commercial strength to allow them to become materially involved in the bid situation if they chose. Certain relevant information was also requested and obtained from some of these companies. Finally, IRC obtained the views of the Post Office, the Electricity Generating Board and the British Railways Board.

In the course of these discussions, a number of alternative concepts of the desirable structure for the electrical/electronics industry were put to IRC. All these concepts, including a merger of English Electric with either Plessey or GEC, were carefully considered by IRC, having regard to the opportunities for rationalisation and development which they afforded and to the likely ability of the managements concerned to make the most of these opportunities. In considering Plessey's bid for English Electric IRC gave full weight to the possibility of certain subsequent rationalisation measures involving the hiving off of parts of the merged enterprise. IRC concluded that, of all the practicable alternatives, a combination of the businesses of English Electric and GEC appeared most likely to assist the economy of the UK. This conclusion was based on the belief that it must be in the national interest to create the strongest possible companies, in terms of managerial, financial, technical and other resources, to compete in international markets, and also on the industrial case for such a merger, the arguments for which are summarised in general terms below:

1 On the *electrical engineering* side, the potential rationalisation benefits are substantial as the following examples demonstrate. In *turbo-generators*, the merger would achieve at one stroke a situation which IRC and the CEGB have been trying to bring about for many months, namely the rationalisation of the industry into two groups with roughly equal shares of the home market. In the case of *power*

transformers where the CEGB and IRC have again been concerned to effect a reduction in the number of suppliers, the merger would bring together the English Electric business with approximately 25% of the home market and the GEC business with around 20% and would thereby offer substantial rationalisation opportunities without creating too dominant a supplier. The same is true of *distribution transformers*, where the fragmented state of the industry has caused severe problems. There would also be scope for rationalisation both in *grid switchgear* and *smaller switchgear* where the combined concern would have around 70% and 40% of the home market respectively. The existence of a monopoly home buyer and another substantial supplier mitigates the effect of the dominant position in grid switchgear. In the ranges of both *large electrical machines* and *small motors* there is again much overlap between the businesses of GEC and English Electric which together would have approximately 40% of the UK market. The merged enterprise would nonetheless still face strong competition over the full range of electrical machines and motors. Finally, in *traction equipment* the two companies would together have a dominant position at home with possible monopoly disadvantages to offset the rationalisation benefits. However, in this case the one large home buyer, British Rail, already has its own workshops and both companies are in any event heavily reliant on export business on which they have been co-operating successfully for some time.

2 On the *electronics* side, the merger offers much scope for the development of a powerful position in international markets with attendant opportunities for rationalisation at home and overseas. It was in this area that the industrial case presented by Plessey was at its strongest but even here IRC considered that the same general arguments applied with even greater force to a combination of the businesses of GEC and English Electric. In *telecommunications*, for example, the business of GEC may be regarded as complementary to that of Marconi in such a way as to give an excellent 'systems capability' particularly in view of GEC's position as one of the two largest suppliers to the Post Office in the field of transmission and microwave equipment (the other being Standard Telephone & Cables, a subsidiary of the American company, International Telephone & Telegraph). Domestic competition in the telecommunications area would be largely unaffected by a GEC/English Electric merger. In *process control and automation* GEC is not as strong as English Electric, but has much to offer the latter in terms of reinforcement and rationalisation opportunities. Domestic competition again remains strong, not least in view of UK subsidiaries of certain American firms. The fields of *radar, navigational aids and radio communications* are ones in which the English Electric businesses have a larger total turnover than any other UK competitor, though in particular areas other companies may have a competitive edge. Nevertheless, there would be considerable opportunities for rationalisation and development as a result of combining the activities of GEC and English Electric in these fields. Although GEC

allied to English Electric would be very strong, the market is largely international and the competition from foreign companies very keen, particularly in the important area of satellite ground stations. In *electronic components*, GEC and English Electric each have major companies manufacturing industrial types of elecronic valves and cathode ray tubes, which together have more than 40% of the UK market and offer scope for rationalisation since there is a material degree of overlap in their product ranges. Neither company makes passive components to any great extent. In *micro-electronics*, English Electric has a fast-growing operation of its own, while GEC has the semiconductor business acquired with AEI and a one-third stake in the Mullard (Philips) subsidiary, Associated Semiconductor Manufacturers. As far as the particular field of microelectronics is concerned, IRC recognises that there could in some circumstances be greater benefits from Plessey joining forces with English Electric in view of the urgent need to develop the UK effort in this field in the face of strong competition from American firms.

3 Among the other product areas in which a GEC/English Electric merger offers significant scope for rationalisation are rectifiers, electrical instruments, control gear, domestic appliances, and X-ray equipment. Each company has successful independent instrument businesses but in rather different fields which are barely complementary: GEC in electron microscopes and mass spectrometers and English Electric in electronic measuring and test instruments. Among the major product groups of the two companies in which there is little or no overlap are diesel engines, cables, lamps and lighting, and radio and TV sets.

4 In addition to the material improvements in the export capability of the two companies which should result from the merger, there would also be substantial gains to be derived from the integration and development of their overseas manufacturing and selling operations. The elimination of inevitably wasted effort by the two companies in seeking large overseas contracts and the concentration of British technical and sales effort would be very much in the national interest.

In deciding to support a GEC/English Electric merger, IRC took full account of three other important factors: competition, the extent to which the GEC management was still absorbed with the integration of AEI into the group, and the position of the rest of the industry in the event of the merger becoming effective:

(*a*) As regards competition, IRC after careful study formed the opinion that there would be strong and effective competition for the merged company both at home and overseas across the whole range of its products with the sole possible exceptions of electric traction equipment and heavy switchgear, in both of which areas there was a dominant customer at home and the other supplier was part of a powerful group.

(*b*) The integration of the businesses of AEI with those of GEC is a huge task and one which has to be done effectively if the full benefits of the merger between GEC and AEI are to be realised. IRC therefore had some misgivings that a merger between GEC and English Electric would overburden the management to the detriment of the new group. To a lesser extent, IRC was also concerned lest the merger would react unfavourably on the integration of Elliott-Automation into the English Electric group. IRC has discussed its concern with the management of GEC and has had access to GEC's current trading results and to the detailed month by month reports from second and third line management in the areas of GEC's business mainly concerned. It has also questioned the management of English Electric about the progress made in integrating Elliott-Automation into English Electric. As a result IRC is satisfied that the top managements of GEC and English Electric are in a position to devote their attention to the task of making the most of the opportunities afforded by the proposed merger. There is the further point that the integration of AEI into the GEC group continues to require many decisions which could be taken to better effect, and against a background of wider rationalisation opportunities, if GEC merged with English Electric. To this extent, the sooner the merger with English Electric takes place the better the rationalisation which can be achieved. Moreover, the best of the management available in the two companies could be deployed more effectively within the combined enterprise than if the two companies remained as separate organisations.

(*c*) IRC has given much thought to the position of the remainder of the industry in the event of a GEC/English Electric merger becoming effective. It cannot accept the view that the new company is bound to have harmful effects simply because it is larger than any other single company engaged primarily in the electrical/electronics industry. It notes that there are several UK-controlled companies in competitive opposition to the proposed GEC/English Electric group which are themselves of major size and financial strength by any standards. It is also aware of the ever-growing force of international competition and the presence in the UK of large and thriving subsidiaries of foreign-controlled firms, including Philips, IBM, International Telephone & Telegraph and Honeywell. Nevertheless, IRC recognises the importance to the economy of the major UK-controlled firms which will be competing with the new company on the domestic front and is willing to assist these firms and also their smaller competitors in any way it can. To this end IRC is studying the opportunities for constructive rationalisation and development in the remainder of the industry and is ready to enter into discussions with any firm, large or small, in furthering this objective.

Finally, the IRC Board had before it at its Meeting on 6th September certain assurances from both Plessey and GEC. The assurances given by GEC were endorsed by English Electric and referred among other things to the proposed new company's intention (*a*) to confer with the appropriate Trades Unions and Government Departments about any matters arising from the merger which would significantly affect the work people, and with appropriate Government Departments about other action having an important bearing on the Government's regional policies, and (*b*) to accept an IRC nominated Director on the Board of the new company and renegotiate the IRC loan to English Electric.

13th September, 1968

5

Rank, Kent and Cambridge

In May 1965, Mr John Davis, Managing Director of the Rank Organisation, invited Dr Erasmus Barlow, Managing Director of Cambridge Instruments (CI) to dinner. Davis suggested a merger that would combine Rank's instruments subsidiary, Rank Taylor Hobson (RTH), with CI, but Barlow thought the time inopportune (Morley and Jones, 1968). Rank did not renew its approach to CI until the spring of 1968, when it again sought an agreed merger. CI wanted only discussions on technical cooperation and a meeting on 5 April 1968 left Rank 'convinced that Cambridge was not prepared to merge with them at any price. One Cambridge man went so far as to say that the two companies had nothing in common' (Morley and Jones, 1968). Since agreement seemed impossible, on 9 April Rank made a bid for CI which was to launch the IRC into its first, and its most controversial, stock market intervention.

THE IRC AND THE SCIENTIFIC INSTRUMENT INDUSTRY

The IRC had been studying the instrument industry since its formation in 1966. From the beginning, the IRC had seen this as exactly the kind of industry that it should try to reorganise. There was a large number of smallish companies, many of them with excellent technical reputations but lacking both in financial strength and in general efficiency. A great deal of information had been analysed by the IRC covering all the major companies in the industry although, significantly, little detailed information had been collected on RTH. This was partly because Rank's main interests were in other fields but also because RTH's own activities were not seen as central to the industry. It was producing 'laboratory' or 'scientific' rather than 'industrial' equipment. Even so, it had built up substantial and successful interests in lenses and in high quality measuring devices.

The turnover of the industry was estimated at about £180 million per annum and the scope of its activities ranged from producing specialist instruments for laboratory use to the relatively large-scale production of process control devices and instruments for other industrial applications. RTH's turnover was about £11 million and CI's about half this. GEC and EMI had subsidiaries producing similar instruments, as did several American companies, but the largest UK independent company was George Kent with a turnover of about £23 million, chiefly in industrial instruments. Other independent companies included Hilger and Watts (H&W) which, like CI and RTH, specialised in laboratory instruments, and Negretti and Zambra which specialised in instruments with medical applications.

During its investigations the IRC had found a strong prejudice, among the independent companies, against becoming part of a large conglomerate. Their main argument was that this industry, more than most others, depended on the contribution made by a handful of key scientists and engineers who were more likely to flourish in relatively independent organisations. On the other hand, it was widely acknowledged that some concentration of the UK industry was needed if it was to remain competitive in world markets. The benefits on concentration were seen to be (a) greater financial strength – giving an ability to invest more in research and development, which was vital; (b) the greater marketing strength, particularly overseas, that increased turnover would allow; (c) the ability to offer higher salaries and greater opportunities to management and to make more effective use of the best managers in the industry; (d) mutual stimulation in R & D and, perhaps, some savings from rationalisation; (e) benefits derived from the exchange of know-how on production techniques and from the rationalisation of production.

The IRC had already been involved in one successful deal in the industry, helping Nuclear Enterprises to take over the nucleonic instrument business of EMI and Elliott Automation, with EMI keeping a minority interest. Indeed, when the Rank offer was announced, the IRC was still discussing several other proposals. It was inevitable that the IRC would take a view on the merits of Rank's bid for CI and, given the conclusions of its study of the industry, this view was not likely to be one of unqualified approval.

BIDS AND COUNTER-BIDS

The value of the Rank bid for CI depended on its own share price and when it was announced on 9 April it was worth just over 33*s*

(£1.65p) per CI share. It was not an ungenerous offer, pitched about *7s* (35p) above the market price before the bid, and giving a price to earnings ratio of between 20 and 25. The stock market clearly expected some kind of battle and CI's share price soon rose to almost £2. The CI board, predictably, announced that the offer was unacceptable and set about looking for an alternative deal which would block Rank's approach.

The IRC did not take an immediate stand and Villiers's initial inclination was not to take sides. He at once asked Davis to come to the IRC to explain Rank's position. A first meeting took place on 29 April. Davis said that for some time his board had been considering suitable ways of increasing its involvement in the instrument industry. Rank wanted CI because the two firms' product ranges were complementary, Rank could provide considerable drive and the two firms' marketing resources could be rationalised. Davis reported that Rank was also interested in other firms, including H&W, but hoped first to negotiate a settlement with Cambridge.

Rank emphasised that it wished to be included in the IRC's plans for the instrument industry and that it would not need government finance to persuade it to take part in rationalisation moves.

Meanwhile, CI had been active. Having studied alternative solutions, CI's first preference was to negotiate a deal with GEC, involving the Scientific Apparatus Division of AEI (SAD). Negotiations, although friendly, soon broke down because Weinstock would not accept the valuation being put on CI. CI then began discussions with George Kent. On 5 May, while these talks were under way, Rank issued its formal offer document. The next day it told the IRC that it would also be bidding for H&W.

Kent and CI then moved quickly and, after informing the IRC, announced on 15 May that terms had been concluded for an agreed merger. This valued CI shares at 42*s* 6*d* (£2.12½p) against Rank's offer which, thanks to a rise in the price of Rank's own shares, was then worth 35*s* 9*d* (£1.82½p).

On 17 May Rodney Kent, Chairman of George Kent, explained his plans to the IRC. He said that if the deal with CI was successful he would then want to acquire H&W, which he regarded as complementary to CI, and probably Negretti and Zambra as well. He saw Kent as being the nucleus around which an integrated 'British Instruments Corporation' could be formed. He envisaged that he would need finance beyond his company's own resources and asked the IRC to consider a medium-term loan of £5 million. The IRC made no commitment, at this stage, either on support or on finance. It told Kent that the matter would be considered at an IRC Board meeting on 31 May.

Three days later, on 20 May, Rank announced that it would increase its offer. So, when the IRC Board met, it was already clear that a decision to back Kent would involve a fight with a large and profitable company.

DECIDING THE IRC'S STANCE

The IRC executive prepared a brief for the Board's meeting. It set out the events that had taken place since the beginning of April and reviewed the conclusions reached from its own study of the industry. It also made an assessment of the case for the IRC becoming involved with Rank, Kent and CI and of the relative merits of the two bids. The IRC executive argued that (a) the scientific instrument industry was very important both from the point of view of balance of payments and the development of technology in the economy; and (b) in a number of areas covered by the industry, the UK was pre-eminent in world markets and this could be said of very few UK industries. On both grounds it was an industry to which IRC should give the closest attention.

On the merger question, the executive concluded that there was a marginally better case for CI being acquired by Kent than by Rank. Three main reasons were put forward. The first was based on industrial logic. CI's product range overlapped very little with either Rank's or Kent's. However, a greater proportion of CI's turnover was sold to the same markets as Kent's, so that greater rationalisation of marketing effort ought to be achieved. In addition, the IRC put some weight on Kent's claim that its activities in industrial applications meant that it would benefit greatly from CI's strength in advanced laboratory instruments. Today's laboratory instruments, it was argued, became the industrial instruments of five or ten years ahead.

The second argument in favour of Kent was that CI's management had expressed strong support for Kent and strong hostility to Rank. Third, the IRC executive felt that Kent–CI, as an autonomous scientific instruments company, would be a more attractive nucleus for further rationalisation of the industry than would a subsidiary of Rank.

The arguments in favour of Rank were seen as its greater financial strength, possibly stronger management resources, and greater market consciousness. On balance, though, the executive recommended in favour of Kent. Before the Board's meeting, further discussions were held with Rank. Rank had not yet put a value on its new bid, so the IRC tried to persuade it to consider the alternative of a joint company. This could involve Kent, CI, H&W and Rank's subsidiary RTH. Rank would have a substantial shareholding, of possibly 25 per cent.

Rank resisted this idea as well as the suggestion that it should delay its revised bid for CI. It insisted, again, that Cambridge would be a particularly suitable partner for RTH. Davis had initiated friendly discussions, and could not understand why the CI Board would not accept Rank's offer. Nor could he understand why the IRC seemed to agree that Kent's bid must stand, and yet wanted to prevent Rank from making its own promised second bid. This was unfair to Cambridge shareholders. Rank was not interested in a minority stake; management problems always arose where companies did not have clear, dominant leadership. Rank had initiated the merger movement in the scientific instrument field. Why should what was in both its own shareholders' and the national interest be discouraged?

Rank therefore went ahead with its revised offer which was set at 48*s* (£2.40p), about 15*s* (75p) per share above its first bid and about 5*s* (25p) above Kent's. When the IRC Board met, it could hardly have been unaware of the seriousness of Rank's interest. Nonetheless, members if anything took a stronger line in favour of Kent than the executive. The balance of the argument was put at 60:40 in Kent's favour. Given this, the Board felt that the Corporation should use its considerable statutory powers, and its financial resources, to support its judgment.

The IRC had already consulted its sponsoring department, the DEA, and Mintech, which was responsible for the instruments industry. Both were in favour of IRC support for Kent. Board members therefore discussed the form that IRC intervention could take. The options were (a) a direct IRC bid for Cambridge; (b) the formation of a new company to acquire both Kent and Cambridge; and (c) active support for Kent in its own bid. It was estimated that the total cost of IRC intervention, plus support for subsequent rationalisation, could be £10–15 million. Members accepted this, subject to two provisos. First, they decided that the method of intervention should be support for Kent's bid rather than more direct IRC involvement. Second, they wanted a clear maximum to be put on the IRC's financial support, which should be on a scale commensurate with the profits of the combined companies and the likely commercial returns.

With hindsight it can be argued that, even at that stage, the IRC Board should have seen that this second condition could not be met. The revised Rank bid implied a price to earnings ratio for Cambridge shares of well over 30, and Kent would undoubtedly have to go above this to beat Rank. The Board, led by its Chairman, Kearton, was taking a decision of principle hedged by a sensible practical constraint that was almost certain to be ignored. It seems that Villiers would have favoured a more cautious line of action. After all, the case for supporting Kent against Rank was arguable and the price of doing so was certain to be high. Villiers had, however, been in his job only for a few months and had probably not yet gained the full confidence of the Board. Once the decision had been made, though, he deployed all his own and his organisation's skills in ensuring that the IRC won its first takeover battle.

IRC SUPPORT FOR KENT – THE BATTLE JOINED

The IRC Board had met on the Friday before Whitsun 1968 and a series of meetings was held over the bank holiday weekend. These chiefly concerned the tactics for Kent's counter-bid and the proposed management structure for the Kent–CI group, but they also involved H&W. Three meetings were held on Whit Monday, 3 June. The first was with the Chairman, Managing Director and Finance Director of H&W to discuss their provision of up-to-date financial information on which an offer for the company could be based. Like CI, H&W expressed a strong preference for joining Kent rather than Rank. The second meeting was with Barlow, then Chairman of CI, and his Managing Director, Webster. The purpose of this meeting was to enable the IRC to hear their views on the detailed discussions of management structure that had been taking place over the weekend. This is an example of the care taken by the IRC to ensure that there should be no misunderstanding between those involved in the mergers it backed. Peter Wilsher later reported in *The Sunday Times*:

> The largest amount of time was taken up in preparing a full, detailed plan for the management structure, organisation and commercial policies of the new Kent–Cambridge company. . . .
>
> In all its recent interventions . . . it [the IRC] has refused to commit a penny until it has down on paper, and agreed among the boards and senior managers of the firms involved, a specific timetable and chart showing who is going to move where on what date to do what job, with a clear understanding that anyone not prepared to fit in will be expected to fade swiftly from the scene . . . (Wilsher, 1968).

In this case, the IRC's care was reinforced by a concern about the management strength of both companies. While existing managers were capable of running their own parts of the company there were still doubts about their ability to handle the necessary rationalisation measures and there was a clear possibility that a new chief executive would have to be found from outside the group.

Nevertheless, the IRC was now committed to supporting Kent and, at the third meeting on 3 June, Rodney Kent and his Chief Executive, Hartop, joined Barlow, Webster and their financial advisors to work out the terms of Kent's new offer. It was decided to match, but not to exceed, the value of Rank's second bid. This would be done by adding 5*s* (25p) per share to Kent's original offer to bring it up to about 48*s* (£2.40).

Further meetings were held on 4 June, when it was decided that Kent had sufficient resources to make the increased offer without immediate financial support from the IRC. Kent's bankers agreed with this and both the IRC and Kent drafted press announcements for release, with the new offer, at 16.00 on the next day, 5 June. Before this, however, the IRC made a final attempt to reach agreement with Rank. Kearton and Villiers went to Rank's offices to see Davis and his advisors on the morning of 5 June and told them what was planned. Davis said that Rank's position was unchanged. Villiers also went to see Lord Aldington, Chairman of GEC, to explain the IRC's action and to make it clear that the IRC had no general prejudice against conglomerates. GEC accepted this assurance and was, in any case, quite unperturbed by the IRC's support for Kent.

Kent's revised bid went ahead. The IRC was well aware that this was unlikely to be the end of the fight and that if Kent's offer had to be increased again IRC money would be needed. Any use of its funds in the takeover battle would have serious political implications. So, also on 5 June, Villiers went to see the Leader of the Opposition, Edward Heath. Heath thanked him for the advance warning but could say only that he disliked the prospect of the use of public money in this situation, which raised issues to which his party would have to give serious consideration.

The battle, which had been simmering through April and May, now came rapidly to the boil. CI's financial advisors, who had been buying CI shares in the market, urged the IRC to do the same. In particular they suggested that the IRC should try to buy a block of about 600 000 CI shares owned by the R.W. Paul Investment Trust (PIT). At first, the IRC hesitated because it did not want to push the CI share price above the value put on them by Kent's bid, but it soon became clear that Rank was not going to withdraw and that Kent would not win without active help. So on 11 June, the IRC met the trustees of PIT at the Royal Society and offered 50*s* (£2.50) per share for their holding. The next day, before they had reached a decision, Rank announced that it would increase its offer to 55*s* (£2.75p) per share.

However, CI's financial advisors had now acquired about 8 per cent of CI's equity and this, together with the CI Board's substantial holding, put them in a strong position. It was therefore decided that Kent should again match Rank's bid and that the IRC would then make every effort to ensure that this was successful. The IRC's support took three forms. First, to finance an increased bid it was necessary for Kent to issue new shares and the IRC agreed to underwrite 25 per cent of this issue. Second, the IRC would buy as many CI shares as possible at a maximum price of 55*s* per share. Third, the IRC would also buy Kent shares in the market, if necessary, to keep up their price.

On 13 June at 10.00 the IRC executive went back to the Royal Society and this time succeeded in acquiring the PIT holding for 55*s* per share. During the rest of that day the IRC holding was increased, through purchases on the stock market, to just under 20 per cent of CI's equity.

Also on 13 June, Rank and H&W announced that they had reached agreement on terms for a merger. Since Kent was now likely to be stretched both financially and managerially by the bid for CI, it was decided that no action should be taken by the IRC to oppose Rank over H&W.

On 14 June Kent issued a press announcement giving details of its revised offer, matching Rank's bid. The IRC's acquisition of CI shares was also announced. During the day the IRC bought a further 2 per cent of CI's equity and at 21.00 Kent's financial advisors were able to announce that 'acceptance and assured acceptances of the Kent offer have now been received in respect of more than 50 per cent of the CI shares'.

During the next few days the IRC bought several large blocks of Kent shares in the market, spending almost £750 000, to keep the price at a reasonable level until the fuss died down. On 18 June, Kent was able to issue its formal offer documents and, as it had assurances of over 50 per cent acceptance, to declare the offer unconditional, subject to the shareholders and the Stock Exchange approving the issue of the necessary new shares. On 19 June Rank formally withdrew and the battle for the control of CI was over. (Appendix 5.1 sets out the timing and the value of the successive bids.)

THE POLITICAL REACTION

The IRC's action had been conducted in a massive glare of publicity. Not only had every move been analysed in the City pages but all the serious press had long features on the issues involved and most had leading articles too. Even the Archbishop of Canterbury felt moved to write a long letter to *The Times* in support of the IRC's action. Mintech also appeared very pleased. It felt that it was a major achievement to have decided a takeover battle on grounds of 'industrial logic' rather than financial strength. But other comment was by no means generally favourable and the CBI expressed concern. The issue was one of principle. Should the IRC have used public money to intervene in the market in this way? John Davies, Director General of the CBI, pointed out that business had been suspicious about the activities of the IRC from the beginning, but he had tried to allay these suspicions. The IRC, which had already done valuable work and would no doubt continue to do so, must not damage its reputation with industry at large. Later, in preparation for a further CBI Council discussion of Kent—Cambridge, CBI officials summarised the issues as they saw them.

The CBI's summary can be described as follows.

The IRC case was that the Kent–CI group would provide a nucleus for further amalgamation in the scientific instrument industry; that there had been an agreed merger between Kent and CI, which did not wish to enter the Rank empire; and that a large group like Rank, with wide interests, was not the best vehicle for rationalising the industry. On the other side, there were disquieting issues; the IRC had manipulated public funds as if it were a merchant bank; and it had clinched victory by securing a sizeable CI holding from the PIT, though, of course, Rank could have done the same. The IRC might argue that public interests should prevail over commercial ones, but it had been bidding against Rank on a remarkable 40-times price to earnings ratio. This might be acceptable so long as members of the IRC Board were reputable figures, but a future Board, composed of less industrially experienced and more doctrinaire members, could use the Rank–Kent–CI fight as a dangerous precedent. Moreover, the IRC was not open to detailed public interrogation.

Their conclusion was that, thus far, the CBI's suspicions had been allayed, but that there must always be room for argument over how far the substantial sums of public money readily available to the IRC were used to its own advantage. The CBI would continue to watch the IRC's actions. Its public status, it was argued, required it to operate more carefully than its directors would perhaps be accustomed to do, in similar circumstances, in the conduct of their private affairs.

The Conservative Party, despite the IRC's efforts, was more openly hostile and called a parliamentary debate early in July. Villiers had followed up his meeting with Heath with a long explanation and justification of the IRC's action. He emphasised that the IRC had observed the 'City Code' in letter and spirit (indeed, the City's takeover panel had resisted attempts to persuade it to make a formal inquiry into the IRC's action). Moreover, the IRC had deprived no-one of money, but had paid a fair price, as between willing buyer and willing seller, for all the shares it had acquired. More important, the IRC had assured a future structure for the instrument industry which, in the business judgment of all the IRC Board members, was the one most likely to bear fruit. The IRC had no quarrel with Rank, but the judgment had been made that Kent was the central company in the UK instrument industry. If it was to develop a capacity to make and sell systems, and to compete internationally with Honeywell and Foxboro (its leading US competitors), it had to acquire CI. If CI had gone to Rank the industry would have become unbalanced, Villiers argued. A critical moment for changing its structure would have passed, leaving only a second-best solution.

The IRC also briefed other leading Tories for the debate, as well as its own Minister at the DEA, Peter Shore. The Tories' motion 'That this house, while upholding the independence of the IRC, deplores its action in intervening with public money on behalf of one bidder in a merger operation, and regards such action as a dangerous precedent for the future' was defeated by 307 votes to 223. Perhaps the Conservatives never forgave the Corporation for its arrogant interference with market forces.

THE IRC'S COMMITMENT

The IRC had paid about £4.3 million for approximately 30 per cent of CI's equity. In addition, it had bought £700000 worth of Kent shares. It was due to receive £1 million of disposable Kent loan stock as part payment for its CI shares, but it had a further potential commitment of up to £2.8 million for underwriting Kent's share issue. It had also promised up to £2.5 million to assist with the rationalisation and further development of the new group. By the time financial arrangements for the merger had been completed the IRC was likely to be holding almost 25 per cent of Kent's enlarged equity and the IRC Board considered the position at its meeting on

28 June. The Board wholly approved the action that had been taken and decided that the IRC should have at least one, and preferably two, members on the Kent Board. It was agreed that Mr C.R.E. Brooke, the IRC's most senior executive and also its Deputy Managing Director, should be appointed immediately. If it seemed necessary, Kent would accept the further nomination of a person suitably qualified in terms of general business experience and specific knowledge of the instrument industry. Brooke's job was not to take part in the day to day management of Kent but to look after the IRC's interests and to monitor progress on the rationalisation and development of the group. The second appointment would be made later, if required, to support him.

An IRC press announcement (included as Appendix 5.2 to this chapter) was released a few days later. It set out the extent of the IRC's financial commitment to Kent, announced Brooke's appointment and explained the IRC's reasons for supporting Kent. If things had then gone as planned, this chapter could have ended here. Unfortunately, they did not.

THE DECLINE OF KENT–CAMBRIDGE

It was soon apparent that, at best, the process of rationalisation would be more difficult and take longer than had been hoped. Webster, the Managing Director of CI, was over sixty and it had been anticipated that he would retire and make way for someone younger. When he went, towards the end of 1968, this seemed to create more problems than opportunities. Deficiencies were gradually becoming apparent in CI's production planning and inventory control systems and these were to be exacerbated by the problems of rationalising its activities with those of Kent.

It did, however, seem that some progress was being made and, in late 1968 and early 1969, the IRC reopened merger discussions. It obviously had to take account of Rank, which remained a major factor in the industry. Early in January 1969, the IRC met Davis and a colleague for discussions. The meeting was friendly, everyone agreeing that to pursue a vendetta would be absurd. The merger between RTH and H&W had gone through and a new Rank subsidiary had been formed, called Rank Precision Instruments (RPI). It would be some time before RPI was earning substantial profits, and factory closures were necessary, but Davis talked about the possibility of rationalising production between CI and an enlarged RPI. Indeed, Davis thought he had agreed a price at which he could buy SAD from GEC. The IRC, however, saw no reason to disturb the existing situation. It reiterated its wish to see Kent–CI become part of a growing British Instrument Corporation, which would have the benefit of all the work being done to rationalise CI, and it saw no reason why RPI should be better able than Kent to cope with the problems of a £50 million group.

About a week later, IRC executives met Weinstock of GEC. Despite Davis's claim to have agreed a price for SAD, they discussed its sale to Kent. Negotiations for this had so far failed because GEC wanted £7 million, and Kent had decided not to offer more than £5 million. Weinstock said his preference was *either* to sell SAD, *or* to buy both Kent *and* RPI, but Rank would not sell. The IRC came away with the impression that Weinstock would sell SAD for something between £5 million and £7 million (giving a price to earnings ratio of between 15 and 22 on the earnings forecast for 1969) and that he would probably prefer to deal with Kent.

During the spring of 1969 there was a 'teach-in' for the IRC and Kent's top and middle management, which concentrated on Kent's corporate planning. To improve managerial performance, each executive director was to be given responsibility for a division. Outline objectives had been approved a month before and, at the 'teach-in' line managers and executive directors were asked to explain in detail how they would achieve these objectives. A major aim was to get commitment and understanding from the non-executive directors and from the IRC.

The IRC executive saw the 'teach-in' as successful, and thought that morale in the group was good. While older managers had reservations, the younger ones totally accepted the need to appoint divisional directors. Indeed, there was now a feeling that the opportunity to buy SAD for about £7 million should have been seized. However, this feeling was distinctly premature because Kent still had fundamental problems, including, in the IRC's view, the need to find a new chief executive.

Soon after the teach-in Brooke's two-year term at the IRC came to an end and he was replaced on the Kent Board by another IRC executive, Michael Knight. The latter learned that Kent's pre-tax profit for 1968/69 would be only £1.85 million, nearly £700000 below the forecast made at the time of the bid for CI, the biggest single reason being that inventories at CI were worth £300000 less than had been thought. This supported Knight's view that the whole production and planning structure at CI was unsatisfactory. CI had run into serious problems in introducing a new production control system and in coping with the movement of about half its activities into the Kent instrument division.

While one may doubt whether Kent could at this stage have faced yet more rationalisation, talks about a Kent–SAD merger continued. The Kent Board's main reservation seems to have been that it did not want anything to happen which would enable the IRC to acquire an even larger stake in Kent. GEC for its part, believed that it would gain from links with Kent–CI because of their electron microscope and their R&D and marketing expertise and perhaps also from Kent's process control business. No progress was made in these discussions while, during 1969, the IRC became more and more concerned about the internal situation at Kent.

Prospects were worsening rather than improving and Kent's share price had fallen to a low point of 18*s* 9*d* (94p) compared with 32*s* (£1.80) at the time of the merger. The IRC felt that an injection of new senior management was essential for Kent's recovery. The Corporation suggested to Rodney Kent that it should help in the search for a new chief executive and this was agreed.

Meanwhile, Knight persisted with his efforts to improve the group's profitability, suggesting that Kent should seriously consider selling some assets. In the six months to July, Kent's profits had been only £900000, substantially below expectations, and CI had earned nothing. A major problem was that, because the two firms made quite different products, production could not be integrated, and this was causing more management difficulties than had been anticipated. Some rationalisation of marketing was possible, but CI was bound to remain a largely separate entity. Partly because of the impending changes in Kent's top management, even senior managers were becoming restless and morale was low. Nevertheless, it was some months before a consultancy firm was appointed to seek a new managing director. At the end of 1969, it was agreed that Rodney Kent would remain as Chairman only until March 1970.

The IRC Board was given a progress report in January 1970. The Corporation still held 25 per cent of the enlarged Kent equity, which had cost £6.5 million but was now worth only £4.8 million. Kent's share price had recovered somewhat to 25*s* (£1.25) but could well fall again. However, a candidate for chief executive had at last been found. He was Mr John Lutyens, Managing Director of Pressed Steel, an experienced industrialist who was keen to take on the challenge of managing Kent.

In mid-March, the IRC Board was told that Kent's profits for 1969/70 were likely to be close to the amount forecast at the time of the bid for CI; that Hartop, the Managing Director of Kent would take over its chairmanship from Rodney Kent; and that Lutyens was to begin work as chief executive on 1 May. The IRC Board was sceptical about the profit forecast but agreed that the Corporation should retain its investment in order to be in a position to fulfil its primary objective of restructuring the scientific instrument industry. In particular, it should resist attempts by other companies to obtain Kent shares, except where this was likely to change the structure of the industry in ways of which the IRC approved. In some cases, Kent might see the acquisition of a minority holding in its equity by a large firm as a protection but, where it raised the prospect of a later takeover, such an acquisition might simply demoralise the Kent management.

In July 1970, Kent reported a profit for 1969/70 of £2.06 million. This was £700000 below the forecast, and CI accounted for about £400000 of the shortfall, but it was better than had been feared. The auditors reported that control of inventories at CI remained inadequate, that there might still be substantial amounts to write off, and that Kent itself needed to weed out obsolete and slow-moving products. The IRC Board forcefully emphasised the need for better results in the current year, perhaps to be achieved by a considerable reduction in overheads. But what probably discouraged the IRC most was that, contrary to what it had been told at the time of the merger, there was no evidence that the advanced scientific instrument technology of today was the process control technology of tomorrow. One of the main arguments put forward in favour of the merger did not seem to be valid.

Kent's problems worsened rapidly in the new financial year and a trading loss of about £400000 was reported for the first quarter. However, with the Conservative Party returned to power there seemed little likelihood for further IRC moves. Indeed, partly because of this, Rank reappeared on the scene and during the summer of 1970 built up a holding amounting to 18 per cent of Kent's equity.

POSTSCRIPT

Kent's subsequent history has not been happy. From the profit of a little over £2 million in 1969/70, there was a dramatic fall to around £1 million in 1970/71. There was a recovery to £1.6 million in 1971/72 but then a further catastrophic fall to £133000 in 1972/73 and to a loss of £100000 in 1973/74.

Kent's solution was to try to undo most of the merger. It approached a private company, Metals Research, to acquire CI's business in laboratory instruments but negotiations failed because this business was losing money. With Kent itself in difficulties, in 1974 the Swiss electrical group, Brown Boveri, offered £6.1 million for a majority stake in a new holding company which would take over Kent's process control activities, but would exclude CI's laboratory instruments. GEC made a counter-bid of £5.8 million, aiming to buy the whole of the Kent equity and to put the whole of Kent into a new holding company. The Labour government, then back in power, controlled the IRC's stake in Kent, and decided at first to support GEC in order to prevent Kent from effectively passing into foreign control. Rank, which still held 18 per cent of the Kent equity but had decided not to go ahead with a full scale bid itself, took the same line.

At this stage, Benn, Labour's new Secretary of State for Industry, with his enthusiasm for employee participation, called for a vote to allow Kent employees to decide who was to acquire 'their' company. A majority voted in favour of a merger with Brown Boveri, though, perhaps significantly, former CI employees voted solidly for GEC. Nevertheless, Benn accepted the majority decision and used the government shareholding in Kent to back Brown Boveri, with Rank again following suit. This decided the result. Brown Boveri made the government's switch of policy easier by reducing its proposed shareholding in the new group to 49 per cent. Each Kent share was exchanged for one new share in Brown Boveri–Kent plus one share in another new company, Scientific and Medical Instruments (SMI), which took over the bulk of the old CI business.

Brown Boveri–Kent shares were immediately listed on the stock exchange and, in early 1979 were trading at about 46p, giving a capitalisation of about £25 million.

SMI, whose shares remained unlisted, ran into immediate trouble. In November 1974 the government gave guarantees of £2 million to enable the company to increase its already high borrowing but, with financial problems continuing, it was announced in October 1975 that SMI would merge with Metals Research. The government, not Metals Research, would effectively finance the merger. SMI shareholders acquired a little under 10 per cent of the equity of the new group though, to judge from its accounts, they contributed the greater part of its assets. The government increased its own equity stake to about 28 per cent, paying £1.25 million to do so. It provided a further £2.35 million by loans, which were to be interest-free for at least two years. The new shares had an asset value of only 3.6p, but the alternative seemed to be liquidation.

The fact that this move reversed much of what the IRC had attempted was underlined only too clearly when the merged SMI–Metals Research immediately renamed itself The Cambridge Instrument Company. *The Times* thought the real point was 'that the Government will have spent about £7.5 million by the end of the day in solving the problems of Cambridge (not including the bank guarantees) when Rank initially, or GEC later, might have found a commercial solution' (Rowley, 1975).

COMMENT

The Kent–CI merger was a departure for the IRC in two respects:

(a) It forced the Corporation into an active battle in which it not merely made the controversial recommendation to support Kent and not Rank, but actually used public funds to take a direct stake in the equity of a company in order to outbid a competitor.
(b) Because of the substantial equity stake that it acquired, the IRC was forced into a degree of management responsibility. This step was regarded by many in the IRC at the time as important, even inevitable, but it was one for which the Corporation was ill prepared.

The IRC never did anything quite like this again (the ball-bearing case described in Chapter 6 differed in an important way), but it never had to. After Kent–CI, the IRC was incontrovertibly a force to be reckoned with. Its actions over Cambridge created many enemies for the Corporation and they were important, perhaps crucial, in bringing about its later dissolution. More immediately though, industrialists could not ignore the power which the IRC had always had and which in the Kent–Cambridge merger it had shown that it was willing to use. This almost certainly changed attitudes towards rethinking the structure of UK industry.

The analysis, thus far, begs the question whether the Kent–CI merger was an appropriate one on which to have taken such a stand. Both the executive and the board of the IRC had originally agreed that the case for supporting Kent was marginal. Moreover, the Board had explicitly stated that commercial considerations should be paramount. In the event, a stake was taken at a price to earnings ratio of about 40 for a company whose record and prospects were mediocre. And the price was paid by a not very large, and not very strong, company. Without the IRC's assistance Kent's bid could not have been pushed so high and it was Kent that subsequently had to carry the high cost of the acquisition.

The IRC also underestimated the management problems it was taking on. It had acted so decisively during the merger battle, and had acquired such a large stake in Kent, that the company's management waited fearfully, expecting the IRC to take control. With its tiny staff and limited experience the IRC lacked the ability to do this, so that valuable time was wasted. It was almost two years before a new chief executive was appointed and by then too much time had been lost.

The 'industrial logic' which was one plank of the IRC's case for supporting Kent, was in part misconceived. Both the IRC and Kent diagnosed wrongly the potential advantages of bringing together the laboratory instruments of CI and Kent's interests in industrial applications. There never was any significant technological or marketing relationship between the two activities and the management skills required in the scientific end of the business were quite different from those to which Kent was accustomed. Indeed, the scientific instruments activities were hived off again in 1974 under the merger arrangements with Brown Boveri.

CI's industrial business – temperature controllers, recorders and analytical instruments – did, however, fit in well and became an important and profitable part of Kent's process control business. Nor is it clear that Rank would have handled the management problems inherent in the takeover of CI any more successfully than Kent did.

Overall, despite Kent's recovery after the link with Brown Boveri, the verdict must go against the IRC on at least three counts. First, it allowed itself to be drawn into a situation where it encouraged too high a price to be paid for CI, with a consequent loss of public money. Second, having forced the merger through and taken such a substantial stake in Kent's equity, the IRC was too slow to recognise that it had to take a firmer line with Kent's management. Clearly the Corporation did learn from this experience and was more aggressive in ensuring that management changes were made in ball-bearings (Ch. 6), in Rolls-Royce (Ch. 12) and especially in Cammell Laird (Ch. 13). Third, whatever the secondary advantages to Kent, the benefits from the merger were misconceived. The deal was not, it turned out, the key to restructuring the UK instrument industry.

APPENDIX 5.1

The value of successive bids for CI by Rank and Kent are given in the following table:

Date	*Rank offers (price per CI share)*	*Kent offers (price per CI share)*
9 April 1968	33*s*	
15 May	(35*s* 9*d*)	42*s* 6*d*
30 May	48*s*	(44*s* 6*d*)
5 June	(48*s* 6*d*)	48*s* 9*d*
12 June	55*s*	
14 June	(55*s* 6*d*)	55*s*
18 June	(56*s* 6*d*)	(56*s* 9*d*)(unconditionally)
19 June	Rank withdrew	

Both companies' bids were made up partly of shares and so the value of the terms offered fluctuated. Figures in parentheses indicate the approximate value of successive bids at the market prices of Kent's and Rank's shares on the dates shown.

[*Note*: One new penny (1p) is equivalent to 2.4 old pence (2.4*d*); twelve old pence (12*d*) equalled one shilling (1*s*) and twenty shillings (20*s*) equalled £1 sterling. Thus, for example, 56*s* 6*d* = £2 16*s* 6*d* = £2.82½.]

APPENDIX 5.2

This appendix comprises the IRC's statement on the completion of the acquisition of CI by Kent.

IRC STATEMENT ON THE ACQUISITION OF THE CAMBRIDGE INSTRUMENT COMPANY BY GEORGE KENT 5TH JULY, 1968

The IRC announces that it now holds, or is entitled to receive, not more than 4 295 000 Ordinary and Deferred Ordinary Shares in George Kent Limited (Kent) which represents 24.9% of the enlarged equity. These shares have been acquired with the approval of the Board of Kent either direct, or through the market, or as a result of IRC's sub-underwriting participation in the offer by Kent for Cambridge Instrument Company Limited (Cambridge). The Panel on Takeovers and Mergers have authorised the IRC to say that in its view the IRC has conformed to the Code.

The IRC has undertaken to consider making funds available to Kent, in amounts and on terms to be agreed, for the further development of the Group. The Directors of Kent have invited Mr C.R.E. Brooke as nominee of the IRC to join the board of Kent and have agreed to make another seat available to the IRC if required.

The IRC intervention in connection with Cambridge was made after detailed study of the likely future prospects of much of the instrument industry. Kent was already established as the largest independent British owned company making industrial and process control instruments. To enable it to expand at least as fast as its international competitors it needed to gain access to the latest technologies emerging from academic and other laboratories and to develop a scientific instrument capability. This will be achieved by the merger with Cambridge. In addition Cambridge make a number of industrial instruments which will increase Kent's systems capability and give rise to rationalisation opportunities in both companies in production, marketing and R & D. Finally, the establishment of the new group creates a nucleus for further rationalisation and for the continued development of Kent's successful policy of logical acquisitions.

The bid by the Rank Organisation Limited (Rank) for Cambridge precipitated the proposal to merge by the boards of Kent and Cambridge. The IRC was in touch with all three companies and carefully considered the arguments put forward by Rank. However, whilst noting the achievements of Rank and the strengths of its Taylor Hobson Division, the IRC Board concluded that if Cambridge were to be acquired by Rank, without Kent, the opportunity for the best possible development of the industry would have been missed. As it is, the high technological contribution of Cambridge will reinforce the industrial capability of Kent and, in the judgment of IRC, with which the Ministry of Technology concurs, this produces a sound structural base for this part of the instrument industry.

It is and has always been the IRC policy to reach agreed solutions to such problems. Unfortunately in this case agreement could not be achieved. In view of the strategic significance of this case for the future of such an important sector of industry the IRC Board decided to back its judgment with financial support. The Department of Economic Affairs, as the sponsoring Ministry, has been kept informed throughout, but the IRC acted, as it is entitled to do by the IRC Act 1966, entirely within its own discretion.

The IRC intends to retain its shareholding in Kent for a limited period only until the benefits of the merger have been realised. The IRC does not intend to participate in the day-to-day management of the new Group.

6

The Ball-Bearing Industry

Unlike the events described in the previous two chapters, the ball-bearings case provides an example of an industry where IRC went beyond supporting the moves of particular companies and devised its own plan for restructuring. It also illustrates the IRC's approach to a situation involving a major foreign company. Even here, however, where IRC action can be seen at its strongest, the Corporation's first involvement came as a reaction to events rather than as their cause. This chapter outlines the moves behind the IRC's initial involvement. It describes the problems and disappointments faced by the IRC before it succeeded, with the help of Mintech, in creating a major British company in this industry.

THE STRUCTURE OF THE INDUSTRY

Ball-bearings are a small but vital component in all kinds of equipment ranging from pumps to machine tools and from bicycles to aeroplanes. Almost everything man-made that moves or has moving parts requires ball-bearings (or roller-bearings). In the late 1960s, about 10 per cent of UK sales of bearings were imported. The rest of the market was equally divided between three UK-owned producers and four multinational bearing manufacturers. The approximate sizes and market shares of these companies are given in Table 6.1. Thus it can be seen that 45 per cent of the market was in the hands of UK companies and 45 per cent was supplied by foreign-owned companies based in the UK.

Skefko, the UK subsidiary of the Swedish company SKF, was already the largest producer in the industry, and the other foreign companies were subsidiaries of multinational producers. SKF had world sales of over £300 million in 1968, twice those of the second-ranking company, Timken. Fafnir and Torrington had sales of £43 million and £31 million respectively, still two or three times that of the largest UK bearing manufacturer, and the UK market was coming under increasing pressure from European, and especially Japanese, imports.

Table 6.1 *Structure of the UK ball and roller bearing industry in 1968*

Company	*Approximate market share (per cent)*	*Sales (£ million)*	*Ownership*
UK-owned			
Ransome and Marles	19	14.4	Public company
Hoffmann	15	11.5	Brown Bayley
Pollard	12	9.5	Public company (30 per cent owned by Chairman)
Overseas-owned			
Skefko	27	17.8	SKF, Sweden
British Timken	7	5.3	Timken, USA
Torrington	6	5.0	Ingersoll Rand, USA
Fafnir	5	4.0	Textron, USA

FOREIGN DOMINATION

The IRC's first involvement in the industry came in May 1968 when it learned that Ransome and Marles (R&M) had been talking to SKF about a merger with Skefko. It seemed that R&M might be prepared to agree terms which would give SKF 55 per cent of the equity in a joint company. The IRC was told that both Hoffmann and Pollard were also talking to foreign firms. There was a significant chance that the whole of the UK bearings industry would come under foreign control. If this were to be prevented, action would need to be taken very quickly. The position was reported to the IRC Board when it met on 17 May. It decided that the importance of the industry, and the danger that there could soon be no major UK bearings company, clearly warranted IRC involvement. The Board also noted that, compared with the industries in Western Europe and North America, the UK industry appeared excessively fragmented, which also brought it directly within IRC's sphere of activity. The IRC executive was therefore instructed to make a detailed examination of the industry.

IRC'S INVESTIGATION

By now, the pattern of the IRC's approach to the study of an industry was clearly established. It informed itself on the companies concerned, using the accounts both of parent companies and of all their subsidiaries, as well as industry statistics. It visited the main manufacturing units in the industry. It held extensive discussions with the chairmen, chief executives and senior managers of all significant producers and many customers. In addition, it kept in close touch with the government departments most directly concerned with the industry, in this case Mintech, the DEA and the Board of Trade. Simultaneously, the IRC collected and analysed information on the structure of the industry in other industrialised countries and on the trading characteristics and relative efficiency of ball-bearing companies in Western Europe.

It was clear at the outset of the investigation that the IRC would have to devise a proposal for a UK-controlled grouping that R&M would see as an acceptable alternative to its arrangement with Skefko. This would probably mean a deal with Hoffmann or Pollard, or both; however, a UK-owned group with a minority holding for Skefko was also a possibility. The first steps were therefore to examine the potential benefits from rationalisation and to discover the attitudes of Hoffmann and Pollard.

Hoffmann was controlled by Brown Bayley Ltd (BBL) which also owned a private sector steel maker, Brown Bayley Steels (BBS). The IRC had been concerning itself with private sector steelmakers since nationalisation in 1967 and so already had contacts with BBL. It now learned that Hoffmann was worried about the competition it might face after a Skefko–R&M merger and would favour a Hoffmann–R&M link. It was open-minded about the possibility of Pollard being added to the group at a later stage.

Pollard was effectively controlled by its chairman, Mr John King, who owned 30 per cent of the company's equity. He gave the initial impression of being an aggressive entrepreneur who was determined to enlarge his share of the bearing market and confident that he would do so. Indeed, Pollard believed that if Skefko and R&M merged it would be able to take business from them. On the other hand, it saw considerable scope for rationalisation if all three UK companies were merged. Even a Pollard–Hoffmann merger could yield significant benefits, but Pollard's liquidity position prevented it from taking the initiative in negotiations.

The underlying economics of the industry and of the various possibilities for rationalisation were examined, using cost information supplied by the companies concerned as well as comparisons based on data about international bearing manufacturers. The UK industry was certainly relatively fragmented. In West Germany two companies, SKF and the domestically owned Kugel Fisher FAG, shared over 80 per cent of the market. In France and Italy, SKF alone had a market share of about 70 per cent, and there was a similar pattern in the Scandinavian countries.

The reason for such high levels of concentration is that the economic size for a bearing manufacturer is very large, relative to most national markets for bearings. There are economies of scale in research and development and in production. The major international bearing manufacturers were able to finance research into both the production and uses of bearings on a far larger scale than any of the UK-owned companies and this was one of the attractions to R&M of a link with Skefko. In production, the advantages of rationalisation and of long runs were substantial. This was illustrated to the IRC, in detailed cost breakdowns both for different manufacturing units and for production runs of varying lengths. Rationalisation would also achieve cost savings in the manufacture of component parts and through the reduction of stock levels.

The conclusions of the IRC investigation were that rationalisation was necessary if UK-controlled manufacturing capacity was to be retained in the bearing industry; that rationalisation was desirable in order to obtain the benefits of economies of scale in R&D and in production; and that rationalisation was possible, provided that fairly rapid action was taken to prevent the R&M–Skefko merger.

SCHEMES FOR RATIONALISATION

Whatever the arguments in favour of a Hoffmann–Pollard deal, the IRC executive felt that there was no time to pursue this immediately and that it should at once set about arranging a UK merger attractive to R&M. It had discussed this with Mintech, whose officials were, understandably, in a difficult position. Mintech favoured the establishment of a strong UK-owned company but felt that it would be wrong to take any action against Skefko which was a well established business that had been operating in the UK for a considerable time. The IRC Board considered the report on the executive's investigation in July. It endorsed the view that the IRC's objective should be to establish a strong UK company (with or without minority participation by Skefko), but decided that the best approach would be to try to link Pollard and Hoffmann. This would provide a stronger position from which to approach R&M. The executive was instructed to pursue this course, but to be ready to react quickly if events started to move against them.

Visits by the executive confirmed that Pollard had, in general, more modern and more efficient plant than Hoffmann. In King, it also had a chief executive who appeared to be keen to expand his activities. Much of the product range of the two companies overlapped, so that there was considerable scope for cost savings from rationalisation. As the executive had feared, however, there was no time to pursue a Pollard–Hoffmann merger. Discussions had to be started at once with R&M if it was to be prevented from going ahead with its deal with Skefko.

IRC executives paid a visit to R&M in early August and this was soon followed by a meeting at Pall Mall with Senior, Chairman of R&M. R&M regarded Skefko highly. It felt that it either had to tie up completely with Skefko or had to find a very attractive alternative, because it foresaw increased competitive pressure from Skefko if the deal fell through. R&M did not relish the thought of facing a more hostile UK-based competitor together with the increasing pressure from Japanese imports. Several possible schemes were discussed. R&M thought that an attempt to link with Hoffmann would provoke a direct takeover bid from Skefko, but was also intrigued with the idea of an R&M–Hoffmann–Pollard company. This, it thought, really would produce a powerful unit, with enormous scope for rationalisation.

The IRC suggested to Senior that R&M would be the best 'vehicle' for restructuring the UK bearing industry and emphasised the help that Senior could give as the 'statesman' of the industry. At this stage, Senior still felt he had to pursue the Swedish link-up, but his interest was clearly aroused by an IRC suggestion of enlarging this to create an Anglo-Swedish company with a majority UK interest. He wondered whether this would be acceptable to the Board of Trade – it would mean a substantial reduction in the number of separate companies manufacturing in the UK. But, if it were acceptable, he thought he might be able to come to terms with SKF.

The IRC felt it had to keep open all possible options. It was not against a Skefko–R&M–Hoffman–Pollard amalgamation so long as control remained in the UK. But this was a vital proviso because it would be a significant change in policy for SKF to accept a minority stake. Moreover, the task of bringing the four companies together was daunting. If the Anglo-Swedish scheme could not be arranged, a merger between all three UK-owned companies appeared to be the most sensible alternative. But there were a large number of ways of achieving this. The IRC brought in the merchant bank, Rothschilds, to work out the details of some of these possible schemes. The IRC Board's directive was still to link Pollard and Hoffmann if possible, but, although this was becoming increasingly unlikely, Rothschilds were asked to look also into a scheme for a Pollard bid, underwritten by the IRC. The other two schemes put to Rothschilds both involved a completely new role for the IRC. The first was an R&M bid for the whole of BBL, with a commitment from the IRC subsequently to buy BBS, the private steelmaker, from R&M. The second was even more radical and involved a cash bid by the IRC for BBL. These moves were yet to be considered by the Corporation's Board members.

Before the IRC Board could meet, the situation was complicated further by a story which appeared in *The Sunday Times* on 25 August. This revealed the IRC's interest in the bearings industry and went on to suggest that Pollard 'was already being considered as a possible focus for restructuring'. The article was written by the paper's City Editor, Richard Milner, and it speculated that 'Pollard will make an issue of shares at well above their market price to IRC in return for cash to be used for purposive acquisitions'. Pollard's Chairman, King, was said to be 'preserving a discreet silence, referring questions to Charles Villiers' department'. Whatever the source of the story, it at once made relationships between the companies more difficult, and possibly put back a meeting between Senior and King.

The IRC Board met at the end of August and considered the position at length. It was told that Mintech was now strongly sympathetic to the IRC's aim of creating a strong UK-controlled company and that the Board of Trade had indicated that it would not oppose an R&M–Hoffmann and/or Pollard merger. On the other hand R&M had just submitted revised proposals to SKF and if these were accepted an R&M–SKF deal could rapidly be concluded. The executive argued that, far from being neutral, a Skefko–R&M merger would wreck any potential of forming a viable UK ball-bearing industry. A merged firm would have access to SKF technology but it would not be allowed to compete with SKF's operations overseas, while rationalisation within SKF might increase imports into the UK.

The executive therefore argued that the IRC must, at the least, merge R&M and Hoffmann. The main problem would be to satisfy

R&M shareholders that they would not lose a good deal, in the short run, by joining Hoffmann rather than Skefko. The long-term advantages would be enormous. A merged Hoffmann–Pollard, though with great potential, would probably not be big enough to survive in the medium term. Without R&M, the IRC would be dealing with only a very small part of the problem.

It was not unprecedented for the IRC to support a merger of the leading UK-owned producers in an industry, but in the earlier case of the motor industry there had been only two British companies and Leyland might have made a bid for BMH, sooner or later, without IRC assistance (see Ch. 7). The ball-bearing scheme was very much of IRC design and the IRC might well have to buy one of the companies outright to push it through. But lack of confidence was not one of the IRC's weaknesses and the Board decided to pursue the R&M–Hoffmann–Pollard deal. It agreed with the executive that the essential first step was now to link R&M and Hoffmann. It seemed reasonably certain that Pollard would 'wait in the wings' while this was done, whereas if Pollard were moved first, R&M could slip away before the IRC had time to tie up the Hoffmann deal. The simplest procedure would be an R&M offer for Hoffmann, but there were two snags. First, R&M felt morally committed to explore the SKF link, though a Minister might tell Senior that the government disapproved of a merger with SKF and that the UK grouping would be more beneficial to R&M's shareholders. Second, the market ratings of R&M and Hoffmann were such as to make it difficult to find acceptable terms for a merger, if R&M were the 'vehicle'.

Despite R&M's preference for the SKF deal, Senior made no immediate move and, while this prolonged the uncertainty, it also gave IRC some breathing space. Indeed, the executive even considered using Hoffmann as the merger vehicle. The IRC would perhaps have to underwrite such a move, but would thereby obtain greater control over the situation, and a bigger say in the details of any arrangement.

BBL's attitude posed a big question. Would BBL want a minority stake in a large bearing group? Would it be prepared to liquidate its holdings and distribute the proceeds to shareholders? In the end, it was to be tax considerations which suggested that the best approach for BBL shareholders would be a cash bid for the company by IRC. This would give the Corporation control, not only of Hoffmann, but also of BBS, one of the leading special steels producers, giving the IRC a key position in that industry too. But before such a move could be made, agreement had to be reached with R&M.

DEALING WITH THE SWEDES

Senior planned to visit Sweden soon, but first talked again to the IRC. Skefko had come closer to R&M's suggested terms and the IRC had to agree to consider including Skefko in a merger, though it pointed out that SKF would probably then have to break its rules and accept a minority shareholding.

By the end of the month, Rothschilds had reported on possible terms for a Hoffmann–R&M–Pollard merger. They feared that Hoffmann might not find these very attractive because, as recently as 1963, its pre-tax profits had been larger than those of R&M. On full conversion, the proposal divided the equity in these proportions: Hoffmann 25 per cent; R&M 51 per cent; Pollard 24 per cent. The IRC lost no time in telling Senior what Rothschilds proposed for R&M. The scheme valued R&M at much the same price as did the Skefko proposals, but provided more income and gave R&M at least 51 per cent of the enlarged equity, against a maximum of 49 per cent through Skefko. In addition Villiers hinted that a continued 'flirtation' with Skefko might mean a headlong collision with the IRC and the government.

Meanwhile, Villiers made a move which, though seeming innocent enough, brought matters to a head. He telephoned Wallenberg, Chairman of SKF, who was in Sweden, explained that the IRC was likely to be in competition with SKF over ball-bearings, and emphasised its hope for an agreed solution. But the industry needed restructuring and the IRC intended to see that this happened. The IRC later discovered that this telephone call had put the cat among the pigeons because SKF had never previously been frustrated in an attempt to control a company.

Even so, SKF at least went through the motions of considering taking a minority holding in the merged British company. With the IRC pointing out that the situation would not keep indefinitely, Senior agreed to tell SKF that the IRC would consider a four-company merger, but that if this were impossible, it would merge R&M, Hoffmann and Pollard. Mintech appeared pleased at the possiblility of SKF participation. While SKF was something of a 'Trojan horse' it could be an advantage in the long term to have it as a friend, not an enemy.

On travelling to Skefko at Luton and expecting to be impressed, the IRC's visiting executive was not disappointed. Turnover was £18 million, though Skefko's 'balance of payments' was in deficit by about £1 million. The executive reported that the way the company was laid out was really most impressive by comparison with any UK company's factories that he had visited to date. The management team, aged 30–45, seemed to show more enthusiasm than their counterparts in the UK-owned companies and could be valuable to the new bearing group. But Skefko had been upset by the suggestion that it would consider doing anything not in the interests of the UK, and by not being consulted earlier. The executive therefore explained at length to Skefko what the IRC's motives and plans were.

On 21 October a crucial meeting took place. Villiers had hoped to visit SKF in Sweden but instead was asked by Sir Richard Clarke, Permanent Secretary at Mintech, to attend a meeting there. SKF and Skefko were represented in force. Wallenberg was present himself, as was Lord Goodman, who had been retained to act for SKF. Skefko's Chairman, Sporborg, and Managing Director, Dickinson, were also both in attendance. SKF had refused to meet in Sweden, being very irritated to learn that the IRC had already decided to issue a press statement, on the very day of the meeting, announcing that the three British companies were considering a merger.

Goodman explained SKF's attitude to the restructuring of the ball-bearing industry in the UK and said that, although the IRC had spoken in a friendly way about including SKF in a new grouping, its actions, especially over the planned press release, were unfriendly. Mintech explained that the government wanted to see a restructuring of the bearing industry, covering as wide a field as possible, and that it reacted unfavourably to the whole industry being controlled from overseas. It had no wish to be hostile either to SKF or to Sweden, but if SKF and R&M merged, the whole UK industry was likely to become foreign-owned. Under pressure, Villiers agreed not to issue the IRC press release, and offered to re-open talks with SKF on an equal footing. Wallenberg was not impressed and insisted that where he invested he controlled, but he must have realised, at this meeting, that if this were so he would not be investing in R&M.

The IRC executive's reaction to the meeting appeared to be that SKF's prime objective had been to spoil the three-way merger and then get together with R&M after they had broken up other negotiations. However, SKF argued that, to regroup the industry successfully, all major voices should first be listened to with care. As the largest unit in the UK industry, SKF recognised its responsibilities, and felt that it had an important role to play in any UK grouping. But proper discussions would be impossible if Skefko was confronted with an alliance already constituted against it of three other units. This presupposed unwillingness to allow Skefko to rank on the same footing as any other British operating company. SKF wanted rights according to its strength and ability to contribute – not in accordance with previously established group alliances. It was keen to examine the merger objectively with government representatives, but not against the background of an attempted *fait accompli*.

In an effort to cool down the situation, the IRC immediately responded to Sporborg saying that it was very distressing to see that its attitude to Skefko had been misunderstood. The IRC had a high opinion of SKF and still hoped that an agreeable solution could be found, but the government felt that the right course was to merge the three British companies, leaving room at every stage for SKF participation. Because of Stock Exchange rumours, it was essential to begin negotiations very soon.

Despite some misgivings, the IRC continued to keep the door genuinely open to SKF. Late in October Villiers told the IRC Board that the conversations with SKF had resulted in the offer for R&M being put on ice and in SKF agreeing for the first time in history to consider a minority participation in a major overseas territory. He therefore sought agreement that the IRC should try to negotiate a four-way merger, subject to safeguards from SKF. Some Board members feared that SKF might have to be asked for so many safeguards that it would not find participation worthwhile, whereas others felt that participation would hamper the new group's export effort. In the end, the board agreed to the executive's proposals. However, Board members emphasised that they saw no reason to put IRC money into a new ball-bearing company.

There was now a series of meetings. At the first, at Mintech early in November, it was agreed to forget the earlier misunderstandings and differences. Nevertheless, SKF described the IRC's plan as clearly unrealistic, since it presupposed that the three British companies would agree and it had learned that at least one British company had serious misgivings. It transpired that this was not R&M but Hoffmann and that its reservations were exactly the same as the IRC's own about the difficulty of competing successfully with SKF. Goodman added that R&M had approached SKF and not vice versa, but that the negotiations with R&M were over and each company was now a free agent.

During the meeting, Villiers continued to maintain that the IRC would willingly investigate a four-way merger, provided that it knew the parameters and if SKF would take a minority stake. The meeting ended, however, with the IRC saying that it must continue to discuss the formation of a three-way group, though leaving room for SKF.

A few days later, the IRC turned down a request that SKF should have an opportunity to present its views in detail to the Board of the

IRC, but a further meeting was held between IRC and SKF representatives. This went over all the familiar ground and ended with a formal invitation to SKF to embark on discussion with the IRC about restructuring the industry on an open basis and with no precommitments.

By now it seemed clear that SKF would not, in the end, agree to join any UK-controlled grouping. The IRC therefore told Senior that it would press ahead with the R&M–Pollard–Hoffmann merger. No alternative would provide a viable British company. While Senior still saw SKF taking a minority interest, he conceded that the best alternative would be to group R&M, Hoffmann and Pollard. It was, however, unlikely that R&M would be willing to make the first move. The IRC therefore brought in the accountants, Peat, Marwick, but even now they were *not* asked to evaluate a merger – merely to present the accounts of R&M, Pollard and Hoffmann on a comparable basis. Once this had been done, SKF was once more invited to examine proposals for reorganisation. So the IRC and SKF met yet again, but this meeting turned out to be crucial. It finally became absolutely clear that the stumbling block to bringing in SKF was its unwillingness to join a British company as a minority shareholder.

The IRC's protracted negotiations with SKF had succeeded only in delaying its plans for restructuring the UK bearing industry. With SKF now apparently off the scene, they could now go ahead. It was clear, however, that this would not happen unless IRC not only took the initiative but actually put itself in a position to determine events. This set the stage for the Corporation's first, and only, acquisition of a public company.

THE BROWN BAYLEY BID

The IRC's interest in the ball and roller bearing industry had been public knowledge since the *Sunday Times* article in August, and it was now late in the year. The Corporation was itself anxious to get results and it was also coming under indirect pressure from the trade unions to clarify its position, via the MPs of those constituencies most likely to be affected by reorganisation. The idea of the IRC bidding directly for BBL had been mooted for some time, and it could be seen as a logical development of the Corporation's activities. The first step had been to support one company, GEC, in an opposed bid (see Ch. 4); the second was market intervention to buy shares, which were then pledged to Kent in its bid for Cambridge Instruments (see Ch. 5). An outright IRC bid would be a further move along the path of direct intervention. There were many objections to it, not the least of which was the possible alienation of many industrialists who would see the move as 'back door' nationalisation. However, if IRC was ever to bid for a company, BBL provided almost the ideal case. The IRC had clear plans for the immediate disposal of one of its two subsidiaries. These plans had been developed in collaboration with the other leading UK companies in the industry and had the support and encouragement of the government. The other subsidiary, BBS, was in a sector where the IRC had already been active and this should help to convince sceptics that the IRC's aim would be to dispose of this, too, as rapidly as possible. The acquisition of BBL would thus give the IRC an ideal opportunity to illustrate that it was using public money to promote rationalisation, not to acquire ownership and control. Other objections related to the financial risk to the IRC of undertaking such a venture. Most of the IRC's financial transactions involved borrowing money from the government and then lending it to a company at a marginally higher rate of interest. The conditions varied and the loans were often unsecured, but the Corporation risked losing its money only in the unlikely event of the complete collapse of the borrower. In the present case, however, the IRC would be putting money into shares which could not easily be resold. It could recover its investment only if it could successfully dispose of both Hoffman and BBS at sufficiently attractive prices. Even the sale of Hoffmann could not be 100 per cent guaranteed, and there were no firm plans at all for selling BBS.

The IRC Board met to consider the situation on 24 January 1969. They acknowledged the risks involved and considered the possibility of a counter-bid for BBL. They felt that the case for the IRC making its first acquisition was both strong and logical and decided to go ahead.

Having made this decision the IRC Board set up a sub-committee comprising its Chairman, Deputy Chairman and Managing Director, and authorised it to negotiate terms within limits set by the Board. Lockwood and Villiers went to see Peter Shore, Minister of State at the DEA, to inform him of the IRC's position. Shore's initial reaction was unenthusiastic, although he accepted the Corporation's right to make the bid. The IRC's motivation was explained at length and Shore finally agreed to give his support.

Rothschilds, who had devised the original R&M–Hoffmann–Pollard scheme, now advised the IRC on the details of its bid for BBL. They suggested that the bid should be at the lower end of the range set by the IRC Board, 45*s* (£2.25) against a current share price of 35*s* (£1.75) which approximately matched the underlying asset value of the company. Rothschilds also accepted an idea which came from IRC to offer, in addition, 'units of participation'. These would be warrants issued to BBL shareholders who accepted the IRC offer, entitling them to any profit that the IRC might make in disposing of BBS and Hoffmann. It was hoped that agreement could be reached with the Brown Bayley Board before any announcement. But the day before the IRC sub-committee was to discuss terms with BBL the news broke in the press. On 30 January 1969, *The Times* reported that the IRC's attempt to reorganise the bearings industry centred on Hoffmann and Brown Bayley. Having pointed out that if BBL sold off its subsidiaries it would be left either with shares it did not want or with cash it would find expensive to distribute, *The Times* concluded that a bid for BBL, with the bidder left to do the dismembering, was the obvious solution. BBL was worth at least 50*s* (£2.50) per share and a bid could not be long delayed.

The report did not surprise the IRC, which had already been told that it would be published as a result of a clumsy City conversation. However, it forced the sub-committee to abandon its plan to allow a week or two for discussions. Instead, BBL was told of IRC's intentions on 30 January and asked to co-operate. The bid was announced on the same day, and the IRC issued a press release explaining its reasons for making the offer and outlining its intentions in the ball and roller bearings and special steels industries (Appendix 6.1).

Discussions revealed that BBL's bankers – Lazards – would probably recommend the offer, subject to reservations about minority shareholders and about price. After some haggling, the IRC agreed to pay 48*s* (£2.40), automatically reducing the potential value of each unit of participation, but only if the offer was recommended by the BBL Board, and accepted for their own shareholdings. This was done later the same day, 13 February, and the bid went through without a hitch. As a result, on 11 March, Villiers was made Chairman of BBL and Cant, an IRC Board Member, was also appointed to BBL's Board. Subsequently Cant and Ewart, an IRC executive, were made Board members of Hoffmann and authorised to begin merger negotiations with R&M.

The bid had been precipitated by a press leak, but the subsequent press comment was, perhaps surprisingly, neutral. The facts were reported, the IRC press release was summarised, and the terms of the offer were assessed. There was one cartoon where the name of the IRC's office door was altered to Industrial Nationalistion Corporation, but this theme was not taken up by reporters or editors. It seemed that IRC's explanation of its bid was accepted or, at least, that the press was content to wait and see what the next moves would be.

SKF'S LAST THROW

Having acquired BBL, the IRC was anxious to move as quickly as possible. Discussions were resumed and at the IRC Board meeting on 14 March the executive was able to report that things appeared to be going smoothly. Skefko had said that it accepted the future existence of a combined R&M–Hoffmann–Pollard group and intended to intensify its own competitive effort to meet it. This was welcomed as an additional spur to improving efficiency in the new group. The Board was also told that R&M were ready to go ahead with a merger with Hoffmann and Pollard. The position had been cleared with the Mergers Panel of the board of Trade and the IRC's initial stake in the new group was estimated at 20 per cent.

Peat, Marwick were again working on the accounts of Hoffmann and R&M (this work having been suspended by agreement during the IRC bid for BBL), but Senior was becoming concerned about Pollard's position. King was invited to meet IRC Board members at the beginning of April and agreed to rejoin the negotiations subject to discussions with his financial advisors. He confirmed this on 8 April and so his announcement, later the same day, that he had reached an advanced stage in negotiations with SKF came as a considerable shock. King told the IRC that, during their recent meeting, he had not been free to reveal that he had been approached by SKF with a view to discussing a merger. Terms had now been agreed for SKF to take 15 per cent of the Pollard equity for £1.6 million, buying new shares for considerably more than their market price. In the immediate future, this would give Pollard cash on very favourable terms, reducing its short-term indebtedness substantially. In the longer run, it would allow an exchange of directors and of information about research and development, as well as providing bigger outlets for Pollard's products. This strengthening of Pollard was, according to King, undoubtedly in the interest of his shareholders. King argued that the scheme made the technical skills of SKF available to part of the British industry, did not give immediate control of any British company to SKF and would lead to two bigger groups, namely R&M–Hoffmann and Pollard–SKF. Since this achieved so much of what IRC originally intended for the industry, King confidently suggested that he should receive the Corporation's blessing.

This final comment may have been intended as facetious, but the hopes which King expressed were certainly not fulfilled. The IRC Board was to meet on 11 April and the executive set out alternative courses of action, which did *not* include support for the Pollard—SKF link. Indeed, the position was not unlike that which had existed when IRC first became involved with the industry. Members felt that the SKF link with Pollard would effectively prevent the proposed three-way merger, by giving King and SKF approximately 45 per cent of the Pollard equity; would probably lead to ultimate Swedish control of Pollard; and might well reduce R&M's interest in a merger with Hoffmann alone.

On 13 April, a Sunday, IRC officials met Senior and were assured that R&M would go ahead with its bid. On Tuesday 15 April, Tony Benn and IRC representatives met Senior, while Lockwood and some of his colleagues met SKF. Inevitably, the latter meeting went yet again over the familiar ground, with Lockwood suggesting that all parties should look at the four-way deal, and with Goodman referring to suspicions in Sweden.

The meeting with Senior was the more important of the two. Benn described Pollard's defection as regrettable but not disastrous and three possibilities were discussed: first, an R&M–Hoffmann merger, which would achieve most of the government's aims; second, an R&M–Hoffman–Pollard merger, perhaps through a bid from R&M strongly supported by the IRC; third an R&M–Hoffmann–Pollard–SKF merger. Benn asked Senior, as Chairman of the leading British company, to pursue these ideas with the IRC. He said that he would certainly like to see the R&M–Hoffmann merger consummated as quickly as possible, and would ask for the issue of Pollard shares to be postponed until then.

R&M were firmly of the opinion that Pollard should be included in the UK group and the IRC executive agreed with this. This view was endorsed by a special IRC Board meeting on 21 April, at which it was agreed that the IRC would underwrite a bid for Pollard by R&M. However, not least because of his large holding in Pollard, King was to be informed before the announcement was made. King was in the USA but, having returned, on 28 April he was told that R&M would bid for Pollard, offering 22*s* 6*d* (£1.12½) per share. He was given forty-eight hours to consider this situation with his advisors. When forty-eight hours expired, at mid-day on Wednesday 30 April, nothing had been heard from King, and Villiers informed King that because of pressure on the Pollard share price, Ransome and Marles felt obliged to announce the offer, the terms of which had been left with him the previous Monday.

After the formal offer, the *Financial Times* argued that the IRC's main problem was to prevent Pollard spinning out the time until its own proposals to link with SKF came up on 14 May, and that its best hope was for Pollard to postpone the meeting. Since R&M might later dilute its earnings by acquiring Hoffmann, a way of avoiding difficulty would be for Pollard shareholders who accepted the R&M bid to be given an overriding say on any proposals emerging from R&M–Hoffmann negotiations (*Financial Times*, 4 May 1969).

The Times took the line that 'Ransome's formal offer document has an air of panic about it'. Pollard holders should vote against the SKF deal at this juncture, wait on events during May and assess the R&M bid on its merits nearer the closing date.

Pressure was put on King to postpone his deal with SKF but, despite a meeting with Stokes and Benn and a personal plea from Villiers, he refused to put off the shareholders' meeting fixed for 14 May which was to vote on the share issue. Indeed, King wrote assuring shareholders that the commercial and financial benefits to be obtained over the years to come to Pollard and its shareholders from the association with SKF and Skefko would be greater than those to be obtained from the present R&M offer. R&M were offering 22*s* 6*d* (£1.12½) whereas SKF would pay 25*s* (£1.25) for only 15.6 per cent of Pollard's equity.

Anxious not to be defeated now, the IRC consulted with R&M who, on 13 May, announced an increased offer of 27*s* 6*d* (£1.37½), in cash, for Pollard shares with a Convertible Loan Stock alternative. The IRC would purchase any Convertible Loan Stock not taken up and would lend R&M up to £3 million. Inevitably, the Pollard meeting now had to be adjourned to allow shareholders time to consider the new offer, while the IRC told King that if the R&M offer was not formally made, or if it lapsed, the Corporation would itself offer 27*s* 6*d* (£1.37½) per Pollard share. There were still fears in the IRC that SKF would improve its terms and, if it did, that R&M would probably refuse to chase the price up further.

A meeting between Senior, IRC representatives and King on 15 May did not remove this anxiety. Senior offered to welcome King to the Board of the new group in semi-executive role, but King hinted that he would prefer the SKF deal.

For once, the fears were unjustified. On 21 May, the Pollard Board recommended shareholders to accept R&M's revised offer and the IRC at once issued a long press statement on the UK ball and roller bearing industry (Appendix 6.2). King explained that he wanted to end his service agreement. While he would not join SKF, he wanted to acquire a Pollard subsidiary, but would remain with the new group long enough to help it off to a good start. 'Ex-Kings are better in exile', he was reported as saying. Later in the year, Mr King did buy a subsidiary of Pollard – R and J Dick.

THE NEW GROUP

During the negotiations with Pollard, discussions had also continued between R&M and the IRC on Hoffmann. These had resulted in an agreed merger on 15 May. So, subject only to the formal ratification by the shareholders of the three companies, the IRC press statement was able to announce the formation of the new UK ball-bearing company – Ransome, Hoffmann, Pollard. The negotiations had taken almost exactly a year and had ended with IRC holding a substantial financial interest in the new group. It had paid £5.4 million (plus the units of participation) for BBL and, although part of this would be recovered following the merger of Hoffmann, it had subscribed for over £6 million of R&M convertible loan stock, as well as lending the company a further £3.1 million. The IRC's concern was now to do all it could to ensure the success of the grouping it had done so much to bring about.

The Corporation was well aware that substantial changes were essential. The average output per man-year of the three companies was 30 per cent below the average for foreign-owned bearings manufacturers operating in the UK. The position at Hoffmann was particularly bad and Cant had undertaken a complete review of its management. The results of this were reported to the IRC Board on 30 May and were not encouraging. The most pressing need was to find a chief executive for the new group. King had been considered for this position but it had become apparent that he would not want, nor would he be able, to work successfully with the managements of the other companies. Now he had announced his intention of leaving the industry altogether. The IRC Board had asked Stokes to co-ordinate the search for a suitable man to take on the job and he reported on progress at the Board Meeting on 30 May. Members discussed this and felt that the challenge posed, plus an attractive salary, should be sufficient to attract candidates of the right calibre. (A salary of £20 000 was mentioned, i.e. the same salary as that of Villiers, the IRC's Managing Director). In the event a suitable candidate was found by management consultants in August. He was G.W. (Bill) Barlow, whom Stokes described as an outstanding young British executive with a proven record of success and a brilliant future. He had management experience, both in the English and the American styles, and was attracted by the challenge of the industry.

Mr Barlow's appointment as chief executive was made public on 14 October, when it was also formally announced that the group was to be named Ransome, Hoffmann, Pollard Ltd (RHP). The main responsibility for RHP's success now passed to Barlow, but the IRC still took an active interest in the firm, with Cant and Ewart both remaining directors.

Barlow decided very early that RHP should be run as a unified business, which would be organised into divisions aimed at the main markets – general bearings, transmission bearings and aerospace bearings – rather than into product groups. Rationalisation was necessary to increase productivity. These views were outlined in a leaflet issued by the company in May 1970, which set out plans for each manufacturing site. The effects of the consequent fall in employment were kept to a minimum by consultation and by a temporary ban on recruitment, but a few senior men were replaced, especially in finance and personnel. Factories and equipment were reorganised to give long production runs and to use higher-speed, more specialised equipment. About £3.5 million was spent on investment in the two years to September 1971. Resistance to a decision to reduce the overall number of types of bearings sold by RHP from about 45 000 to about 15 000, a good deal of it from within RHP itself, was overcome.

There were many people who doubted whether RHP could become successful, but events proved the IRC right and the doubters wrong. In the year to 30 September 1971, RHP had a turnover of £44 million and a net profit before tax of £2.5 million. In the next two years, turnover fell and rose again, with profit reaching a low point of £850 000 in 1972/3. RHP then developed well. Turnover rose to £52 million in 1973/4 and to £64 million in 1974/5. Within this total, export turnover increased from £9 million in 1970/1 to £12 million in 1974/5. The improvement in profit was rapid. It rose to £2.8 million in 1973/4 and to nearly £6 million in 1974/5.

Rationalisation must have had a significant effect, with the labour force down from about 14 500 in 1970 to a little over 10 000 in 1975. A five-year programme of investment transformed factories into well equipped modern units with excellent working conditions.

Subsequently, turnover and exports continued to rise, to almost £100 million and £30 million respectively in 1979/80. Profit stagnated, reflecting difficult market conditions, but RHP maintained its market position against intense international competition.

Indeed, two extracts from an article in the *Financial Times* in January 1979 illustrated the relative success of RHP: 'SKF's problems in Britain are due partly to the fact that in RHP it is up against a strong indigenous producer' and 'As the leading supplier to the British market the group [RHP] managed to maintain its market share in the face of intense competition . . .' (Duffy, 1979).

COMMENTS

The ball-bearing industry had first come to the IRC's attention when it was told about the discussions between R&M and SKF. Its own detection mechanism had not identified this sector as one in need of help or intervention. Even so the formation of RHP must be judged as one of IRC's successes.

Once it became concerned with the industry, the IRC Board decided that it raised important issues and that an urgent study of industry was needed. Within two months, the Board had decided to try to link Pollard and Hoffmann, enabling it to talk to Ransome from a much stronger position. The IRC had already concluded that it would be undesirable to allow a significant increase in foreign control of British ball-bearing manufacture and was expecting events to move quickly. It believed that, far from being neutral, a Skefko–R&M merger would wreck any possibility for forming a viable UK-owned ball-bearing industry.

By this time, Mintech had been persuaded to agree that the IRC should seek a merger, but Mintech was much more cautious than the IRC. As late as October 1968, Mintech was suggesting that SKF would be better as a friend than an enemy, and was torn between a desire to create a strong British ball-bearing producer and an anxiety not to annoy Sweden. Different elements in Mintech, and indeed in Whitehall as a whole, had been emphasising different aspects of the problem. In the discussions with SKF at the beginning of September 1968, Mintech felt it must insist that the firm would be welcome as part of a four-way merger, but had simultaneously set conditions that effectively ruled this out. The IRC's problem was either to bring the Swedes in on acceptable terms or, if they must be left out, to do so while giving them minimum offence. It is therefore unfortunate that, even after Villiers's telephone call to Wallenberg had shown how sensitive the Swedes were, the IRC should have planned to issue a press release and, even worse, given SKF wind of it in advance. The role played by Goodman is an interesting one, but entirely consistent with his almost unique position in British public life. As if this needed further ironic illustration, his appointment to the IRC Board was accepted and confirmed during these negotiations.

One cannot help feeling a good deal of sympathy for SKF and, given the treatment it received, one can hardly be surprised that it should have responded to 'losing' R&M by trying to link with Pollard. The IRC executive's words on SKF – including what it said to its own Board – did not always match its actions. However, while they were embarrassing and tricky, the negotiations with SKF did not hold events up for long. They lasted from October to January and were unavoidable.

The IRC also had its problems with Pollard, especially over the proposals to link with SKF and over King's decision to leave the industry rather than take up a management position in the new company. His going robbed the industry of a man of both energy and colour. Fortunately his talents were soon taken up by Babcock & Wilcox, and subsequently by British Airways.

If the IRC found King increasingly difficult to accommodate, Senior became increasingly amenable. The 'statesman' of the industry, he played a role consistent with that position. In particular, he steadily moved away from his initial enthusiasm for a merger with SKF and did this more in a desire to help the national interest than because his own inclinations had changed.

The negotiations themselves were characterised by intrigue and by the pressure of events. Twice, the IRC had to act against deadlines imposed by potential deals with SKF, and twice its hand was forced by leaks to the press.

More than with the studies in the two previous chapters, the IRC found it difficult to know where to start in fostering this merger. It had no choice but to form a bigger British firm from some combination of R&M, Hoffmann and Pollard, even though SKF appeared from time to time as a possible element. With none of the firms eager to set off the process, different starting points were inevitably proposed at different times. The starting point finally chosen – the IRC takeover of Brown Bayley Ltd – was largely determined by the Corporation's doubts about R&M's willingness to detach itself from SKF and about using Hoffmann as the takeover 'vehicle'. As it turned out, it was fortunate that the IRC's concern with special steels gave it an interest in the remainder of Brown Bayley. Even without that, a bid for Brown Bayley, to be followed by its dismemberment, must always have been a possibility.

Setting the terms for acquiring Brown Bayley, Hoffmann and Pollard proved easy. The IRC's problem, especially over Pollard, was not so much how to determine the right price as that R&M might not be willing, or indeed wise, to chase the price up far enough to outbid SKF. Later there were difficulties with the dissident Hoffmann shareholders and over the anxieties of trade unions representing Hoffmann's employees, but these were handled relatively easily. Perhaps because their firms were in better financial shape, there were fewer difficulties with the employees of R&M or Pollard.

The main event of this chapter might well have been IRC's decision to make its first and only bid for a company, but this went surprisingly smoothly, and was generally accepted as a step towards rationalisation rather than as an attempt to extend state control. The main issues in this chapter therefore concern the IRC's problems over personalities and over plans. How to persuade Senior to abandon the idea of a link with SKF; how to avoid antagonising the Swedes, while keeping the ball-bearing industry British; how to persuade Hoffmann and Brown Bayley to play the roles the IRC wanted; how far to push R&M in bidding for Pollard; and, not least, whether there was any way at all of handling the ebullient King. Each of these was immensely difficult. The IRC threaded a way through the maze, giving some pain to everyone but producing a solution which has stood the test of time. And for once the issue is relatively clear because if there had been no IRC there would now be no major UK-controlled ball-bearing company.

Only one nagging question remains. Given SKF's manifest excellence, was there really *no* way to give it a larger role in the British ball-bearing industry?

APPENDIX 6.1

The statement in this appendix was issued by the IRC on 30 January 1969 in association with the IRC's bid for BBL, and following a press leak in *The Times*.

IRC STATEMENT ON THE OFFER FOR BROWN BAYLEY LTD 30TH JANUARY, 1969

Following studies of the ball and roller bearing industry and of the independent special steel producers, thé Industrial Reorganisation Corportaion ('IRC') has concluded that both industries would benefit substantially by restructuring. In order that restructuring can be carried out with the least delay and to the greatest effect, the IRC is proposing as a first step to make an offer through N.M. Rothschild & Sons for the whole of the issued share capital of Brown Bayley Limited ('Brown Bayley') in view of the latter's controlling interests of 60% in the equity capital of The Hoffmann Manufacturing Company Limited ('Hoffmann') and 50.1% of Brown Bayley Steels ('Steels'). Hoffmann is a leading manufacturer of ball and roller bearings in the UK and Steels is one of the largest independent UK producers of alloy or special steels.

The IRC has informed the board of Brown Bayley of the details of the offer and has explained the reason why it is taking this step. The formal offer will be despatched as soon as possible. In the event of the IRC offer being successful, it intends to do everything possible to safeguard the interests of the staff and employees.

It is the IRC's purpose in making this offer to achieve substantial industrial restructuring in conjunction with other major companies in both the bearing and alloy steel industries, which is expected to result in subsequent disposal of Brown Bayley's controlling interest in Hoffmann and Steels. In undertaking this action the IRC will also take account of the interests of the existing ordinary shareholders of Brown Bayley by obtaining the advice of independent financial consultants as to the terms of such disposals; it will also ensure that equivalent terms are offered to the minority shareholders in both Hoffmann and Steels. If immediately following these subsequent disposals, the net asset value per share of Brown Bayley exceeds a sum equal to the total of 45*s* plus stamp duty, expenses and interest incurred by the IRC in acquiring and holding the share capital, the excess will be paid in cash to Brown Bayley shareholders who have accepted the IRC offer. Pending any such payment, accepting shareholders will receive 'certificates of participation'. It is intended to arrange for the certificates to be dealt in on The Stock Exchange, London.

The UK Ball and Roller Bearing Industry

The IRC has been studying this industry since last summer. The total value of production of the UK Bearing Industry is currently about £70 million. Exports in 1967 were £15 million while imports were £9 million. The motor industry is the largest single customer, accounting for about 30% of annual production. In recent years the UK industry has been dominated by six leading manufacturers; three of which are controlled from within the UK and three of which are foreign controlled. From its studies, factory visits, discussions with customers and others closely associated with this industry, the IRC is of the opinion that there is a strong case for rationalisation to strengthen the UK industry. The major manufacturers and customers in the UK concur with this conclusion. The Ministry of Technology has been involved in these discussions from the outset and fully supports the views of the IRC.

A substantial proportion of each manufacturer's range of bearings overlaps with that of other manufacturers. Restructuring will make possible greater standardisation of product lines, and longer runs of individual items. A certain amount of competition will be eliminated by regrouping but at the same time continuing effective competition would be assured in the UK by the pressure of imports and the presence of substantial foreign controlled companies. A larger ball bearing group will also be better able to support, and benefit from, a combined research and development effort. Though the overall balance of trade performance of the industry is positive, the UK industry has an adverse trade balance with the rest of Europe; the UK's share of total European imports is only 6%. A larger, UK based company should be better able to mount the initially costly overseas marketing effort required to penetrate export markets effectively. In these respects comparisons with the industry in other countries point to the benefits of large companies deploying considerable resources and exploiting large production units.

The IRC has concluded that it is both practically possible and strategically sensible to promote a strong ball and roller bearing industry under British control. The IRC wishes to acknowledge the co-operative attitude of the leading bearing manufacturers in the UK and others closely associated with the industry during the discussions with the industry.

The Private Sector of the UK Alloy Steels Industry

The UK alloy steel producers developed in smaller units than those of common steel producers. Consequently since nationalisation in 1967 was based on a tonnage measure of production, only the largest alloy steel producing groups were incorporated into the British Steel Corporation ('BSC'). Approximately two-thirds of the UK's alloy steel making capacity is now owned by the BSC. The remaining third is owned by a number of private sector steelmakers, including Steels, which is one of the three largest producers of alloy steels in the private sector.

The BSC's alloy steel-making capacity is concentrated into three major and two minor units. In the private sector, however, the industry is still highly fragmented and the capacity of even the largest of the private sector producers is less than one half of the largest units being operated by the BSC. Although alloy steels are specialised products and are required in smaller quantities than normal or carbon steels, concentration within the private sector could yield production economies and enable future investment in larger plants to be undertaken on an economic basis. In addition, there exists benefits to be reaped from the fuller integration of the steel making and re-rolling processes in this industry.

The IRC has been in contact with the private sector of the steel industry since late 1966. In October, 1967, the IRC announced its support for a merger between Dunford & Elliott (Sheffield) Limited, a leading re-roller of bar and rod, and Hadfields Limited, an alloy steel maker with its own forge and a smaller re-rolling activity. In the course of its investigation of the alloy steels industry, the IRC has maintained regular contact with the BSC and is fully aware of the importance to the private sector of the current BSC pricing proposals. The BSC is aware of and is in agreement with IRC's intention to effect reorganisation.

The IRC was entrusted by its Act to promote the greater efficiency and international competitiveness of British industry. If the offer for Brown Bayley is successful, it will consult with all interested parties to ensure in disposing of its investments that it achieves these aims in the industries concerned.

APPENDIX 6.2

IRC STATEMENT ON THE UK BALL AND ROLLER BEARING INDUSTRY

The Board of the Pollard Ball & Roller Bearing Company (Pollard) announced today 21st May, 1969, its intention to recommend the offer made by Ransome & Marles Bearing Company (Ransome & Marles), for the ordinary share capital of Pollard. Earlier it was announced that terms for a merger had been agreed between Ransome & Marles and The Hoffmann Manufacturing Company (Hoffmann). Provided these merger proposals, which are recommended by the Boards and their financial advisers, are ratified by the shareholders of the respective companies, the basis will have been laid for a viable British owned ball bearing industry which it has been the purpose of IRC policy over recent months to promote. IRC is publishing this statement in order that the public should have a comprehensive account both of the industrial reasoning behind IRC's policy and of the complex negotiations which have brought that policy to fruition.

Early in May 1968 IRC's attention was drawn to impending developments in the ball and roller bearing industry (henceforth referred to as the ball bearing industry). The situation was considered at the IRC Board Meeting on 17th May, 1968, and for three reasons it was decided that a detailed investigation of the industry should be undertaken by IRC staff. In the first place, the ball bearing industry is a large sector of engineering technology, making an essential input to major exporting sectors such as the motor and aircraft industries; secondly, compared with the industries in Western Europe and North America the structure of the UK based industry appeared fragmented and thus fell directly within IRC's remit; and in the third place the possibility of a merger between Ransome & Marles and The Skefko Ball Bearing Company (Skefko : a subsidiary of SKF of Sweden) could mean that there might shortly be no viable British owned company in the industry.

In its study of the industry IRC followed its established pattern of informing itself about the companies concerned, visiting their various manufacturing units and conducting an extensive dialogue on all aspects of the situation with the senior management of the producing companies and their main customers. IRC wishes to record its appreciation of the full cooperation that was extended to it by all those companies with whom it was in contact. IRC also had the benefit of working closely with the Department of Economic Affairs, the Ministry of Technology and the Board of Trade. This work was supported by a detailed examination of relevant reports from government agencies and private institutions from which useful information was obtained on the structure of the industry in other industrialised economies and on the trading characteristics and performance of companies in Western Europe. Although much of the factual information made available to IRC is strictly confidential and cannot be published, the principal considerations which impressed themselves on IRC in reaching its conclusions can be stated.

The characteristic structure of the industry in other advanced economies shows a very high degree of concentration. In Germany two companies, SKF and Kugelfischer FAG share over 80% of the market; in other countries, notably France and Italy, the market is dominated by SKF with approximately 70% of the market. The pattern is similar in the Scandinavian countries where the market for bearings is again largely supplied by SKF. The factors that have made for this concentrated structure are principally the need to gain maximum economies by optimising the lengths of production runs, and the need to limit the range of bearings to be produced. The economies of scale to be reaped from volume production were demonstrated to IRC in detailed breakdowns of various cost structures for different manufacturing units. There are, of course, particular applications where the small specialist producer is able to compete. But to supply ball bearings efficiently and profitably for the wide range of applications in the electrical and mechanical engineering industry, particularly the motor industry which takes over 30% of the UK production, all the successful companies have insisted on the necessity for volume production supported by advanced production engineering know-how.

It was against this background that IRC considered the situation in the UK industry. In 1968 total UK based production amounted to some £70 million of which £15 million was exported. Imports accounted for £11 million making total UK consumption of £66 million. There were six major manufacturers, three of whom are wholly owned subsidiaries or operating divisions of foreign groups: Skefko, British Timken (Division of the Timken Roller Bearing Co., USA), Fafnir (subsidiary of Textron Inc., USA). The three other major manufacturers were UK controlled: Ransome & Marles, Hoffmann and Pollard. The share of domestic consumption held by the three UK owned companies is approximately 35%. Skefko supplies about 27% and the rest is shared between the other companies and imports.

There was an identity of view in the industry that with the possible exception of tapered bearings, where production is shared by Skefko and Timken alone, there were too many companies producing in sub-optimum manufacturing units an excessive range of bearings in too short runs. The fragmentation in the industry was one major factor causing low productivity which international comparisons made clear: output per employee in Europe is on average approximately £3000 per annum; in the UK owned companies the comparable figure averages only just over £2000 per annum. The performance of the UK industry has reflected these limitations. In 1963 the value of our exports was over 75% more than the value of our imports; in 1968 exports were only 36% more than imports and the UK had increasingly heavy deficits in our balance of trade with the advanced economies of Western Europe and North America. The existing surplus is based on our established position in the slower growing Commonwealth markets. The UK's share of European imports was only 6%.

One of IRC's overriding considerations in promoting industrial reorganisation is to assist British industry to improve its export potential. Amongst those European countries for which information was available IRC observed that apart from Sweden, the only country with a strong surplus in its trade in ball bearings was Germany. The independent German company, Kugelfischer FAG, made a strong contribution to this surplus. IRC was also aware that SKF, as with any strongly based international group, acting in the interest of its own efficiency and profitability might well find it advantageous to rationalise its production facilities, locate its R&D, buy its raw materials and machine tools and direct its marketing policy in ways which would not necessarily benefit the UK economy.

For this reason IRC, whilst in no way excluding cooperation with Skefko, went deeply into the possibility of creating a strong British controlled element in the industry out of the three British owned companies, Ransome & Marles, Hoffmann and Pollard. The three companies, with combined sales of over £30 million, offer considerable possibilities for rationalisation and development. The two largest companies each manufacture between 7000–13 000 different types of bearings and a major proportion of all three companies' products overlap. Rationalisation would make possible standardisation of product lines, the concentration of production of the component parts – balls, rollers, cages and races – and a reduction of stocks. The resulting volume of sales and economies of scale could be expected to generate a cash flow for new plant and machinery, for sustaining a strong development effort in advanced production engineering techniques and mounting an extensive overseas marketing effort. Thus a strong British owned group would be formed, and the position of Skefko, firmly established in the UK market and with the backing of SKF's international operations particularly strong in the tariff-free EFTA market, would not be prejudiced. The result would be a balanced industry ensuring effective competition of benefit to producer and customer.

The Board of IRC decided accordingly on 27th September, 1968, to support the formation of a British owned company comprising if possible the three British owned ball bearing companies. IRC was aware that a strong group would have to include Ransome & Marles, the leading British owned company, and that it would therefore be necessary to request SKF not to proceed with its merger arrangements. Equally IRC was aware of the great contribution SKF could make to the efficiency and technical development of the industry and was anxious therefore that the possibility for an association should be left open. IRC was supported by the Ministry of Technology and the Department of Economic Affairs in these decisions and in the subsequent negotiations that have taken place to give effect to them.

The views of IRC were expressed to SKF at meetings which took place during October 1968 and which were attended by Senior Government Officials and the Chairman and Managing Director of IRC.

On 31st October the Managing Director of IRC wrote to the Chairman of Skefko setting out IRC's position in the following terms: 'The IRC Board has always had the highest opinion of Skefko in all its manifestations and I have gone out of my way at every meeting concerned with the problems of this industry to stress how desirable IRC considered it to be that SKF – in some way to be defined – should participate in the rationalisation of the British-owned ball bearings industry. . . . The IRC Board feels that the right way to proceed is through a grouping of the three British-owned Companies in the ball bearings industry, leaving room at every stage for SKF participation. Such participation would, of course, involve assurances of a type which I expect you have already discussed with Ransome & Marles, and there may be others which we would propose. It would also involve a survey of the manufacture of the whole range of ball bearings and rationalisation of production in this country. There would, of course, also be questions of management, and the financial problems would be formidable. We remain, however, of the opinion that if agreement can be reached between all the parties concerned the foundations will have been laid for an important Company, which will benefit not only the shareholders concerned but also the British balance of payments and the productivity of British Industry'.

On this basis the Chairman of the three British owned companies were invited by IRC on 18th November to participate in an investigation by an independent firm of Chartered Accountants which would collect and analyse financial information on the three companies as the basis for the detailed merger negotiations which would take place later. In a letter of 4th December from the chairman of IRC, Skefko were also invited to participate in the Accountants' investigation on the same basis as the other companies and to continue discussions with IRC on possible ways in which they could be involved in a comprehensive scheme for reorganisation. In this letter IRC listed the questions on which satisfactory arrangements would need to be negotiated. These were 'such important issues as control, market share, the industry's contribution to the Balance of Payments, commercial freedom, rationalisation of production and, of course, management structure'. The subsequent discussions with SKF broke down almost immediately on the question of control.

By January 1969 progress in the discussions with the companies was slowing down and the Board of IRC decided that reorganisation could be achieved to best effect and with least delay if it had itself a firm base from which to negotiate. Accordingly IRC made a cash offer on 31st January for the shares of Brown Bayley Ltd, which owned 60% of the ordinary shares of Hoffmann. At this juncture it was agreed with IRC that Pollard should withdraw from the negotiations. A revised IRC bid, recommended by the Board of Brown Bayley and its financial advisers, became unconditional on 28th February. Immediately thereafter IRC invited Pollard to discuss terms on which that business could be brought into the proposed three-company group. However, since withdrawing from the IRC sponsored negotiations, Pollard had held negotiations with Skefko and announced on 8th April that terms had been agreed for Skefko to take a 15.6% interest in Pollard by subscribing for new shares at a price considerably above the then market price. The arrangements were also to provide for an exchange of Directors and of technical developments in design, manufacturing and engineering research.

At this point in a long and complex negotiation, Ransome & Marles and IRC had to decide whether to settle for a two-way grouping or to proceed with an offer to the shareholders of Pollard for all their shares. IRC was particularly influenced by the judgment of the Board of Ransome & Marles as the focal point in the reorganisation. Both Ransome & Marles and the management of Hoffmann considered that there were important industrial and commercial arguments in favour of including Pollard in the group. The decisive considerations were that Pollard's output was strongly concentrated on the standard range of bearings where the economies of volume production were particularly applicable, that Pollard had useful additional market outlets in the UK and abroad, and that with Pollard the British group would have a market share enabling it to stand up to strong foreign based competitors.

Accordingly IRC gave full support to Ransome & Marles' offer for Pollard. A first offer was announced on 30th April and a revised offer of 27/6 in cash per Pollard share was subsequently recommended by the Pollard Board on 21st May. The three-way grouping had thus been achieved.

IRC is conscious that the successful conclusion of this negotiation does not in itself create a viable commercial enterprise. IRC is a major shareholder in the new group and intends to see that the funds it has made available are turned to good account. As before, IRC is prepared to consider participation by SKF or another large international ball bearing company in the enlarged group on arrangements similar to those envisaged between Skefko and Pollard, subject to the necessary consents being obtained from the Board of Trade. IRC is keen to promote joint industrial ventures on terms that can be seen to be beneficial to the parties concerned and it is currently considering various possibilities in ball bearings and other fields.

IRC is convinced that the management and engineering skills can be found in British industry to build up a group with the required technical competence and financial strength to compete at home and in world markets. IRC is firmly supported by Lord Stokes, Chairman of British Leyland, who has agreed to advise on building up a management team. The success of this venture will be determined by the ability and will of those involved in the industry to seize the opportunities that reorganisation has created for the integration of the three existing businesses. IRC intends to use its shareholding to see that this is done and to dispose of its holding as soon as the new group has demonstrated its viability in markets at home and abroad.

21st May, 1969.

7

The British Motor Holdings – Leyland Merger

British Leyland was formed in April 1968. It was the culmination of a whole series of mergers of UK-owned motor companies. These mergers had brought together Leyland, AVC, Standard, Triumph and Rover on the one hand and Austin, Morris, MG and Jaguar on the other. So the creation of the British Leyland Motor Corporation, albeit after protracted and often tortuous negotiations, can be viewed as but the final move in the concentration of the UK industry in the face of international competition. Given this, the merger was probably inevitable, at some time or other, and the IRC influenced only its terms and timing.

The IRC was much less heavily involved in the British Leyland negotiations than it was with the GEC, Kent and RHP mergers, but this was an important deal for the IRC for several reasons. First, it was one of the earliest and one of the largest of the IRC's mergers. Second, the IRC advanced more money, an initial loan of £25 million plus a further £10 million later, than in any other case. Third, the BL deal illustrates what was probably the IRC's most consistent and effective skill. This was its ability to facilitate (using cash if necessary) and to push through a merger which had been suggested by other people but which had run into problems.

In this case, and in many others, the IRC was reacting to events rather than imposing its designs on the companies involved. Its reaction was well prepared, constructive and in the event successful, at least in ensuring that the merger went ahead. Whether, with hindsight, the merger itself can be seen as the best way ahead for the UK motor industry at the time is more debatable and is considered further at the end of this chapter.

THE EARLY DISCUSSIONS

Leyland and British Motor Holdings (BMH) had been talking on and off about a full or partial merger since 1964. The full story, based on access to British Leyland Board minutes and to internal documents, is told in Graham Turner's comprehensive and detailed book, *The Leyland Papers* (Turner, 1971; see Ch. 7 therein, 'The grand alliance – opening moves', for details of the early discussions). In this chapter, we shall concentrate on the involvement of the IRC and the government in the negotiations leading up to the merger and in the events which followed.

The IRC's first public deal had been, at the government's request, to take a financial stake in Rootes Motors and to act as a public watchdog following the extension of Chrysler's holding in the company to over 50 per cent (see Ch. 3). During the talks on the future of Rootes, Tony Benn, the Minister of Technology, had told the IRC that the government favoured a merger between Leyland and BMH. He said that both he and the Prime Minister, Harold Wilson, had made this known to the chairmen of the two companies in personal discussions. This was in December 1966 and the IRC at once held talks with the companies, both separately and together, but without any immediate results.

The next move came from the companies themselves. Partly at the prompting of Benn they had been considering some form of co-operation in overseas markets. It was decided that Ceylon would make a good starting point. So, in February 1967, Benn made a statement in the House of Commons saying that Leyland and BMH were having exploratory discussions and that all parties agreed that the IRC would be an ideal intermediary. A meeting was arranged and the possibility of a joint assembly plant in Ceylon was explored. Talks on this drifted on through the summer and were finally abandoned in October. By then, however, more progress was being made on other fronts.

Even in the spring, the IRC was looking beyond limited collaboration and, at its April Board meeting, the IRC executive argued the case for a full merger between the two companies. Its concern was for both the short-run financial position of BMH and for its long-run survival and growth. The company's profits had fallen from over £20 million in the early 1960s to zero in 1965/6 and it had lost £7.5 million in the first half of 1966/7. It had a poor investment record, only limited plans for new models, and increasing liquidity problems. The IRC could not see how, if it remained on its own, BMH could raise the cash required for the investment and rationalisation necessary to restore it to reasonable profitability.

Leyland's profits, on the other hand, had quadrupled in the four years from 1962 to 1965 and were £17 million in 1966. Stokes himself had acquired an impressive public reputation and, significantly, was an IRC Board member. (He was, of course, excluded from all discussions at IRC Board meetings relating to his company and its competitors.) He was therefore seen as having the vision and management drive required to improve BMH fortunes, given the economies and greater financial strength that a merger could bring.

Despite these factors, the argument presented to the IRC Board was by no means one-sided. Potential benefits were said to include the rationalisation of designs; the production economies of long runs; the merging and streamlining of the marketing and distribution networks – to give the advantage of offering a full range of both cars and commercial vehicles; the concentration of management skills; and a pooling of research and development expertise. Doubts were, however, expressed about the wisdom of concentrating the greater part of the British motor industry in one company, and about the bad effect that this might have on labour relations. It was pointed out that high quality management was spread somewhat thinly in both companies.

The IRC Board decided that, despite their reservations, the possibilities for a merger should be investigated further. It also agreed to consider the case for providing IRC finance if this was necessary, to bring forward rationalisation and investment following the merger. Both companies were then formally approached for more information about their operations and financial position. According to Turner, Stokes and the Chairman of BMH, Sir George Harriman, discussed this on the phone on 12 May and

> they agreed that there would be no objection to the IRC examining their figures, providing they were of the kind available to any stockholder; they also came to an understanding that they would regard this merely as a private investigation which did not imply negotiations of any sort (Turner, 1971, p. 114).

The IRC, however, took the initiative and Kearton asked two merchant banks, Warburgs and Lazards, to draw up merger proposals based on the information which the companies had provided. They did this very quickly and, before the end of May, Kearton showed the results of their work to Stokes and Harriman. The bankers felt that, partly for tax reasons, one of the companies should be used as a 'takeover vehicle'. They drew up two schemes, using each company in turn; however, both schemes gave each firm 50 per cent of the equity of the combined company.

In discussions which followed, the proposals were approved by the Leyland representatives, subject to their obtaining full authority to proceed from their management, but Harriman was not nearly so enthusiastic, and wanted to wait a year or eighteen months. BMH was trading at a loss, and it may well be that Harriman thought a merger at that time would look too much like a rescue operation, and that his company would be in too weak a bargaining position.

STOKES TAKES THE INITIATIVE

When merger talks had first begun, Leylayd had been clearly the junior partner. BMH was larger in terms of assets and sales and, up to the mid 1960s still had higher profits. By the summer of 1967 the picture was significantly different, with BMH making a loss while Leyland was forecasting an increase in profits to about £20 million. When the first IRC initiative broke down Stokes began to think seriously about making a bid for BMH rather than waiting, perhaps indefinitely, for an agreed deal.

Stokes still had some doubts about the advantages of the merger, but two actions were taken to prepare the ground if the decision to bid was eventually taken. The first was a technical issue relating to Leyland's share structure. It had just over 50 million £1 shares whereas BMH had approximately 250 million 5*s* (25p) shares. The Leyland Board decided to split the £1 shares into four and make a one for four scrip issue, thus creating about the same number of shares in Leyland as there were in BMH.

This was seen to have two advantages. First, it would make the technicalities of any bid simpler and the terms more readily understandable. Second, and more important, if the timing of a bid was right, such that it could be combined with a suitable profit forecast, it might well take Leyland's market capitalisation above that of BMH. Contingency plans were therefore made to undertake the share split.

The second preparatory action was to clear the ground with the government. This scarcely seemed necessary as the government and the IRC had been pressing for the merger, but Stokes felt it possible that there would be a different reaction to a Leyland takeover bid opposed by BMH. Stokes therefore went to see Benn at the end of July and asked for an indication that the government would not refer a takeover bid to the Monopolies Commission.

Benn pointed out that the decision rested with the President of the Board of Trade but agreed to raise the matter confidentially with the Monopolies and Mergers Panel. This was a committee made up of representatives from relevant Whitehall departments. It was responsible for examining situations which appeared to come within the scope of the monopolies legislation and then advising the President of the Board of Trade. Benn arranged for the Panel to give an informal and provisional view and this gave Stokes the answer he wanted.

Having made these two moves the Leyland Board decided to wait until after the publication of its 1966/7 preliminary figures, due in the second half of October. Before this took place there was further top level political intervention.

Both Benn and Wilson were anxious for progress to be made and well over six months had now passed since the first talks between the companies and the IRC. So, at the beginning of October, Harold Wilson invited Harriman and Stokes to join him and Benn for dinner at Chequers. The story of the evening at Chequers and the impression it made is told in Graham Turner's book (Turner, 1971, pp. 120–122). All that need concern us here is that both men, and Harriman in particular, seemed to come away from it with an increased desire to find a way to an agreed merger.

It was arranged at Chequers that representatives of the two companies would meet again on 20 October. A few days before that, Leyland's results became available and its Board decided to go ahead with the share split. The effect on Leyland's share price was all that had been hoped for and when the meeting took place the market value of Leyland's shares had overtaken that of BMH.

Even so, Leyland took a very constructive approach at the meeting. First, Stokes agreed that he would not make a unilateral bid for BMH. Then, when the discussions seemed to be bogged down on differences on management structure and other issues, Leyland suggested bringing in a neutral arbitrator. The Prudential Assurance Company was a major shareholder in both Leyland and BMH and seemed the ideal choice to make an independent assessment of both companies' figures and forecasts and to suggest reasonable terms for a deal.

The 'Pru' was approached and agreed to take on the task. When it gave its views in November, it was clear that more weight had been given to BMH's asset value and recovery potential (backed up by bullish forecasts) than to its current profitability and market values. The Pru's suggestion was that BMH shareholders should be given 55 per cent of the combined company – more than the merchant bankers had proposed in the previous spring, despite the fact that BMH's relative position had deteriorated significantly since then.

So Leyland's approach had misfired: under no circumstances was it prepared to accept the Pru's proposals. Moreover, the differences between the two firms on how the group should be run seemed irreconcilable. BMH wanted a loose federation of the existing businesses under a holding company. Leyland insisted on a clear, strong command structure under Stokes as managing director and chief executive. So, by the end of November, Stokes had again come round to the view that an outright takeover bid from Leyland would be the best answer. The two chairmen had agreed to discuss the matter again with Benn before any final decision was made, and they did this just before Christmas. Benn suggested that negotiations should not be broken off and that Kearton should be brought in to act as mediator. So the IRC came back into the centre of things.

Now that there really was pressure, either for an agreed deal or for a Leyland bid, the IRC had several important advantages. First, as a government agency, it could reinforce the political pressures for a merger. Second, Kearton and his executive could devote much more time than could Wilson or Benn to the details of the negotiations and to long bargaining sessions. Third, the IRC had cash to offer, on appropriate terms, and it was clear that the combined company would need a substantial capital injection if it was to undertake major rationalisation and development. Stokes' position as an IRC Board member was also important. It meant that the IRC knew him well and it constrained him, to some extent, to listen to the views of the Corporation and to co-operate with it as far as possible.

So, once more, Leyland's plans for a unilateral bid were postponed and negotiations resumed on an agreed merger. A preliminary meeting was held between all the parties on 8 January 1968. Kearton next met most of the key people in both companies individually. Then, on the evening of Sunday 14 January, he acted as a go-between, with the Leyland team in Stokes's flat in St James and BMH at the Hyde Park Hotel (again a detailed account of the meeting that Sunday evening is given in Turner, 1971, pp. 145–147). The key issue to be settled was still management structure, but by 01.00 the next morning Kearton's patient negotiating skill had helped to produce an agreement, although the atmosphere between the two sides was still strained. Nevertheless, the companies arranged to go back to the IRC later the same day to set out their respective forecasts and to begin the bargaining process on the financial terms for the merger.

When the parties had gathered at the IRC's Pall Mall offices on the Monday morning, BMH revealed that it had significantly reduced its profit forecast for the current year. The Leyland side were not surprised by the direction of the change but were taken aback by the magnitude of the revision as compared with the figures given to the Prudential Assurance Company only two months earlier. They asked for more detailed information and the meeting was adjourned until the late afternoon.

At this second meeting, BMH gave a full account of its financial position. Among other things it revealed that its overdraft had risen to over £50 million, making it certain that IRC cash would be an essential part of any merger deal. BMH answered detailed questions on its figures but Leyland decided that it must have a fuller examination by merchant bankers before it could go ahead.

Leyland's regular Board meeting was held the next day, Tuesday 16th January, at which the progress that had been made was reviewed. The issues on management had been settled satisfactorily, with Harriman as Chairman but Stokes as Managing Director and effectively chief executive. The revision in BMH's forecast had removed any chance of BMH acquiring more than half of the new company and a 50:50 basis had been agreed. The major concern was the seriousness of BMH's Financial position but the Leyland Board gave authority for provisional heads of agreement to be signed, subject to a more thorough examination of the figures.

That evening, the Boards of both companies met at the IRC. Their respective bankers had spent the day going through the figures and were reassured that the position seemed no worse than that which BMH had reported the day before. The final details of an announcement were discussed and agreed. There would be an equal number of directors from Leyland and BMH on the new Board and the Chairman would not have a casting vote. Harriman would be a full-time chairman and it would be made clear that his responsibilities were quite distinct from those of Stokes as Managing Director. The new group would operate as a single autonomous unit, not as a holding company – this was another victory for Leyland's point of view. And the IRC would consider a loan of £25 million on terms and conditions to be agreed. The formal document incorporating these terms was signed and announced the following day. So it seemed that the UK was to have a new giant motor corporation to take on the rest of the world.

FURTHER ARGUMENTS AND FINAL RESOLUTION

The agreement, announced in the glare of mostly favourable and optimistic press comment, was of course subject to the approval of the shareholders of both companies. This was scheduled for March 1968 but before then the merger came very close to being called off.

There were still serious frictions over the management hierarchy in the new company, and particularly over the relative positions of Stokes and the BMH Managing Director, Joe Edwards. Whether or not this problem could have been resolved is not clear, because it was overtaken in February by a row over another downward revision in BMH's profit projections. The final result for the year ending in July 1967 had been a loss of about £4 million and it now seems that BMH would, at best, break even in the first half of 1967/8 (before taking into account exceptional items such as benefits from the 1967 devaluation of sterling). Prospects were little better for the second half of the year. So, instead of a profit forecast that had varied from £12 million to £20 million, it now seemed that BMH might fail to make a significant profit for 1967/8 as a whole.

Leyland Board members were very disturbed by this, as they were by BMH's continuing sluggish production and high stocks and its consequent failure to reduce its substantial overdraft. The two sides met again on 14 February, with BMH's merchant bankers and legal advisors present. Stokes told the meeting that, in view of the latest information on BMH's financial position, Leyland could no longer recommend the provisional terms of the merger to its shareholders. Moreover, as Leyland's annual general meeting was fixed for 20 February, it was important that a final decision should be made very quickly. The BMH side indicated that they felt that Leyland was overreacting but, if the agreed terms were not now acceptable, there was nothing left to be done but to draw up a press statement announcing that the merger had been called off. In fact, after several hours of drafting, the two sides failed to find a mutually acceptable form of words for the announcement and the meeting broke up in disarray. This gave Kearton one last chance to retrieve the position, and at 23.30 Stokes was asked to attend an emergency meeting at the London flat of his senior financial advisor. When he arrived he found that Kearton was there and that a senior partner from BMH's merchant bankers was also expected.

Kearton was brought up to date on the position between the two companies. He said that the IRC was not prepared to see the merger slip away. An announcement that it had been abandoned because of a deterioration in BMH's financial position would be very damaging not only to the company itself, but also to its component suppliers and indirectly to the reputation of British manufacturing industry as a whole. If no compromise could be found, Kearton indicated that the IRC would support an immediate takeover bid by Leyland for BMH.

This put BMH in a very difficult position. If it lost a takeover battle it might face worse terms for its shareholders and have little or no say in management. Even if it fought off the bid, the public battle was likely to be very damaging. According to Turner, the advice from BMH's bankers was that it should aim to stick to the terms of the merger but should compromise on management, and Harriman was prepared to accept this advice (Turner, 1971, p. 167). Leyland, for its part, was prepared to accept the additional risk implied by BMH's revised figures, provided that it had full management control once the new company was formed. Certainly, this was how things worked out. Private letters were signed under which Harriman would resign as Chairman within six months and Stokes would take over as Chairman and Chief Executive. The merger went ahead. It was approved as planned by the stockholders of both companies in March 1968, and British Leyland was born.

The resignation of the BMH Managing Director, Joe Edwards, was almost inevitable and came in April. Stokes was therefore assured of a clear majority on the combined Board. He had achieved almost all the crucial points he wanted from the deal without any of the harmful publicity that a bitterly fought takeover battle would have produced. He was, however, glad to make one concession. This was to undertake that BMH's Jaguar subsidiary would remain a largely autonomous unit under the management of its founder, Sir William Lyons, and Stokes and Lyons worked together increasingly closely.

It is possible, but no means certain, that the link-up would have happened through a bid, even if the IRC had not intervened. The difference would then have been that the squabbles between the two managements would have taken place in public and not in private. Two points should, however, be remembered. First, Graham Turner, who studied the situation closely, and with full access to the company papers, says of the potential takeover bid: 'It is at least doubtful whether Leyland would in fact have launched one: Stokes had grave doubts as well as ambitions' (Turner, 1971, p. 171). Second, British Leyland needed IRC money if it was to have any chance of carrying through a rationalisation programme. One of BMH's fundamental problems had been its low level of investment. It had half the capital per man of Vauxhall or Rootes and only a third of that of Ford of Britain. If the merger was to produce a company fully able to compete internationally, it was essential for investment to be stepped up, and this meant more money. The group's combined overdraft was more than £60 million and the prospect of obtaining sufficient cash from any source other than the IRC was remote.

Indeed, the IRC was asked to increase the amount of money it had agreed to make available. It declined to do this, taking the view that its role was not to refinance the group's existing borrowings but to provide additional finance to facilitate the integration of the activities of the two companies and to enable investment to take place. The IRC did, however, make two important concessions to British Leyland. First, it agreed that the £25 million which it supplied would be in the form of unsecured loan stock. Second, it made this available at slightly below the market rate of interest.

The second concession was unusual and indicated the importance IRC attached to the merger. Indeed, in its own Annual Report and Accounts the IRC said that '. . . the merger between Leyland and British Motor Holdings is of cardinal importance . . .' (IRC, 1967/8, p. 10).

The terms of the loan also allowed for a supplementary rate of interest of 2 per cent per annum to be paid over its entire period. This supplement would come into effect if, for any year during the seven year life of the loan, Leyland paid a dividend on its ordinary shares in excess of 10 per cent. This condition was introduced to ensure that the concessionary interest rate was not used to finance a higher dividend, or to provide a better return to the IRC if the group's performance was really exceptional. (For details of the loan see Appendix A at the end of this book.)

Finally, the provision of such a substantial sum implied, at least as far as the IRC Board was concerned, the need to follow up the merger to see that it succeeded. The recipients of IRC cash did not always agree with this attitude, however, and British Leyland was the earliest example of the IRC's continuing difficulty in following up mergers it had helped to arrange, to ensure that the anticipated benefits were realised. By the spring of 1968, there was a strong feeling among the IRC's executives that this would be almost as vital a part of the Corporation's role in any merger as arranging the original deal.

FOLLOW UP

At one time it had been felt that the IRC should have a director on the British Leyland Board, as it had with Rootes. In the end, it was decided to rely instead on regular contacts with the company and on studies of its figures. In April 1968, Villiers therefore went to see Stokes. He suggested that there should be a meeting every quarter between British Leyland and the IRC to discuss progress, and he asked Leyland to supply detailed, quarterly figures to the IRC so long as the IRC loan to British Leyland was outstanding. Stokes was extremely reluctant to give the IRC any information which a firm's bankers would not demand in a similar situation, but he did agree to send to the IRC, quarterly, the overall sales and profit figures for the group.

Between 1968 and April 1971, when the IRC was abolished, there were only two full-scale meetings between the company and the IRC, though there were a number of less formal contacts. The first meeting, a presentation by British Leyland executives to the IRC executive, did not take place until November 1969. The IRC prepared itself well for the meeting. The executive was particularly concerned about British Leyland's continuing industrial relations problems and about the group's low productivity as compared with that of its international competitors. They estimated that to reach the level of sales per employee of Volkswagen, British Leyland would need to cut as many as 47,000 from its workforce of 188,000. Yet no redundancies had been announced. On the contrary, the IRC estimated that the company's workforce had actually risen by 8,000 in the previous year, while Rootes built car bodies with half the man-hours required in British Leyland. How much the meeting achieved is questionable. One IRC executive complained that the presentation was no more than a public relations exercise with no chance for detailed questions, let alone a more positive IRC role.

In the following February, however, the IRC devised a scheme which, as a by-product, could have given it a new lever with which to influence British Leyland. Its purpose was both to provide more cash for the company and to give a stimulus to the ailing UK machine tool industry. The proposal was for the IRC to lend £10 million to British Leyland on the condition that this was used to advance its purchases of UK machine tools.

The rationale of this arrangement, which might have been extended to other major companies, is discussed in full in Chapter 8. Its aim, in relation to the machine tool industry, was to encourage major customers to order in advance of an upturn in the economy. In this way, it was hoped to reduce the bunching of orders, lengthening delivery times and loss of business to imports. It was also designed to provide a more stable basis from which the UK machine tool industry could develop more sophisticated products.

As far as British Leyland was concerned the rationale of the scheme was two fold. First, it was designed to add to the company's cash flow and thus enable it to up-rate its machine tools more quickly than would otherwise have been possible. Second, it was hoped to negotiate agreement that, at least as an informal condition of the loan, British Leyland would provide the IRC with more detailed and regular information on its plans and performance.

While arrangements for the loan were being discussed, the IRC

Board, which was concerned about the progress and prospects of British Leyland, asked Stokes to arrange another formal presentation of his company's position. He agreed and the meeting took place in May 1970. Stokes again refused, however, to give the IRC any information that was not available to British Leyland's shareholders. Indeed, although the new loan was by no means unwelcome it was not essential, and British Leyland was still sufficiently profitable and liquid for Stokes to resist IRC pressure. Profits in 1967/8 had been well above expectations at £38 million and in 1968/9 they were £39 million. Moreover, since British Leyland had paid a dividend of 11 per cent for 1967/8, the interest rate on the original IRC loan had automatically risen to 7½ per cent – which was in line with commercial rates at the time of the advance. So, although the IRC executive was no more impressed by the second meeting than the first, the new £10 million loan went ahead. It did so as part of the IRC's machine tool strategy, but without any other special conditions for British Leyland. (For details of the loan, see Appendix A at the end of this book.)

The IRC's main concern was that, while British Leyland had made manifest improvements in its marketing and product plans, its management had still not solved the fundamental problem of productivity. It was also worried about the absence of any new models in the Austin–Morris volume car division which would be capable of sustaining that division's share of the market. The IRC came to feel that it had been a mistake to think that any one man could carry out the roles of chairman and chief executive in such a large and complex organisation, and it therefore urged Stokes to appoint a new chief executive. In the summer of 1968, the IRC itself began to make enquiries aimed at discovering whether there was anyone available with the right experience and ability since it felt that outsiders should be considered, in addition to anyone within the company who might be thought to be capable of taking on the role.

Leyland announced its own reorganisation in September. Some of Stokes's tasks were delegated, and a much bigger role was given to George Turnbull. But IRC executives were disappointed that there were no new faces among British Leyland's senior management. They also pressed the company to accelerate the process of integration. When the 1969/70 results were announced soon afterwards, they revealed a loss of £16 million for Austin Morris and a profit of only £4 million for the group as a whole. The reasons for the IRC's concern were now clearly apparent in the company's financial results.

COMMENT

It does not seem that the IRC had much success in using its influence to ensure that what it thought should be done within British Leyland was done. Despite the two loans it had provided, the IRC lacked the effective levers which would have been required to make changes which the British Leyland Board did not see as necessary. Stokes had set himself against large-scale redundancy from the very outset of the merger. This was partly because he wanted to avoid disruption among the workforce and partly because his optimistic outlook led him to believe that the problem of low productivity could be solved by expanding sales rather than by reducing the number of people employed. Stokes was also initially reluctant to disturb the more successful parts of his group. In 1970, in a long conversation with the IRC, he explained that if a plant was operating profitably he preferred to leave it alone. Reflecting on this, the IRC executive argued that it meant that many opportunities for improving the profitability of the group as a whole could be missed. In an extreme case, and where there was excess capacity, it could pay to close down a profitable plant, if this resulted in a larger improvement in higher profitability elsewhere in the group, thus taking advantage of what has become known as the 'systems effect'.

Stokes, however, held fast to his step-by-step policies, though some outsiders were eventually brought into senior positions in the company. For example, British Leyland reinforced its team responsible for labour relations in 1970 with the appointment of Pat Lowry, former head of the Engineering Employers' Federation. Under his leadership the company began in the following year to replace the piecework system of payment with measured day work at one or two of its factories (though not then at Longbridge) and combined this with some improvements in work methods.

Some special factors inhibited the IRC from taking a firmer line with British Leyland. First, the company's problems, or at least the results of them, did not become serious until 1970, and the Conservative Government had then come to power. Even if the IRC had survived, the Conservatives had made it clear that they would expect it to be less interventionist. The second problem was the unique position of Stokes himself. By the time the severity of British Leyland's problems had become clear, Stokes had been made Deputy Chairman of the IRC, and he had been one of its most influential Board members from the beginning. He had impressed the other IRC Board members and executives alike and the IRC's support for the merger was in no small part support for Stokes's management ability. Once the merger had taken place it was recognised quite quickly that the combined job might be too much for Stokes alone, and probably for any one man, but by then it was not easy to do anything to change matters.

It is always difficult to persuade a chairman/chief executive to change course and almost impossible if he has, as Stokes had, the majority of his Board behind him. Difficulties are compounded, and embarrassment acute, if he is the deputy chairman of the body seeking to persuade him to relinquish some of his responsibilities.

Special factors aside, there are some lessons to be learned from the British Leyland case. The IRC might have been tougher when the machine tool loan was made. The Corporation was advancing £10 million at special interest rates to British Leyland and reasonably expected the company to make some commitments in return. However, the loan was not essential at the time, and Stokes, who was not, in any case, particularly keen on the idea, would have been unlikely to accept stringent conditions. Moreover, this tactic would have run counter to what was apparently the basic predilection of the IRC, namely to choose the man they wanted to carry out a particular piece of restructuring and then leave him to get on with it. That was a sound basic philosophy, so far as it went, because the IRC was not staffed to take on the actual job of managing a number of enterprises, many of them large. Nor was it ever intended that this should be the IRC's role. What *was* required, as is clear from the British Leyland case, was a more effective way of exerting an influence when events did not work out as the IRC hoped. Like anyone else engaged in business strategy and in selecting top managers, the IRC was bound to make mistakes. It therefore needed some way of ensuring that these mistakes came to light as quickly as possible and that, when they did, there was some means of correcting them. But this problem is endemic to British industry and there is no easy solution. It was certainly not a problem specific to the IRC.

The most basic question of all is whether the merger of Leyland and BMH was the best answer to the problems of the British motor industry. By the mid-1970s the merger had brought no apparent benefit. The company's market share had fallen from 41 per cent in 1968 to about 30 per cent, and its management was swamped by the intractable problems of the Austin–Morris volume car division. British Leyland then accepted government finance on a scale which gave the government control of the firm. Old problems were tackled anew, with large amounts of government money. And the government took the opportunity to make a series of management changes culminating in the appointment of Michael Edwardes. The question is, therefore, whether different action by the IRC in the late 1960s could have left the UK motor industry in a stronger position.

With hindsight many people now doubt the wisdom of merging Leyland with BMH. Was it impossible to succeed in this? Would it have been better to have reconstructed the BMH management and to have left Leyland as a relatively strong, independent force in the UK and in world markets? The voices raised against the merger in 1967/8 were, however, few and faint. The Leyland management was convinced that their company was too small to thrive against international competition. Moreover, the problems of raising sufficient funds for the development of new models were likely to have been insuperable for Leyland operating alone.

BMH was in an even worse position. Villiers was closely involved with the company before he joined the IRC, because his merchant bank was BMH's financial advisor. He had been approached by Harriman to help the company to find a way out of its financial problems and, among other things, had tried to find an overseas partner for BMH. By early 1968, when he moved to the IRC, Villiers felt that, in the absence of the Leyland deal, there was a very real possibility of BMH being forced into liquidation. The disadvantages of the merger therefore have to be weighed against the strong possibility of the demise of BMH and the stagnation of Leyland.

The difficulty which the IRC found in taking action once the merger began to go wrong has already been spelled out. Only very drastic action, probably before 1970, could have avoided the need for the subsequent government intervention in the mid-1970s and huge financial assistance it has provided since then. The only alternative course would have been to intervene much more directly in the company's affairs, as the IRC did later with Cammell Laird (see Ch. 13). The IRC *was* worried about British Leyland, but not that worried. In any case, would the company's Board, its shareholders or indeed the government have supported such intervention at the time? Even if they had, could a new management capable of taking the action needed to maintain British Leyland's profitability through the 1970s have been found? And if it could have been found, could it have been persuaded to take over the job of running British Leyland?

8

Machine Tools

On 20 November 1969, Charles Villiers was one of the principal speakers at the annual dinner of the Machine Tool Trades Association (MTTA). The main message in his address was that the IRC was anxious to assist the industry, and individual firms, in whatever ways were most helpful. The performance of the industry was at the best patchy. There were some successful firms but, as a whole, it was insufficiently profitable and was losing out to foreign competition both in the UK and in export markets. The problems of the investment cycle, which meant very substantial fluctuations in the demand for machine tools, still seemed intractable and the downturn in the current cycle had been more severe than ever.

Villiers acknowledged that mergers which increased the size of companies were not necessarily the answer, although he argued that deals, involving subsidiary companies, to achieve product rationalisation could be helpful. The IRC was prepared to assist with such deals and was ready to consider providing finance for investments by individual companies. Indeed, by 1969, the IRC had been involved in negotiations involving full and partial mergers and schemes to encourage investment. Its involvement with the industry had begun, three years earlier, with yet another type of support arrangement, under which various credit schemes were promoted to help to spread orders over time and to dampen the demand cycle. This chapter begins with a review of these schemes, which were largely initiated by the government, and then considers the IRC's own attempts to help to improve performance in the machine tool industry.

CREDIT FOR MACHINE TOOLS

The IRC's involvement began towards the end of 1966, when Mintech was examining a scheme to help to provide more machine tools for machine tool manufacturers themselves. At that time,

Mintech was particularly concerned about a sharp increase in imports of machine tools and wanted to discuss with the industry how the government could help, perhaps by encouraging rationalisation, or perhaps by buying more advanced machine tools and loaning them to firms. Progress was slow and, towards the end of March 1967, another idea for the development of the machine tool industry was formulated, this time by the DEA. It was argued that the well established cycle in machine tool output was continuing. The downturn had now come, with January orders well below the worst monthly total for three years. The DEA argued that the machine tool industry must have enough capacity to meet the next boom but, with investment grants already generous, new measures to help it should be selective and act quickly, enabling it to expand and modernise. It was therefore suggested that an existing scheme, under which Mintech ordered advanced machine tools and placed them with businesses for evaluation, should be extended. The scheme might be enlarged to cover more designs, even where they did not embody major technical advances. For while the scheme encouraged the use of advanced machine tools, it did not help mass-produced ones. The DEA wanted machine tool firms to expand, scrapping their own obsolete machines and buying new ones, so that they could meet increasing demand when it came. Since extension of the Mintech scheme would require legislation, the DEA suggested that it might be better for the IRC to mount its own scheme as a commercial operation.

The IRC had reservations about becoming involved with a scheme which was not tied to rationalisation, but agreed to talk to companies. On 31 March the IRC Board agreed that the Corporation would try to devise a scheme to encourage selected machine tool companies to expand their capacity, would ask machine tool firms how the IRC could help them, and would then suggest a strategy for the industry.

These developments were followed by a good deal of discussion, both within the IRC and between the IRC and business and financial institutions, the main aim being to identify possible sources of funds for the purchase of machine tools. There were also suggestions that only firms that had been, or were, carrying out effective rationalisation should be supported. Indeed, one of the IRC Board members argued that, compared to most other industries, machine tool companies had already undertaken significant structural reorganisation. This had not always been along the lines that appeared to be most logical from an industrial point of view but, in this sense, the IRC had come on the scene too late. The most purposeful rationalisation was seen as having been carried out by

Staveley Industries; Alfred Herbert; the Cohen '600' Group and Tube Investments (TI). These companies, plus four or five others, accounted for perhaps 60 per cent of the turnover of the industry.

The IRC was in two minds. At this early stage in its life it still saw its role as being primarily to promote mergers, but it also saw little merit in urging further mergers on unwilling partners. It therefore decided to go ahead with a credit scheme that was independent of any rationalisation measures. There were, however, numerous difficulties and sometimes conflicting pressures and objectives. For example, the DEA and Mintech were concerned to reduce the severity of the demand cycle and to improve the competitiveness of UK manufacturers, without directly discriminating against foreign producers. The machine tool companies were more concerned to have a scheme which would give incentives to buy from UK firms. The IRC was therefore caught between its objectives of helping the UK suppliers and its desire to promote the use of the most advanced and efficient machine tools throughout UK industry. Indeed, the IRC doubted whether anything would deter British business from importing sophisticated machine tools in whose production UK manufacturers lagged.

Nevertheless, it pressed on with its attempts to devise an arrangement and decided that the most practical approach would be to set up a joint IRC–City institution–machine tool industry company. This would buy machine tools, at a discount, during periods of recession and lease them to customers who, for the first two years, would pay a notional rent. The scheme was designed to maintain the demand for machine tools and to allow customers to re-equip in advance of the next upturn. A scheme was worked out whereby the IRC would put up 25 per cent of the £4 million capital for a company called Machine Tool Finance Ltd (MTF).

New problems soon arose, however. Discussions with industry led to arguments, especially about the size of the discount to be given to MFT and about which companies should take part. Discussions with government departments revealed that ministers had been considering stockpiling schemes and that Mintech was on the point of proposing one of these to the MTTA. Moreover, the clearing banks seemed to be on the point of launching their own buyer-credit arrangements. The IRC tried to retrieve the situation, objecting that business would simply be confused if there were too many schemes. The IRC Board considered the options. It felt that the stockpiling ideas were unlikely to be useful because the main problem area was specialist machines, which had to be custom-built. Its own leasing idea would work only if it had sufficient support from the machine tool manufacturers and this now seemed unlikely. The buyer-credit scheme seemed sensible but, if it were to be undertaken on commercial terms, there were probably adequate facilities available through the clearing banks of either customers or suppliers. The IRC therefore decided to withdraw from all the schemes. This caused some consternation, but was probably a wise move. It was almost certainly impossible to devise a commercial scheme which would persuade machine tool customers to go against what they saw as their own commercial interests, either by buying earlier than they intended or by buying British rather than importing.

At least three of the bigger machine tool companies were still keen on a buyer-credit scheme and tried to persuade Mintech to sponsor a more favourable one. This did not happen, but Herbert and Churchill (the TI machine tool subsidiary) did launch their own buyer-credit scheme, mainly financed by the clearing banks. This at least vindicated the IRC view that such schemes could be handled through conventional financial institutions.

MERGER DISCUSSIONS

Although the IRC had quickly decided that there was little to be gained from the active pursuit of mergers in the machine tool industry it was very receptive, especially after the failure of its initiatives on credit arrangements, to suggestions from companies in the industry. Its interest was therefore rekindled when, in July 1968, TI told the IRC that it was considering making a bid for John Brown, largely to acquire its machine tool subsidiary, Wickman. TI would not require any cash or support from the IRC but it would appreciate help, if the deal went through, in disposing of some other parts of the John Brown group.

The IRC executive took advantage of TI's approach to look at the machine tool interests of both Wickman and TI's subsidiary, Churchill. Both appeared to be relatively sound companies with, if anything, Wickman's management the more impressive. In the event, TI's interest in John Brown came to nothing but the IRC had begun to consider whether Wickman's management could be encouraged to take on wider responsibilities. This raised the question of whether there was a case for other mergers in the machine tool industry, with the objective of putting the best management teams into more strategic positions.

With this in mind the IRC managed to elicit invitations to study the two largest companies in the industry, Alfred Herbert and Staveley Industries. If the prospects for the industry were to be improved, something had to be done to revitalise one or both of these companies or to persuade them to part with some or all of their machine tool activities. The latter course was not really open to Herbert, which specialised almost exclusively in machine tools, but it was a possibility for Staveley, which was a conglomerate with extensive interests in engineering and chemicals as well.

The IRC's initial review of Staveley confirmed that it was having serious problems with some of its machine tool subsidiaries but that others were successful and profitable. In particular, Staveley had a 50 per cent share in Warner-Swazy-Asquith, which produced advanced machine tools on the basis of designs and know-how provided by its US parent company. Other subsidiaries also had good products and line managers. The IRC felt, however, that it was possible that the better companies in the division would be held back both by the problems and the poor results of the others and by the consequent lack of finance for expansion and development.

In September 1968, Mintech officially asked the IRC to report on the group. The IRC was able to do this very quickly, largely on the basis of its existing knowledge of Staveley. It argued that Staveley's machine tool division was worth sorting out and developing and recommended that a takeover would be the best way of achieving this. Staveley might be persuaded to sell off its machine tool division but it seemed more likely that it would not. In this event, a bid for the whole group was a feasible alternative. The non-machine tool activities were readily saleable and should fetch prices which left the machine tool division at a reasonable valuation.

The key question was whether or not there were any candidates for such a takeover. Herbert had enough to do with its own subsidiaries and so was ruled out. The most likely contenders appeared to be TI and, less obviously, the Cohen 600 Group (Cohen).

Cohen's machine tool subsidiaries appeared to be well run and its Chairman and Managing Director, Mr Jack Wellings, was well thought of by the IRC. He was described as the sort of tough character who might well breathe new life into Staveley. The Cohen management, however, had little experience of the heavy, more sophisticated Staveley products and the Staveley management was firmly opposed to any link with Cohen. Neither of these points need necessarily have prevented a bid by Cohen, nor the successful integration of the two groups if the bid was successful. But it was clear that a bid would cause quite a battle and, with Cohen's market value barely exceeding the price it could expect to have to pay for Staveley, Cohen lacked the financial resources it would have needed to be sure of winning that battle. Wellings told the IRC that he would not go ahead, and the IRC turned to TI.

TI's market capitalisation, at about £150 million, was five times that of Cohen or Staveley. It clearly had the resources to make a bid and to absorb the group without overstretching itself financially. For a time it looked as though both companies might favour some sort of deal. TI had told the IRC that it would like to expand its machine tool activities to up to three times their present size. It was keen to make a move because it would shortly lose a lucrative merchanting activity. About £6 million of TI's £20 million turnover in machine tools came from sales under a licencing arrangement with the US company, Cincinatti. Cincinatti appeared to have decided to set up its own direct sales organisation in the UK and so TI wanted to acquire other interests in the industry as soon as possible.

Staveley's management also appeared to be attracted by the idea of a link with TI. They saw this as a possible answer to some of their financial problems, although they thought that they would be teaching, rather than learning from, TI's management on machine tools.

After separate talks with both sides, the IRC brought TI and Staveley representatives together in November 1968. The meeting did not go at all well and at least two fundamental problems emerged. First, Staveley would want to exclude some of its successful subsidiaries from a merger, perhaps including Warner-Swazy-Asquith. Second, Staveley insisted that any link must be through the establishment of a joint company. To be given cash for its machine tool interests would simply make Staveley a sitting target for a takeover. TI, however, was against a joint company. Their main objection was that the inevitable processes of persuasion would be long and would not enhance decision making. TI was even more opposed to a joint company which excluded Staveley's most profitable subsidiaries. The talks became bogged down in detail and the only option with a real chance of success was a complete takeover of Staveley by TI.

TI was undecided whether a bid for the whole of Staveley would be worthwhile, and resolved to wait until the group's 1968 results were announced. These appeared in February 1969 and revealed that Staveley's pre-tax profits had fallen to only about £½ million compared with £2 million in 1967. The machine tool division had made a trading loss of £120 000 in 1968, compared with a profit of £680 000 in the previous year and over £1 million in 1966.

The results did nothing to encourage TI's management to go ahead with a bid, but the IRC decided to make one last effort to persuade them to move, the IRC executive undertaking a complete valuation of Staveley. They calculated that the company could now be acquired for about £20 million, though when outstanding debt was taken into account the total outlay would amount to £36 million. On the IRC's calculations, Staveley's chemicals, abrasives and electricals divisions could be sold to realise a total of just over £20 million, while selling a major trade investment was likely to realise a further £2 million. The effective price for the machine tool division would therefore be between £10 million and £15 million.

Even if these calculations were accurate, of course, the idea of paying between £10 million and £15 million for assets currently losing £120 000 a year could hardly seem very appealing. However, the IRC set out a valuation of the machine tool division, company by company. It argued that if some of the loss-makers were to be wholly or partly closed, they could be included at a zero rather than a negative valuation, because the disposal of assets would easily cover closure costs. Then, even on a conservative valuation, the machine tool division would be worth £15 million and this did not include any assessment of the potential improvement in performance from better management.

TI appeared to accept these calculations, but still decided that the margin was too small to make a bid for Staveley worthwhile, especially since Staveley made it clear that they would oppose a takeover. Given all the risks and uncertainties, TI felt that this was too indirect a way to achieve its objective. TI told the IRC that it would still be interested in a direct purchase of some or all of Staveley's machine tool companies, but both TI and the IRC accepted that these were unlikely to be for sale unless Staveley's position deteriorated still further.

Villiers reported TI's decision to a meeting of the IRC Board on 28 March 1969. Members considered alternative courses of action, including the possibility of the IRC making a bid for Staveley, but decided that this would not be appropriate. In particular, they felt that some of Staveley's machine tool subsidiaries must be closed and that it would be preferable for this to be done, not by the IRC, but by a company that could offer countervailing developments and employment opportunities. The IRC Board decided that, for the moment, there was nothing it could do, though it did instruct its executives to be ready to act if there was further deterioration in Staveley's position.

Six months later, in September 1969, Staveley was clearly in trouble. It had made a loss in the first half of the year and its Chairman and Managing Director, Mr Denis Haviland, had retired. The new Chairman, Mr Spieler, was having problems finding a chief executive, and Staveley's share price had dropped from 30*s* (£1.50) at the beginning of the year to 17*s* 6*d* (87½p), giving a market capitalisation of about £8½ million compared with net assets of just over £16 million.

The group was clearly vulnerable either to a takeover or, if its position deteriorated still further, to a severe liquidity crisis. Spieler had approached the Cohen 600 group, whose advances had been rejected at the end of 1968, and said that Staveley would now be in favour of a complete merger if reasonable terms could be worked out. Wellings felt that, despite the change in Staveley's attitude and his interest in some of its machine tool subsidiaries, it would not be in Cohen's interests to take on the whole group.

The IRC Board asked its executives to re-open discussions with Staveley and to discuss once again the possibility of arranging the sale of its machine tool companies. The executives suggested a number of disposals which would reinforce the specialisation pattern of the leading UK machine tool manufacturers. They argued that this would not only remove some of Staveley's problems, but would provide cash to pay off short- and long-term debt and so improve the financial security of the remainder of the group. These discussions ran into all the familiar problems, however, with Staveley wanting to keep the more profitable, and hence saleable, companies.

The IRC looked yet again at the possibility of a complete takeover of Staveley. Despite the potential profits from splitting up the group, few industrial companies were interested, not least because they had problems of their own. The IRC therefore worked out a scheme with Slater Walker. The IRC took a less extreme view of Slater Walker than some commentators, believing that it had achieved significant industrial improvements in several of the companies it had acquired. The IRC was therefore prepared to back a bid by Slater for Staveley, provided that the subsequent rationalisation of the group was undertaken jointly with the IRC.

Not surprisingly, Staveley was totally against this. Moreover, Spieler had found a new chief executive, Dr A. Frankel, who came from GEC. Spieler told the IRC that losses were already being reduced and that Frankel would undertake a complete review of the group to achieve much needed rationalisation and to reduce or remove loss-making activities. The IRC and Slater hesitated and, as Staveley's performance continued to improve, the chance for either an agreed merger, or a takeover on sufficiently attractive terms, receded. Frankel began to rationalise the machine tool division's product range and its production facilities, and so started to achieve some of the results that the IRC had been seeking. After eighteen months of frustrated negotiations, the IRC abandoned its attempts to re-organise Staveley.

DIRECT INVESTMENT

Although the IRC had been involved in merger talks on Staveley until late in 1969, it had decided long before that its main course of action must be to support direct investment, where this was needed to strengthen individual companies in the machine tool industry. It could do this, in the absence of a merger, under Section 2(1)(b) of the IRC Act. Two loans were advanced, under this section – to Herbert-Ingersoll (HI) and to Kearney and Trecker (K & T). Both companies had brought American expertise in machine tool design and manufacture to the UK. K&T was a wholly owned US subsidiary and HI was owned 51 per cent by Alfred Herbert and 49 per cent by Ingersoll Milling Machine, a leading USA producer of 'transfer' machine tools.

In addition to these '2(1)(b)' schemes the IRC made two further loans, tied to previous mergers. The first was to a UK unquoted company, Marwin Machine Tools. The second was the controversial deal with British Leyland (BL) whereby the IRC provided £10 million for BL, with the condition that BL would use the money to bring forward its purchases of UK machine tools.

HERBERT INGERSOLL

Of the four deals, the loan to HI was probably the most straightforward and the least successful. HI was set up in 1967 on a 'green field' site in Daventry and was designed to overcome many of the problems seen to be the cause of the UK industry's poor performance. The factory was purpose built, well laid out, clean and spacious. Conditions of work were carefully agreed with the unions and there were no 'class divisions' and no separate management and workers' canteens. The link with Ingersoll, a world leader in its field, provided the most advanced designs and manufacturing techniques. Moreover, Ingersoll was effectively transferring to HI the substantial market position that it had built up in Europe and in the Commonwealth countries.

The project seemed to be going ahead successfully. Turnover had been built up to about £3.5 million in the first full year of operation. £2 million was for export and UK sales also benefitted the balance of payments because the large and up-to-date transfer machines, sold chiefly to the motor industry, had until that time been imported. HI's order book, when the company approached the IRC late in 1968, was £4.5 million – with £2.5 million destined for export markets. The two parent companies felt that their joint venture was sufficiently successful to warrant the expansion of the Daventry factory and asked for the IRC's help in financing this expansion.

The IRC discussed the scheme with the Ministry of Technology and was told that it had their full support and encouragement. The IRC then asked each of the parents why they could not supply the money for expansion themselves. With some justification, both claimed that they were in a difficult position financially. The downturn in the machine tool demand cycle had been severe and, although HI had a good order book, the profitability of both parent companies had been poor for a year or two. They wanted, nonetheless, to go ahead with the expansion of HI, to ensure that it would be ready to cope with the next upturn in demand. As this was exactly what the IRC had been advocating, it was predisposed to help. Despite some misgivings among Board members that the HI factory was over engineered, and so carried too great a burden of capital and interest, the IRC approved the loan to HI in December 1968.

The first of a series of delays then occurred. As this was a '2(1)(b)' project, the IRC needed a specific request to undertake it from the Secretary of State at the Ministry of Technology. Instead of agreeing to make this request, Mintech decided to take over the scheme itself, and to advance the loan under the Industrial Expansion Act (IEA). The loan had, therefore, to be vetted by an Advisory committee, set up under the Act, which gave its approval in March 1969. It then took the various government departments concerned no less than six months, until October 1969, to draw up a provisional loan agreement.

HI had estimated that its expansion would cost £2 million and had asked for a loan of £1.5 million. By October 1969, almost a year after the original application, the cost was estimated at £2.5 million. Moreover, Richard Young, Chairman of Alfred Herbert, had been to see Kearton. The IRC's first chairman was now Chairman of the IEA Advisory Committee, and was told that the parent companies now wanted to borrow the whole of this amount.

Kearton reviewed the situation. He thought the scheme was still a good one and felt that, given the state of the machine tool market, Herbert and Ingersoll were justified in asking for this additional support. He feared that it would take too long to deal with a new application under the IEA scheme and therefore wrote to Lockwood asking if the IRC would provide the additional £1 million.

The IRC Board agreed to this on 24 October 1969, but there were still delays. Negotiations between Herbert and Ingersoll and Mintech became bogged down on the question of security for the

IEA loan. Mintech wanted a guarantee from both parents but Ingersoll argued that this was impossible, given its financial position and the controls over outward investment from the USA. Eventually a way was found around the difficulties. Then HI's clearing bank asked for a guarantee from the parent companies for its £4 million overdraft, but Ingersoll refused to give guarantees on either the overdraft or the IEA loan. There was stalemate again. Mintech once more turned to the IRC, since the latter had much more flexibility in the terms on which it could advance money. It was agreed that the IEA scheme would be dropped and that the IRC would take over the whole of the loan. By this time it was March 1970. A full 15 months had been spent on trying, and eventually failing, to negotiate the first loan under the Industrial Expansion Act.

By this time, the IRC was also concerned about the position of Alfred Herbert and had started discussions on the financial position and organisation of the group. Nevertheless it decided to go ahead, albeit cautiously, with the HI loan. It was decided that it would not be prudent to advance £2.5 million as an unsecured loan without guarantees from the parent companies. Moreover, it now seemed that the expansion programme needed to be phased more gradually and that only £1 million would be required initially. So, having been approached in late 1968, the IRC at last advanced £1 million to HI on 3 June 1970. Half was provided as equity in the company, and half as a loan at a commercial rate of interest and with joint and several guarantees from Herbert and Ingersoll. The IRC's equity interest amounted to 13 per cent of the company and Ben Cant was appointed as the IRC representative on the HI board.

The announcement of this arrangement included a statement that the IRC would consider further finance of £1.5 million if this was required, on terms to be negotiated, but no more money was advanced before the IRC was wound up. Nor was the expansion programme completed. In June 1972 HI went into liquidation.

The directors of HI argued that the firm had failed financially because the volume of business available in the United Kingdom had been consistently disappointing and the total workload had not been sufficient to enable the company to trade at a profit. *The Times* took the view that the timing of the launch of the firm had been 'disastrous' since the British machine tool industry was moving into its worst recession since the Second World War (*The Times,* 6 June 1972).

Losses by Herbert-Ingersoll over its life were about £4 million, on a total turnover, including its order book at the time of the failure, of some £13 million. During 1970/1 orders had been only £2 million, all but £100 000 for export. Alfred Herbert had already provided in full for its initial investment of £1.78 million in the company and for the guarantee that the IRC had secured on its £500 000 loan. For this part of its money, the government was covered.

HI was ultimately a failure, but Herbert itself was not much more successful. Towards the end of 1975 it was announced that the government was to provide over £25 million in share capital and loans to prevent the firm falling into the hands of the receiver. Herbert was to be put under the National Enterprise Board, and the responsibility for re-organising it was to be given to Mr John Buckley, largely because of his success in putting Davy Ashmore back into profitability (see Ch. 11).

MARWIN

In terms both of ownership, and of the source of its financial difficulties, Marwin was the complete opposite of HI. The majority of its equity was held, not by parent companies, but by its managers. Mr Ernest Hopwell, Marwin's Chairman and Chief Executive, held 52 per cent and his Vice-Chairman, Mr Joseph Denham, 15 per cent. Together with some of their fellow directors, they had founded the company in 1963 and still owned all the equity, apart from a holding of 28 per cent taken up by Industrial and Commercial Finance Corporation (ICFC) as part of a package of financial support.

Marwin did not approach the IRC for further financing because of a lack of orders or profits, but simply because it was growing fast. Starting from nothing in 1963, its machine tool turnover reached £1.5 million in 1967 and £4.5 million in 1969. Pre-tax profits were £73 000 in 1966 and £350 000 in 1969. Part of Marwin's growth had come from the acquisition in 1968 of Ashwell and Nesbitt, one of its principal component suppliers and subcontractors. The ICFC, which had a substantial interest in Ashwell and Nesbitt, approved the acquisition and, as well as taking an equity stake, advanced £1 million through loans and preference shares. However, as a matter of policy, the ICFC was not willing to increase its commitment to Marwin. Instead, at the end of 1969, it supported the company in its approach to the IRC for a loan of £1.5 million.

Marwin's main business was the production of specialist, numerically controlled (NC) machine tools chiefly for use in the aircraft industry. It was one of the largest producers of NC machine tools in Europe and exported almost 50 per cent of its turnover. It was a public, but unquoted company, and its rapid growth was causing continued cash flow problems, because it had to finance both capital expansion and the build-up of work in progress. When Marwin approached the IRC, it had reached a position where any further expansion would have meant significant financial risk, and it was already having problems with suppliers because it had extended its trade credit too far.

On the face of it, this was exactly the type of company that the IRC thought should be encouraged. It therefore responded positively but, before making any commitment, felt it must check three things. First, were Marwin's management and products as good as they seemed? Second, why could it not obtain the finance it needed from other sources? Third, if IRC money was required, in what form could it be best made available?

IRC executives visited Marwin's factories and met Hopwell and his top management team. They found that Marwin's main UK customers were BAC and Hawker-Siddeley and that its machine tools had been supplied for use in manufacturing Concorde and the Trident. The IRC therefore talked also to the production directors in both these companies and to Minetch. All this confirmed Marwin's reputation and potential. Indeed, the IRC learned that Marwin was using its experience in NC machine tools to develop and market cheaper versions of these for the general engineering industry. This was another measure which had the IRC's full support.

The IRC's financial investigation revealed that Marwin had extended its trade credit to six months, against a normal period of three months, and that suppliers were not unnaturally resisting this. In addition, Marwin had been receiving favourable progress payments, especially for its work on the Concorde, but these were expected to decline. As it expanded into the general engineering market, Marwin could expect no progress payments at all. It had already borrowed heavily and neither its clearing banks, not the ICFC, were willing to increase their loans. The other conventional source of finance was a rights issue, but Marwin's director shareholders were unable to finance this. The alternative was for the company to seek a Stock Exchange quotation but Hopwell argued that it was not the right moment to do so. Marwin had paid no dividends and all its profits had been ploughed back into the business. Public shareholders would certainly expect dividends and, more important, with its present high gearing, the company might not be very favourably received. Its directors emphasised that the company was going through a phase of rapid growth and they wanted this to show in the profit figures before they sought a wider shareholding.

The IRC executive felt that these arguments were reasonable and its executives prepared a case for presentation at the Board meeting in March 1970, setting out the arguments for advancing £1.5 million to Marwin. The executive stressed that Marwin had approached the IRC for financial support because it had grown so rapidly that it had outstripped its financial resources. This was very unusual in the machine tool industry, where most of the companies had insufficient liquid resources because of a declining competitive position.

The executive also reported that every senior member of Marwin's management had been interviewed and that they were a well integrated team whose relative youth was remarkable in the industry. The favourable views taken of Marwin by customers, Mintech and the ICFC were reported, as was Marwin's extensive R&D effort on which its future expansion would be based.

The executive's view was that Marwin should seek a Stock Exchange quotation within the next five years but that meanwhile it was right for the IRC to provide financial support. It recommended that £750 000 should be advanced immediately as a loan that would be convertible into Marwin equity, when the group became quoted. A further £750 000 should be available at a later date, if Marwin continued to expand at the rate it was forecasting.

The IRC Board accepted these recommendations and advanced £750 000 in March 1970 with conversion terms which could eventually give the Corporation 10 per cent of Marwin's equity. A further £750 000 was advanced to Marwin in January 1971.

KEARNEY AND TRECKER

Like Marwin, Kearney and Trecker (K&T) was a leading producer of advanced NC machine tools. In other respects it resembled HI much more than Marwin. Its know-how was derived from a US parent company, Kearney and Trecker Corporation (K&T Inc.) of Milwaukee, which was the pioneer and world leader in the design and manufacture of NC 'machining centres'. These were machine tools which could execute a whole range of machining operations on a component, with a single setting. This removed the need for the expensive resetting for each operation that conventional machine tools required.

Like Ingersoll, K&T Inc. had enjoyed a period of rapid and successful growth, with turnover increasing from $22 million in 1959 to $85 million in 1968, but had been suffering, since 1969, during the severe recession that had hit the industry in the USA. It owned almost 100 per cent of the shares of its UK subsidiary but was not in a position to put any more cash into K&T in the UK where K&T had itself been through a difficult period. In 1966 it had earned pre-tax profits of £280 000 on sales of £5.6 million but profits had declined to £79 000 in 1967, £57 000 in 1968, and in 1969 K&T had made only £34 000 on sales of £6.9 million. This decline in profitability had put a severe strain on K&T's financial resources and, since K&T Inc. was unable to help, the company had turned to Mintech for assistance. Mintech, in turn, asked the IRC to consider a loan to K&T, under Section 2(1)(b) of the IRC Act.

Both Mintech and the IRC saw strong reasons for supporting K&T. NC machining centres had an important part to play in improving the productivity of Britain's engineering industries. The K&T designs were excellent and, as well as competing with imports, the UK subsidiary exported about 40 per cent of its turnover. The combination of US designs and production techniques and UK labour rates was seen as a potentially highly successful way of developing the manufacture of NC machine tools. So the IRC agreed to investigate K&T.

The executive reported to the IRC Board meeting in April 1970, identifying several reasons for K&T's poor performance. The US parent, K&T Inc., had been preoccupied with its own problems, which arose first out of the boom, and then out of the slump, in the USA market. The UK subsidiary had also suffered from an extensive rationalisation programme. This had involved concentrating production on two, rather than four, sites as well as introducing a number of complex products, new to the UK.

The IRC executive reviewed the progress that had been made in tackling these problems. They were satisfied that the consolidation of production at two sites (both in Brighton) had been sensible and had been successfully accomplished. It also seemed that problems in producing the new machine tools had been resolved and that their introduction to the British and European markets was well advanced. A new Chief Executive, Mr Stephen Baker, whom IRC executives had first met at Davy Ashmore, had been appointed and management morale seemed to be much improved. New financial controls had been introduced, on the advice of the company's US accountants.

So the IRC executive recommended that the provision of finance to K&T was a risk worth taking. However, by 1970 the IRC was keen to make its available money go as far as possible, and, as one way of achieving this, wanted to undertake joint financing operations with private sector financial sources. K&T had originally asked for a loan of about £2 million. The IRC executive put their requirements at about £1.25 million and recommended that a scheme should be devised whereby three merchant banks would contribute £300 000 each, while the IRC would supply the remaining £350 000.

The IRC board authorised the executive to proceed on this basis and Mintech indicated that the formal 'request' for a 2(1)(b) project would be forthcoming.

Although IRC finance for K&T was approved on 10 April 1970, no money was advanced until late in December. The intervening months were taken up, partly by a search for private sector partners, but mostly by protracted negotiations with K&T Inc. These concerned the amount of money to be taken out of the UK subsidiary in royalties, etc., and consequently the total external finance that was required. There was also disagreement on this between K&T Inc. and the UK subsidiary's new management. By December, however, the differences had been resolved and K&T decided that it required only £600 000 rather than £1.25 million. On 18 December 1970, the IRC announced that it had advanced half of this amount and the Midland Bank Finance Corporation the other half. The money was provided in the form of convertible preference shares which gave the IRC and the Midland Bank rights, on conversion, amounting to 31 per cent of K&T's equity.

THE BRITISH LEYLAND MACHINE TOOL LOAN

The IRC's £10 million 'machine tool' loan to British Leyland was mentioned briefly in Chapter 7. In the late 1960s, the motor industry bought 30 per cent of the machine tools sold in the UK, so that there was a strong relationship between the two industries. Moreover, for the IRC, the loan was a way of attacking simultaneously two of the UK manufacturing industry's more intractable problems: the weak competitive performance of UK machine tool producers and low productivity at BL.

Negotiations between the IRC and BL started early in 1970. By this time, the machine tool order book cycle was at its peak but most of the UK producers had suffered too severely in the recession to be thinking of investment and expansion. There was consequently a danger that the upturn would produce lengthening order books and would slow down delivery from UK producers, with a further increase in the share of the market taken by imports. As we have seen, the IRC was trying to encourage and support investment in specific individual firms, but it also felt that a wider scheme would be helpful.

We have seen that the IRC's early attempts to devise a general credit arrangement, described at the beginning of this chapter, were not successful. It was agreed that the reluctance of UK machine tool producers to invest was reinforced by an apparent lack of information about their customers' forward requirements. It would therefore be better to try to channel support through major customers and BL was a natural choice. It was one of the largest buyers of machine tools in the UK; the IRC had a close relationship with BL; BL itself needed a further injection of funds to enable it to press on with its own re-equipment programme. If BL agreed to the scheme, then the IRC saw this also as a potential lever for negotiating better 'follow up' procedures with the company, and hence keeping itself better informed on BL's progress and problems.

The scheme was designed to provide a 'rolling facility' for short-term loans which would finance purchases of machine tools from UK producers 'approved' by the IRC. BL had to give the IRC a list of likely requirements of machine tools for as far ahead as possible and to specify its preferred suppliers. The IRC would then indicate which of these purchases it would be prepared to support and the cash would be handed over when an agreed proportion of the approved purchases had been made.

BL spent approximately £10 million per year on machine tools and this was the size of the total facility proposed. Part of this expenditure could be recovered in investment grants, and part would go on purchases from overseas or from companies that the IRC was not inclined to support. It was therefore envisaged that the £10 million would be advanced in four tranches of £2.5 million over a period of about two years. Each loan would be repayable after three years, but could be rolled over if further machine tool purchases were approved. The interest rate would be set to give the IRC its normal, small margin on funds borrowed from the government and so would be slightly lower than the rate that BL could expect from its own bankers.

These proposals were considered by the IRC Board on 1 May 1970. There was some discussion of whether the loan to BL might be seen as discriminatory, but members decided that they would be prepared to consider similar applications from other companies. The main concern, at the Board's meeting, was whether it was desirable to increase the IRC's already substantial commitment to BL. The £25 million advanced at the time of the merger was the largest loan the IRC had made. And, while BL had made some progress, for example in increasing output per man by almost 25 per cent since the merger, it was still uncompetitive by international standards and still beset by industrial relations problems.

The IRC Board approved the loan but set up a sub-committee, under Villiers, to negotiate terms and to try to persuade Stokes to provide the IRC with more information on BL and with more opportunity to review its progress and to discuss measures for tackling its problems. Stokes was not very forthcoming on this. He argued that the loan was not essential to BL and that for BL it was more a question of his company assisting the IRC in its policy towards the machine tool industry. So, when the loan was announced in June 1970, no clear agreement had been reached with BL. The arrangement on machine tool purchases went ahead, however, and BL drew £2.5 million on 1 June 1970, on 15 July 1970, and again on 3 February 1971.

POSTSCRIPT

The day after the IRC–BL machine tool loan was announced, the Machine Tool Trades Association approached the IRC saying that it was concerned about the discrimination that was implied, not only against 'non-approved' UK producers but also against machine tool manufacturers in the European Free Trade Area (EFTA), an international trade group originally set up to counter the EEC. The IRC was more concerned about UK producers than the MTTA members, who were importers or who held agencies for overseas companies. But it was agreed to hold talks with the MTTA and also to consider arranging similar schemes with other substantial UK customers for machine tools. Several approaches were made, but nothing had been arranged before the IRC's own future was put in doubt by the result of the 1970 general election.

Moreover, the upturn in demand that had been seen in 1969 and in early 1970 had now been completely reversed and the industry was heading for its worst post-war recession. This, as we saw in an earlier section, led to the bankrupcy of HI and the problems which meant that Alfred Herbert could not survive without government help. The recession also produced a major reversal in the fortunes of Marwin Machine Tools and stalled Kearney and Trecker's attempts at recovery. Marwin's machine tool turnover, which had been about £4.5 million in 1969 dropped to £3 million in 1972, when a profit of £350 000 became a loss of over £1.5 million. As expected, orders from the aerospace industry had declined but had not been sufficiently replaced by an expansion of general engineering business.

K&T had failed to improve its profitability after its reorganisation and the injection of finance from the IRC and the Midland Bank. In 1972, turnover was down to about £4 million from over £7 million in 1970, and the company was heading for a substantial loss. K&T Inc. sold a 50 per cent share in K&T to W.E. Norton (Holdings), a UK-based machine tool distributor. Norton himself took over as chairman of the company but it was still deeply in trouble in 1973. Norton, together with the ICFC and the Department of Industry, which had inherited the IRC's interests produced a scheme for the merger of Marwin's machine tool subsidiary with K&T.

The merger was announced as a way of bringing together two key high technology companies in the UK machine tool industry. It was said that Marwin would enhance K&T's expertise and that K&T would provide up-to-date manufacturing capacity. Even so, the combined company continued to struggle and in 1974 a further £3.5 million of government money was introduced to prevent its bankruptcy. Vickers was persuaded to take on a management contract to run the company on behalf of the government, on a commission basis.

By 1975 the turnover of the combined company was over £12 million and the losses had been turned into a small profit. Vickers gained some confidence from this and in 1976 took over the company from the government. The terms negotiated by Vickers were generous, with over £6 million of losses written off (£5 million by the government and £1 million by the ICFC) and a further £1.8 million of public money injected as working capital. Since then the position of K&T has improved significantly and in 1978 it had pre-tax profits of £1.5 million on a turnover of £15 million, slightly more than one-third of which was exported.

Staveley also suffered severely from the machine tool recession in the early 1970s. After achieving a small profit in 1970, its machine tool division made losses of £250 000 in 1971, £500 000 in 1972 and £95 000 in 1973. Turnover in each of these years was about 30 per cent below its 1970 level, but Staveley survived this crisis because of the improved performance of its other divisions. When the recession eased, continuing improvements in organisation and efficiency began to show results. The machine tool division's profits climbed to over £500 000 by 1975, over £2 million in 1976 and, in the year ending in April 1979, were £2.7 million.

COMMENT

The IRC failed to make a significant and direct impact on the performance of the UK machine tool industry. This was not surprising because the severe problems of the industry were, in general, unrelated to the size or structure of the member firms. The questions to be answered on machine tools are as follows: first, should the IRC have accepted defeat and refused to devote such a large amount of its executives' time and effort to the industry? Second, did the IRC's activities in the industry make things better or worse?

The answer to the first question is that the IRC had little choice but to be involved. Even if the industry had not been on the IRC's own list of priorities, the Corporation received repeated requests from the government to undertake studies and schemes related to machine tools. The government felt that it would be undesirable for the UK to become totally dependent on imported machine tools, and the performance of UK machine tool producers was very important to the whole of UK manufacturing industry. This was clearly a view shared by the Conservative government in 1973 and 1974, when they continued to support Marwin and K&T and were prepared to inject far larger sums of money than the IRC had committed.

The answer to the second question is that the IRC almost certainly improved the industry's position somewhat. The IRC may not have directly achieved any of its objectives for Staveley, but its continued probing probably contributed to the management improvements made by the group. Of the other companies in which the IRC was involved, HI might have been better off had it been forced to consolidate rather than being given money to expand. However, even if the IRC had refused to become involved, the chances are that at least as much finance would have been provided under the Industrial Expansion Act. Alfred Herbert, Marwin and K&T would all have had difficulties in surviving if they had been left to market forces. It can be argued that market forces should have prevailed, but many of the activities of these companies that were supported remained intact through the 1970s. The IRC contributed to this and, had it remained in existence, the evidence from other cases suggests that it might have engineered their survival at less cost to the public purse than was in fact incurred (as illustrated by the cases of Davy Ashmore, Chapter 11, and Cammell Laird, Chapter 13). The IRC's activities were a relatively small, and sensible, part of the continued government effort to improve the performance of the UK machine tool industry.

9

The Plant Makers – Big Ideas and Small Deals

The IRC was involved with the companies designing, fabricating and erecting process and steelworks plant, from its inception to its dissolution. Both the industrial structure and the range of problems faced by the companies in the industry were complex, and this was inevitably reflected in the IRC's activities. Numerous merger proposals were put forward and protracted negotiations were undertaken that often came to nothing. In this and the next two chapters, we examine the IRC's involvement with the plant makers. Our main objective is to trace the fortunes of two of the leading UK companies, Whessoe and Davy Ashmore. Both companies made acquisitions that were backed by the IRC and both subsequently ran into serious financial difficulties. Both survived these difficulties, at least partly through the help of the IRC. These stories are told in Chapters 10 and 11. To put them into context we begin, in this chapter, with a brief outline of the IRC's initial contacts with the industries and of some of the schemes that were put forward for the IRC to consider. This chapter also covers the deals that were subsequently undertaken with the support or blessing of the IRC and so takes us to the time when serious concern began to develop for the financial positions of both Whessoe and Davy Ashmore.

THE INITIAL DIAGNOSIS

Discussions with leading industrialists in this sector had begun even before the IRC Act received Royal Assent in December 1966. There was no shortage of rationalisation proposals and, in the course of these early discussions, the IRC made its first contact with Sir Maurice Fiennes, Chairman of Davy Ashmore (DA). His company had interests in heavy engineering and contracting for both process and steelworks plant. Initial discussions centred on the steelworks plant companies, and especially on what would be an appropriate organisation for these producers following the renationalisation of the steel industry and the creation of the British Steel Corporation (BSC). The Chairman of another of the leading steelworks plant producers, Wellman Engineering, suggested that there should be only one major UK company, in which BSC should hold an equity interest. The merger of the steelworks plant businesses of the leading companies would also open up possibilities for rationalisation of fabrication and contracting businesses in the process plant industry. Fiennes was opposed to this approach and argued for balanced companies, each with a range of complementary interests. He thought this would give a better chance of a steady workload and would avoid the severe cyclical fluctuations likely to be experienced by businesses supplying only one sector. This philosophy was reflected in DA's own structure. It had engineering and fabrication capacity for designing and producing a wide range of plant and could undertake turnkey contracts in steelworks plant through Davy United (DU) and in process plant through Power Gas (PG).

Fiennes therefore argued for the creation of two steelworks plant companies, both with substantial interests in process plant. He naturally saw his own company as the nucleus of one of these groups. Other companies had varying views on the most desirable overall structure for the industry but in the main were reluctant, in early 1967, to consider disposing of any of their interests. The IRC was still in its formative stage and the Board felt that more information should be gathered before serious moves were considered. Wormald, formerly Managing Director of Fisons, and the IRC's special advisor on steel, was therefore asked to undertake a study of the industry.

Wormald visited most of the major steelworks plant companies, including DA, Wellman, Loewy Robertson (L-R) owned by Tube Investments (TI), and Head Wrightson (HW). His report confirmed the view of the executives. The industry was too fragmented and much capacity was either under-used or could be more effectively employed. There was, however, no general agreement on appropriate rationalisation moves or on the best structure for the industry. There was also much mutual suspicion. The IRC was therefore forced to decide on a pragmatic approach. It would keep in contact with the companies in the industry; it would promote discussion; and it would support and, if necessary, finance any sensible deals that could be arranged.

BUYING AND SELLING

Towards the end of 1967 three deals did become possible, all concerning DA. One of these brought the IRC for the first time into contact with Whessoe, the second company whose fortunes we are to follow. Whessoe had only peripheral interests in steelworks plant but was strong in process plant. It then had a good order book for fabricating heavy plant and was negotiating to buy the Stockton works of Ashmore, Benson and Pease (ABP), a subsidiary of DA.

The deal appeared to make sense for both companies. The Stockton works had relied heavily on working for the rest of the DA group. In the 1950s it had produced 90 per cent of ABP's blast furnaces, but by 1967 this market had almost dried up. The works was little more than half used and was making a loss. Its sale would not only remove this cash drain but would provide resources which would be used to make acquisitions in DA's area of strength. Whessoe, on the other hand, had orders that it could put into Stockton, chiefly for heavy pressure vessels and other process plant. Stockton was entirely suitable for such work but the ABP executives had little experience or expertise in this business. Whessoe's problem was shortage of liquidity, and here the IRC could help.

The IRC made a rapid, perhaps too rapid, appraisal of Whessoe. It was impressed by Whessoe's technical capacity. The company used advanced computer programs in design; had orderly production facilities and good labour relations; and it kept delivery dates. The IRC Board was inclined to support the deal, especially since DA proposed to use the proceeds from the sale to finance two acquisitions in the steelworks plant business.

A series of discussions on merger possibilities had taken place during 1967 between DA, Wellman and HW, but none of these had come to anything. By the end of the year Fiennes had decided that the best policy for his company would be to consolidate its strong position in the rolling mills business. It therefore made an offer for a small specialist company in this field, Brightside Foundry and Engineering Company, and stepped up discussions with TI, which had been proceeding intermittently, on the sale of Loewy Robertson. These moves were both successful. Brightside was acquired for around £1 million and TI, which had earlier told the IRC that it was not willing to sell L-R, changed its position. It now only disputed exactly what should be included in the sale, and the price. DA had sufficient fabricating capacity and did not want to buy more but it did want L-R's engineering design facilities and its continuing business. TI had made some progress in using L-R's manufacturing capacity to produce machine tools but now wanted to sell the works as well as the design and engineering teams. DA had offered a price that covered current assets and work in progress, but TI wanted a price that included a significant payment for goodwill as well. However, both companies were now keen to do a deal and a compromise was agreed.

In the period between 21 December 1967 and 22 March 1968, all three acquisitions were settled and announced. DA bought Brightside and L-R, and sold the Stockton works of ABP to Whessoe. The IRC agreed to advance £3.5 million in convertible loan stock to Whessoe to finance this purchase and the consequent rationalisation. The IRC was also prepared to provide bridging finance for DA, but this was not required. A public commitment was, however, made that the IRC would consider providing finance for DA in the future, if the process of rationalisation meant that DA required longer-term funds. These moves certainly did not constitute the major reorganisation that had been envisaged by some, but the IRC Board saw them as a useful start in tidying up the structure of the two industries and, it hoped, in giving better use of the existing facilities. This process was continued when, in August 1968, DA announced an agreed offer for Armstrong Whitworth, another small company specialising in equipment for the steel and non-ferrous metal industries. Again, DA financed this acquisition from its own resources but the IRC repeated its willingness to consider providing finance for rationalisation, should the need arise.

CAUSE FOR CONCERN

Talks continued on a range of possible moves. The IRC felt that none of the UK companies was large enough to compete soundly and effectively in international markets. It did not, however, take a fixed position on whether there should be one steelworks plant producer only, or two or three companies each covering the whole range of process and steelworks plant. It was willing to discuss any proposals for the industry that made sense in managerial and financial terms, but agreement was as far away as ever. The BSC, as well as DA, were firmly against the establishment of a single UK steelworks plant manufacturer, while Wellman continued to argue the case in favour. Several deals were considered. One was to link Wellman with DA and/or HW; another was to join Whessoe with HW and to join DA with Simon Engineering, a company which was strong in process plant manufacture, including the design and production of chemical and oil refining equipment. Nevertheless, none of the discussions produced results and by the autumn of 1968 they began to be overshadowed by financial problems that were becoming apparent, first in DA and then in Whessoe. Initially, these were seen merely as a set-back to merger hopes, but it was gradually realised that the position of both companies was very serious, and the IRC became more concerned to ensure their survival than to assist further acquisitions.

The IRC had not thought of either company as being financially strong but had believed this was a result of the depressed market and the unsatisfactory structure of the industry, and therefore a principal reason for promoting its rationalisation. Even so, the IRC had seen no evidence to suggest that either DA or Whessoe was in a dangerous financial position, and the companies' own activities and keenness for expansion had done nothing to suggest this.

The Corporation had therefore undertaken no detailed financial investigation of DA or Whessoe itself, and does not appear to have been alerted to problems by any of the merchant bankers involved in the various deals that had taken place. Its concern over DA was related largely to growing losses on a major contract and this is dealt with in Chapter 11. First, in Chapter 10, we shall follow the history of Whessoe, whose problems arose more directly out of the negotiations we have outlined. In short, Whessoe appeared to have overstretched itself financially by its purchase of the Stockton works.

PART THREE

RESCUES AND RESTORATIONS

10

The Plant Makers – Whessoe

Whessoe's purchase of ABP's Stockton works had been announced in March 1968 and the IRC met its commitment to advance £3.5 million over the period from April to June 1968. The IRC finance was provided in the form of convertible loan stock and this, together with the fact that the Corporation hoped for further rationalisation in the industry, ensured that close contact between the IRC and Whessoe would continue. The company was given an initial period to absorb its acquisition but contact was resumed in October, when a new merger possibility was suggested. This came to nothing but the IRC took advantage of the renewed contact to take a more detailed look at the group.

PERIOD OF DECLINE

At this stage, the IRC's approach was still very positive. It saw Whessoe as a technically outstanding, but financially embattled group. The key question was whether the company's financial position was sufficiently strong for it to undertake further acquisitions and/or mergers which could lead to greater financial stability, or whether its problems were such that a period of retrenchment was desirable. The Corporation was reluctant to rule out Whessoe as part, or even the focus, of rationalisation, and it pursued discussions through the winter of 1968/9.

Early in 1969, however, Whessoe's Chairman, Lord, was becoming uneasy about the Corporation's motives and the IRC's attitude to Whessoe was indeed undergoing a significant change. Its opinion of the group's engineering and technical skills remained high but, as the financial problems became more apparent, the IRC's concern grew over Whessoe's ability to get through its troubles and to handle further expansion.

Stockton was proving to be a major problem, partly because

much less work had been found for it than had been anticipated. Originally, it had been expected to lose £70 000 in 1968/9, but this forecast was increased to £250 000 in October 1968 and to £610 000 in early 1969. The loss was to be written off against reserves but Whessoe also revised its overall profit forecast downwards, chiefly because of the late completion of a contract. Cash flow was therefore becoming increasingly tight. No scheme for an aggressive merger was any longer feasible and the IRC began to consider seriously what it could do to encourage Whessoe to strengthen its top management, since both Lord and the Managing Director, Noone, were nearing retirement. The IRC's initial view was that it should wait for these retirements and use them as an opportunity to suggest its own candidates as their successors.

When the results for the year ending 31 March 1969 were published, they proved to be as bad as had been feared. The trading loss for Stockton was £663 000 and this was written off against reserves as planned. Apart from this loss, the Group had produced a pre-tax profit of £1.25 million, marginally less than in the previous year. More dramatically, the forecast for 1969/70 was revised downwards from £1.7 million to £0.6 million and the IRC feared that even this figure might be too optimistic. Whessoe was also in danger of running up against its borrowing limits. For the first time, the IRC felt that it might soon face a situation where its position as an unsecured creditor was as risk.

POSSIBILITIES FOR RECOVERY

The IRC Board saw two ways out of this situation. First, Whessoe could merge with a company that was financially strong, provided that this also made industrial sense. Alternatively, the IRC could support Whessoe through its difficulties and help it to find key men to strengthen its management. Although a number of the earlier merger possibilities were considered again, it was the latter course of action that was ultimately followed. But it was some time before the company was prepared to discuss the seriousness of its position openly with the IRC.

The immediate crisis was met by Whessoe amending its Articles of Association so as to raise its permitted borrowing limit. This was done without advance notice to the IRC. Whessoe also reopened talks, first with Wellman and then with Clarke Chapman. These and other talks drifted on without results, while Whessoe's financial position continued to deteriorate. In mid-September 1969, the profit forecast for the year was revised downwards again. The first quarter's results had been appalling, with sales of only £2.2 million against a forecast of £5.8 million. Activity was low; completion was slow; and there was a loss on completed work which was only offset by taking profits from continuing contracts. Whessoe's share price fell to a low of 8*s* 7*d* (43p) in 1969 against a high of 30*s* (£1.50) in the previous year. At the end of November, results for the half year revealed a pre-tax loss and little more than break-even was forecast for 1969/70 as a whole. Worse still, the company's overdraft was £3.9 million and rising near to the limit of £4 million. Its clearing bank indicated that it would be unwilling to raise this limit.

The IRC increased its pressure on the Whessoe Board, emphasizing that the first priority must be management not mergers. Indeed, it was hard to see how a merger could be agreed, given Whessoe's precarious position, at a price which would do justice to the company's future potential. But stronger management was needed if that potential was to be realised, which made the task of finding suitable successors as chairman and chief executive even more important. The IRC had proposals on both these issues. Villiers suggested that Lord Erroll, a Whessoe Board member, should be made Deputy Chairman and should replace Lord in the spring. This was a few months before Lord's formal retirement date but the change would nonetheless give an air of orderly succession. Priority should be given to bringing in a new chief executive and the IRC recommended a firm of consultants to find the right man.

The Whessoe Board, meeting in December 1969, accepted these proposals and also appointed an investigating committee to make an independent review of the prospects and profit potential of the Stockton works. No immediate or precise steps were agreed to improve the group's cash flow or profit position, but Whessoe continued to trade just within its overdraft limit. Erroll's appointment as Deputy Chairman was confirmed in January 1970 and at the beginning of March he and Lord came to see Villiers at Pall Mall.

At this meeting there were some signs of returning confidence. Orders had increased, prices were firmer and Whessoe expected to be well inside its overdraft limit for most of 1970. The company's accountants had produced provisional figures, showing a profit, before tax, of £300 000 for the year ending 31 March 1970 and giving a forecast of £500 000 for 1970/1. Whessoe's internal figures were rather different, however, and the IRC felt that little confidence could be placed in either set. Nor could much encouragement be given to Whessoe's persistent merger hopes. An alternative to an outright merger was the sale of particular assets but these would have to include a major activity if the sale were to have a significant effect, and it was difficult to see what could be sold at a satisfactory price. The IRC was encouraged, however, to learn that the consultants it had recommended were pressing on with their search for a new chief executive and that the search had been widened to include other key corporate managers.

When the results for 1969/70 were available, they justified the IRC's lack of confidence in the earlier figures. There was a loss for the year of £251 000, despite a dramatic increase in turnover from £18.7 million in 1968/9 to £36.9 million in 1969/70.

THE NEW TEAM

By the time these figures were published, significant changes had taken place in Whessoe; Lord and Noone had both retired, Erroll had become Chairman on 1 May and a new chief executive had been found. He was William Smart, who had made his reputation in turning round part of the Vickers group, and he was due to join Whessoe in September. Whessoe's cash position was still precarious but a credit arrangement had been agreed with the BSC, at a special meeting with its Chairman Lord Melchett.

The company's merchant bankers were now asked to make an appraisal of Whessoe's financial position. Their review indicated that Whessoe was still in a serious financial position. Initial figures showed the company to be very close to its increased borrowing limit. The report recommended substantial cuts in overheads and tighter cash control. Whessoe's own executive committee made similar recommendations for Stockton, involving significant cuts in employment and R&D expenditure, as well as tighter control of work-in-progress. Action which should have been taken when Stockton was first acquired was taken at last.

By the end of 1970, a clear improvement was apparent. It seemed that Erroll and Smart had won their race against time to introduce sufficient financial discipline before the position became irretrievable. It had been a close run thing and the new management acknowledged the contribution of the IRC in forcing action to be taken just in time. Ironically, it was now the IRC's own future that was in doubt, following the General Election. Erroll had contacted the new Conservative Minister of Technology, Geoffrey Rippon, at the end of July. He felt it would be useful, in the context of the debate on the IRC's future, to let Rippon know of his own experience with the Corporation. He said that he had been given tremendous and worthwhile practical help by Charles Villiers and his colleagues on many matters concerning Whessoe, going far beyond the narrow concept of a lender of money. Though not sufficient to prevent the dissolution of the IRC, this and similar comments seem to have made an impression on the new Government.

Before the IRC was dissolved it provided more important assistance to Whessoe. The £3.5 million lent to the company in 1968 was repayable after not more than five years. In January 1971, Whessoe asked the IRC to consider rephasing this repayment, to give the group more time to build up its financial position. In March, only a month before the IRC was dissolved, it was agreed that repayment could be postponed until 1978. So, having become involved with Whessoe quite early in its life, the Corporation continued its involvement, right up to the time when it was wound up. As Erroll had told Rippon, its role was not merely as a lender but also as provider of advice and support.

COMMENT

Having said this, however, we must ask whether it was sensible for the IRC to have become involved with Whessoe in the first place. The answer is almost certainly no. Even if it had been sensible for DA to sell its Stockton works, it is clear, at least with hindsight, that it was a problematic acquisition for Whessoe. However, at the time of the deal the IRC was still feeling its way. The sale of Stockton to Whessoe by DA must have seemed to provide an attractive chance to start rationalising the industry, but the IRC probably jumped at this chance rather too eagerly and without sufficient regard to Whessoe's financial position.

The second question is whether the IRC should have monitored Whessoe's progress over Stockton more carefully, before encouraging it to enter into further merger negotiations. Again, with hindsight, the answer seems clear. Not only was Whessoe's financial position stretched; it was likely to have difficulty in holding its position, let alone coping with substantial acquisitions. Yet, for quite a time, the IRC seemed to see Whessoe as a vehicle, rather than a candidate, for takeovers.

Perhaps the most important lesson from Whessoe is that it is frequently difficult for any outsider – even one as influential and expert as the IRC – to notice early enough that a firm is in financial difficulties. Managers understandably often prefer to keep their troubles to themselves. Even an IRC nominee on the Whessoe board might not have helped. Full-time directors are always in a very strong position and can, if they wish, conceal a good deal of what is going on from their own part-time colleagues. Significantly, even Whessoe's own merchant bankers and accountants seemed slow to spot the seriousness of the company's position.

Once the IRC had appreciated the extent of Whessoe's difficulties, it acted as quickly and as firmly as could have been expected. At the end of 1969, there were discussions about Lord's successor and by January 1970 Erroll had become Chairman-elect and the IRC was assisting with the search for a new chief executive. These appointments seem to have marked the turning point in the company's fortunes.

Since that time, Whessoe's history has been far from trouble free. It operates in a very difficult industry, where good times are rapidly followed by bad and where cash flow management is very difficult. Nevertheless, Whessoe survived its crisis at the end of the 1960s and its survival would have been significantly less likely without the assistance of the IRC.

11

The Plant Makers – Davy Ashmore

In chapter 9 we followed Davy Ashmore's (DA) fortunes up to the autumn of 1968. By then it had acquired Brightside Engineering, Loewy-Robertson (LR) and Armstrong Whitworth (AW). The IRC had twice made a public commitment to help to finance rationalisation following these acquisitions but DA had not, by then, felt a need to take up these offers. In November 1968, however, DA did approach the IRC to begin negotiations for a loan. It revealed that its cash flow position had deteriorated, largely because of difficulties with a project undertaken by its subsidiary Power Gas (PG). This was a turnkey contract to build a refinery for Continental Oil Corporation (Conoco). It was to transpire that these difficulties were very serious indeed. In this chapter we follow the development of this problem and analyse the IRC's involvement in the steps taken to overcome it.

A REQUEST FOR FINANCE

The IRC was becoming concerned about DA's cash position before the meeting in November. It thought that part of the finance for the company's acquisitions had come from advance payments on the Conoco contract and had heard that the cash flow from this project had subsequently turned against DA. This was confirmed at the meeting, when DA asked for up to £5 million to finance its own rationalisation plus a proposed expansion into the manufacture of plastics machinery. DA said that the cash difficulties on the contract were caused by the labour problems of a sub-contractor, but claimed that they were manageable. The loan was required so the group could continue to develop, despite this temporary setback.

The general case for the IRC providing finance for DA was set out by the company's merchant bank. Net of the money raised by selling Stockton, it had cost DA more than £3 million to acquire Brightside, L-R and AW. DA had since spent over £300 000 on improving L-R and Brightside and would spend £400 000 more on rationalising its roll making, and on closing its foundry at Billingham and at least part of AW's Gateshead plant. DA planned to put a further £1 million into re-equipment at Sheffield, with the ultimate aim of concentrating its steelworks plant business there. It was also talking again of buying HW's blast furnace and steelworks plant business.

In addition to this, DA wanted to develop L-R's plastic machinery business by buying R.H. Windsor, a company which produced injection moulding machines. This, plus further development planned in plastics machinery, would cost up to £2 million. DA was confident that its current difficulties need not upset its development plan and that it merely needed a financial 'bridge' in the form of a medium-term loan from the IRC.

The IRC executive was not convinced. Whatever the financial case for the extension into plastics machinery, the IRC would regard this development by DA as having low priority so far as IRC money was concerned. And, before any loans could be considered, the IRC needed to be satisfied on two points. First, what was the loss on the Conoco contract likely to be? Second, could DA raise some of the money it claimed to need from the market?

DA's financial advisors answered the second question. They pointed out that DA had barely covered its dividend in the previous five years, and that the period up to 1970 looked no better. After that things should be much brighter as BSC's re-equipment programme got under way, but until the profits from this actually appeared in the 1970s, there was no question of any kind of share issue.

The first question was more difficult to answer. The problem was that Power Gas had submitted a fixed price tender for the Conoco refinery, the civil engineering component of which was based on a fixed price contract with Mitchell Construction. Mitchell had gone bankrupt in mid-1968 and Conoco, not Power Gas, had brought in another contractor, which had not been prepared to take a fixed price contract, but had insisted on a cost-plus arrangement. There had then been a period of confusion on the site, and an expensive pressure vessel had been badly damaged in an accident. While insurance would cover the damage, the claim might take a long time to settle and DA's most pessimistic estimate of the loss on the Conoco contract was about £4 million; a 'reasonable' one was £1 million. DA was, however, now bound to have a negative cash flow from the contract of about £3 million between mid-1969 and mid-1970.

Despite assurances from DA, the IRC feared that the position might be even more serious. Rumour had it that the loss was increasing rapidly and that, if Conoco enforced penalties in the contract, this could nearly bust Power Gas. While this was only 'scuttlebutt', the evidence was mounting that the IRC should lend DA nothing until it got much more information.

No agreement was reached at the November meeting and in January 1969 DA put forward more detailed figures on its projected profits and cash flow. These indicated that a loss of £2 million was anticipated in the year ending 31 March 1969 (against profits of £2.1 million and £2.3 million in the two previous years) and that profits were not expected to return to the 1966/7 level until 1972/3. The very worst position on the Conoco contract was now seen to be a loss of a little under £5 million, but this was only if no claims, either on Conoco or on DA's own insurers, were met. The expected net loss was about £1.5 million, but even if all these forecasts were correct, cash flow would still be a significant problem. Deficits were foreseen for the current, and the two subsequent, years.

DA told the IRC that in the light of these figures it had shelved its plans for expansion in plastics machinery and it formally submitted an application for a loan of £4 million to fund the investments it had made in iron and steel plant and roll making. Given the uncertainties over the size and timing of BSC's investment programme, DA asked for the loan to be for seven years.

The IRC recognised that it was committed to DA, not only because of its previous public statements, but because it could not stand by and see Britain's leading steelworks plant and refinery contractor disabled. But DA's forecasts, together with the continuing deterioration on the Conoco contract, left the IRC executive seriously worried. DA argued that its local management was on top of the Conoco situation and that the group as a whole was in no fundamental danger. But the IRC was not convinced that a loan would be a sufficient, nor the best, answer to DA's problems. DA's formal request for a loan had, however, now been made and a detailed case was prepared for the IRC Board for its meeting on 24 January 1969. The executive reminded the Board of the discussions in 1968 between Simon Engineering and DA about a merger between the process plant businesses of Simon Carves and PG, which had ended with Simon unwilling to pursue any variant of the idea. Nevertheless, DA would still be happy to see PG as the nucleus of a larger, more versatile process plant company.

The idea of a merger to form a financially stronger group was strongly supported by Jeremy Bray, the junior minister at Mintech. But it did not seem likely that any acceptable deal could be arranged in time to meet DA's immediate needs.

The executive went on to review DA's management structure and the strengths and weaknesses of its senior management. This review was not very critical and discussions were already being held with the company on how best to strengthen particular areas. A key recommendation was that steps should be taken to reduce the very heavy load imposed on Fiennes because he was both Chairman and Chief Executive. Finally, the executive outlined the financial analysis that DA and its advisors had presented to them. On the basis of these figures, a loan of £4 million would allow the company to consolidate its position in steelworks plant following the acquisitions made in 1968 and allow it to survive its short-term cash flow problems.

Neither the IRC executive nor the Board was happy with the position, but the Board saw itself as commited to providing a loan to DA, even though members agreed that a loan would in no sense be a final solution to DA's problems. It would not end the IRC's involvement with the company but would mark the beginning of a closer relationship. The IRC Board authorised the executive to begin negotiations for a medium-term loan of up to £4 million, but set two conditions. First, the talks on strengthening DA's top management should continue and an IRC Board member, Sir Frank Schon, should join them. Second, the loan would be made in two tranches. The first tranche should not exceed £2.5 million and the balance would be advanced only if justified by a review of DA's position in 1970.

The IRC loan to DA was in fact never to be made in this form, but the Board's decision in January 1969 was to involve the Corporation irretrievably in a rapidly worsening situation. At first, negotiations proceeded reasonably smoothly. Fiennes agreed that the jobs of Chairman and Chief Executive should be divided and that he would give up the latter as soon as could reasonably be arranged. He also agreed to make an early presentation to the IRC of his company's proposals for strengthening other parts of senior management and to follow this up with quarterly meetings with the IRC.

A PARTNER FOR THE IRC

While these discussions were taking place with DA the IRC was also talking to the Finance Corporation for Industry (FCI). For some time, the IRC had felt that it could make its own funds go further if it could arrange joint advances with other financial institutions. The FCI was an obvious candidate, so the IRC approached the FCI

Board and asked if it would consider taking an equal share in the £4 million advance to DA. The IRC argued that DA had shown initiative and skill in obtaining overseas orders and had maintained its technological capacity. Furthermore, the IRC contended that British firms must join the 'big league' in process plant contracting. But, after its experience over the Conoco contract, there could be no doubt that DA was paying for an extreme entry-ticket to this business.

During March the FCI agreed in principle to join the IRC in the loan and, on 3 April, Villiers told Fiennes that detailed negotiations on terms could begin between DA, the IRC and the FCI. These negotiations continued through April, without any mention from DA of a change in the estimated loss on the Conoco contract. On 28 April the following announcement was released to the press:

> In furtherance of a policy of bringing about a greater degree of rationalisation in the steelworks plant industry, and with the express support of the IRC, Davy-Ashmore Limited acquired during the course of 1968 the iron and steelworks plant businesses of Brightside Foundry & Engineering Company Limited and Loewy-Robertson Engineering Company Limited and the rollmaking business of Brightside and of Armstrong Whitworth (Metal Industries) Ltd. In supporting these acquisitions the IRC announced its willingness to discuss with Davy-Ashmore the possibility of financial support for it if it should appear that longer term funds would be required for rationalisation and development.
>
> Following upon these undertakings the Industrial Reorganisation Corporation and Finance Corporation for Industry have agreed to join in making funds of up to £4m available to Davy-Ashmore Limited.
>
> The funds will be available for a five-year period on terms which provide for interest at the rate of 8% per annum and for an option to convert one-quarter of the advances made into shares of Davy-Ashmore at a price of 15/–. It is expected that the first drawings will be made in July this year.

The conversion element was designed to give a profit on the loan if DA was doing as well as it anticipated in the early 1970s. The share price stood at around 13*s* (65p) in April 1969 and had been over 19*s* (95p) in February. However this aspect of the arrangement was soon to seem insignificant.

THE 'CONOCO' LOSS

As soon as the announcement was released lawyers set to work on drafting the formal loan agreement. It was the details of this, or more specifically the clause limiting DA's total borrowings, that was to lead to the revelation of further deterioration on the Conoco contract. Up to the beginning of May, DA had not changed its assurance to the IRC that the maximum loss on the contract would be £5 million and the expected net loss, after recoveries, only £1.5 million. In May, Fiennes told the IRC that a gross loss of £7 million was a possibility but that much of this would be recovered through claims. The IRC braced itself, certain that worse was to come. At the beginning of June the figure for the loss became £8.5 million; a week later, on 13 June, it was put at £10 million; and by the middle of July the estimate was £12 million, with at least 6 months still required for completion of the contract.

The loan negotiations were held in abeyance from the beginning of June; the situation was effectively out of DA's control. The company had to turn to its bankers and creditors and its future depended on what kind of financial package could be arranged between them.

Fiennes resigned as Chief Executive from 30 June, but remained Chairman.

The IRC saw two possible courses of action and worked on them both. The first stage of either scheme had to be the possession of financial support to allow Power Gas to stay on the Conoco site and to complete the contract. This was vital, because DA's future now depended on its success in pressing claims to offset part of the gross loss that was certain to be at least £12 million. If Power Gas had to abandon the work, its chances of recovering substantial amounts from Conoco for 'scope changes' in the contract would be significantly reduced. Both schemes therefore involved obtaining sufficient short-term funds and guarantees to make possible the completion of the refinery. The second stage could then be either longer-term financial support, or the absorption of all or part of DA into a larger grouping of process plant companies.

THE ENTRY OF THE BONDHOLDERS

A new group was rapidly assuming the key position in the short-term financial negotiations. This comprised the bondholders on the Conoco contract. As part of normal commercial conditions, a group of insurance companies had put up bonds, totalling £11.36 million, guaranteeing Power Gas's performance to Conoco. This meant that the bondholders had to meet any obligations on which PG defaulted. In particular, if PG failed to complete their work on the refinery, Conoco could have the work done by someone else and send the bill to the bondholders. If PG had collapsed with six months' work still to be done, this bill would have run into millions of pounds. The contract had been signed in August 1966 but the bondholders, ten American and one British insurance company, said they had not been warned of the mounting losses until June 1969. They had then sent in engineers, and estimates of the £12 million loss, and of six months to completion, were theirs.

A negotiating team was formed and led by Field, of Federal Insurance (USA). A meeting was held with the IRC in July, when Field explained that, although their premiums had been paid by Conoco, their interests lay with PG, or at least in helping it to complete the work. This was partly because PG was likely to do this more cheaply than any newcomer to the site and partly because the bondholders had recourse to PG, and ultimately to DA, for any payments they had to make under the bonds. If PG withdrew, failed in most of its claims and collapsed, the bondholders would not only have to indemnify Conoco for all its costs, but would have little chance of recovering them. On 17 July, the IRC, the FCI and the bondholders met DA, its clearing banks and its financial advisors. It was estimated that, as well as keeping its current overdraft facilities, PG would need an extra £5.5 million to enable it to remain afloat and to complete the contract. Field said that if the clearing banks confirmed the existing facilities, and the IRC and FCI made their advance of £2 million, then the bondholders would find and guarantee sufficient resources to complete the contract. This would be £3.5 million on current estimates, but could be more if necessary. The IRC could not agree to this. Its offer of a loan had been made when the position of DA had appeared to be very different and had been designed to assist with rationalisation measures. The IRC could not go ahead with its original proposals unless it could see clear prospects for the long-term development of the DA group's full potential. It could only offer cash to meet the immediate crisis if this was very short-term money, guaranteed by the bondholders. The IRC's proposal was therefore that it should put up £2 million for three months, with a bondholder guarantee. At the end of this period the position would be reviewed and, if the long-term development of DA could then be assured (possibly as part of a larger grouping), the original negotiations for a five-year loan could be re-opened.

The bondholders, in turn, were not happy with this. They felt that they had been assured by DA and by public statements that the IRC/FCI loan would be available. The clearing banks were prepared to confirm DA's overdraft facilities and to put up a further £3 million under the bondholders' guarantee, but without the IRC/FCI money this would not be enough. The meeting was therefore deadlocked and the parties went away to consider their positions until the following day. On 18 July the meeting reconvened, but no party had changed its position significantly. Little progress was made and the bondholders' representatives consulted their principals in New York.

On 21 July, a further meeting was held. The bondholders now agreed to provide a guarantee both for the banks and for the IRC, provided that the cash was advanced to DA in the form of a debenture. DA already had outstanding debentures of £2.3 million. The clearing banks had insisted on converting their £1.5 million overdraft into a debenture as a condition of its renewal, so that the bondholders' suggestion meant creating a third charge (amounting to £5 million) on DA. It was not clear that to do so would be feasible but the parties agreed to retire and consider the legal and technical consequences of the proposal.

The promise of a solution along these lines quickly evaporated. At the meeting on 21 July, the clearing banks had raised the question of security for their contingent liabilities with DA. These were sureties for certain major contracts undertaken by various parts of the DA group and amounted to £10 million. In the normal course of events, the banks would have been liable if DA defaulted on these contracts and would then have had recourse on DA, but only as unsecured creditors. In the IRC's view this proposal made the whole situation untenable. If the bondholders and the banks, both of whom were normally unsecured creditors, were seen to be demanding prior charges on the company, then all other unsecured creditors would scramble for payment. This would have forced DA into bankruptcy.

THE FINANCIAL PACKAGE

The IRC now felt that it had to take the initiative to break this deadlock, even if that meant going back on its original decision. There was rapid consultation by phone with as many Board members as could be contacted. The executive then put forward the following proposal:

(a) The IRC and FCI would lend DA £1 million for five years, with interest of about 10½ per cent per annum, secured by a second debenture on the assets of the whole group. DA's two clearing banks would rank *pari passu* with this security in respect of their existing £1.5 million overdraft advances and these facilities would be guaranteed for five years.

(b) An additional £4 million would be advanced to DA until 15 November 1969 under a guarantee from the bondholders. This would be made up as follows:

IRC/FCI	£1.0 million
DA's merchant bank	£0.5 million
DA's clearing bank	£2.5 million
	£4.0 million

(c) The clearing banks and the bondholders would ask for no prior charge or security in respect of their contingent claim on DA.

This proposal was discussed at a meeting with all the interested parties on 23 July. To some extent the previous negotiations had been financial brinkmanship. It was in all the parties' interests to put together a financial package and the argument was about relatively small differences in security. The bondholders and the banks may not have expected security for these contingent claims, but by raising this as an obstacle they had encouraged the IRC and FCI to offer to put £1 million of their money at risk.

Substantial agreement was reached at this meeting, subject to the important condition that the bondholders' guarantee to repay the £4 million on 15 November (or any later date agreed by the lenders) should be unconditional and automatic. This meeting was also told that Fiennes had decided that he should resign as Chairman of DA.

This was how the position stood when the IRC held its regular Board meeting on 24 July. The executive summarised these negotiations and also brought the Board up to date on discussions that had been proceeding simultaneously with Simon Engineering and Head Wrightson.

THE MERGER PROPOSALS

It was not surprising that, when the position on the Conoco contract became clear, the IRC should have tried once more to form a stronger grouping of process plant and steelworks plant companies. While this was familiar ground, in one respect, the chances of success were improved because it was thought that DA might be more prepared to consider any reasonable arrangement. The idea was discussed at an IRC Board meeting on 11 July, when the members authorised the executive to pursue the possibility of a deal involving DA, Simon Engineering (SE) and Head Wrightson (HW). The IRC's objectives can be summarised as follows: (a) to ensure the survival and development of the companies making up the DA group; (b) to create a group with sufficient financial strength to play a significant part in the international business of process plant contracting; (c) to create a group capable of handling the substantial increase in orders anticipated in steelworks plant; (d) to put the combined assets of these groups under the best possible management.

Meetings were held at the IRC with each of the companies. The first was with SE on 15 July. Barrett, the Chairman of SE, attended together with his Chief Executive, Brook, and three other executive directors. DA's financial advisor was also there. The IRC explained DA's current position and made the case for a partial, or preferably total, merger of the three groups. SE had not previously been in favour of a merger but recognised that the issues at stake were now more significant. Subject to the agreement of the full SE Board they felt that they should agree to talks provided that it was made clear the initiative had come from the IRC. They also asked for any announcement to infer that SE was seen as the acquirer and to make it clear that it would not be taking over any of the Conoco losses.

A similar meeting was held with John Eccles, the Managing Director of HW, and he too agreed to recommend the IRC invitation to his Board. Since Eccles and Brook were seen as key men in the new group if it were formed, the IRC arranged for them to dine together. They had a cautiously successful evening.

On 16 July, Fiennes came to the IRC. He reacted favourably, even with relief, to the IRC's suggestions and arranged to return the next day with his three divisional managing directors. Their response too was favourable but they clearly also wanted to consider alternative possibilities. It was, however, agreed that they too would recommend the IRC proposals to their Board. So, on 17 July, the IRC was able to write formally to all three chairmen recording the meetings that had taken place and asking for a statement of intent from their Boards to proceed with merger negotiations.

A meeting of the SE Board was scheduled for 21 July and the HW and DA Boards were due to meet on 22 July. Meanwhile, the IRC canvassed and obtained support from Mintech, the DEA and BSC. Indeed, BSC indicated that it would be willing to support the new grouping with early major orders. Events had moved very rapidly but so far everything was on schedule. DA hoped to be able to announce its preliminary results for 1968/9 by the end of July. They would include a massive provision for the likely net loss on

Conoco: allowing for this, the group would be reporting an overall loss approaching £4 million. DA wished to combine this announcement, not only with details of the financial package that was being arranged, but also with a statement that talks were proceeding to ensure the long-term future of the company.

The IRC had received replies from all three companies by the morning of 24 July, when it held its own Board meeting. The only significant qualification then made to the proposals was that SE and DA should meet first, bringing in HW at a second stage. The members therefore had before them not the news of an impasse on DA's financial problems, but agreed short-term measures, and the renewed possibility of the kind of merger which had been envisaged for so long in the process and steelworks plant industries.

The IRC Board members had been kept closely in touch with the executive's actions over the previous two weeks and endorsed the proposals and agreements. Some members felt that Conoco was adopting a very inflexible attitude, but agreed that it was within its rights in doing this. However, all involved had assured the IRC that they would do their best to ensure rapid completion of the contract and that this should be substantially achieved by October. For the second time, but now under very different circumstances, the IRC Board gave approval for a loan to be negotiated with DA.

DA's results were announced on 29 July 1969. The total overrun on the Conoco contract was put at £12 million. The overrun was blamed chiefly on extensive design changes required by Conoco and it was explained that PG would be claiming in excess of £10 million in compensation. An arbitrary figure of £6 million was credited for recoveries and a provision of £5.4 million was put against the results for 1968/9. (A figure of £0.6 million had already been provided in the 1967/8 accounts. This decision had been made by the DA Board in July 1968 and was, in itself, an indication of the degree to which the problem had been underestimated.) DA's loss for the year amounted to £3.7 million. The announcement went on to say that the company was 'negotiating to overcome the resulting acute cash problem' and had made arrangements for immediate loans totalling £5 million.

MERGER TALKS BEGIN

SE had asked for the announcement of the merger talks to follow rather than accompany DA's results and so, two days later, a press statement was released. This said that the IRC had initiated talks between SE and DA aimed at a merger and that Fiennes would relinquish the chairmanship of DA and resign from the Boards of DA and SE. DA had accepted Fiennes' resignation, but had asked him to remain as a consultant during the challenging period ahead. DA's new Chairman was Sir Douglas Bell. Barrett, the Chairman of SE, had resigned from the DA Board because of the merger negotiations.

The merger talks started very badly. Some of DA's managers felt that they were treated very roughly by SE and feared that any arrangement would be very one-sided. They therefore began an extensive lobbying campaign with customers and the government against the merger. The IRC tried to patch matters up, and talks went on through September. By the end of the month, however, progress was still negligible.

Bell was now firmly in position as DA's Chairman but no successor had been appointed to Fiennes as Chief Executive. DA was therefore being run by three joint managing directors, Buckley, Baker and Robinson (who was in charge of PG) and it was these three who came to the IRC with Bell at the end of September. It was clear that they were much less enthusiastic about SE than they had been when talks began and they tried to move the meeting on to consider other possibilities. These included an international link-up and schemes with one or more major customers. The meeting ended with the IRC pointing out snags in the various suggestions but stressing the need for DA to find a stronger financial base.

The IRC tried to revitalise the talks, but soon accepted that nothing would be achieved. DA was now firmly against them, SE somewhat detached and unenthusiastic, and HW not keen to attempt to continue discussions. So, on 8 October, the IRC admitted defeat and put out a press release containing the following statement:

> Detailed and constructive discussions [between SE and DA] revealed that the industrial, financial and managerial positions of the two groups do not fit sufficiently well to justify closer association, and accordingly the discussions have been terminated.

The DA management had felt they had been pushed around by SE and strongly resented this. SE's attitude probably reflected a lack of enthusiasm for DA and the view that if they were to become involved it would be strictly on their own terms. However, the key factor was that, somewhat surprisingly, DA felt strong enough to resist SE's pressure. The financial package and the management changes were proving to be more effective, more quickly, than anyone had anticipated. Paradoxically the very success of the refinancing which the IRC had organised was probably the key feature in its failure to effect the merger it had tried for so long to bring about.

A NEW CHIEF EXECUTIVE

When the short-term financial support for DA had been arranged, the IRC had suggested to DA and its financial advisors that three key problems had to be tackled. First, the group had no permanent chairman and no chief executive. Second, there was a continuing short-term cash problem. Third, DA needed somehow to obtain long-term finance for its investment programme.

By the end of September DA's position had strengthened because progress had been made on the first two of these problems. Bell had emerged as a very solid and steady influence. He told the IRC that Buckley was clearly *primus inter pares* of the three managing directors and would be appointed Chief Executive in October. A new finance director had also been found but, even before he took over, progress had been made on the liquidity problems. DA's cumbersome mechanical engineering group had been dismantled and its expensive central marketing, R&D, and service departments had been closed. Other plans were in hand for the disposal of assets which, though peripheral to the business, could raise significant amounts of cash.

The IRC was not totally convinced that Buckley would succeed and was concerned that short-term cash requirements should not override longer-term considerations of industrial structure. It agreed that repayment of the short-term, £4 million, Conoco loan should be deferred from 15 November 1969 to 31 March 1970, but that DA should be requested to consult the IRC on its progress, and on its top management structure. DA agreed to this and arranged for monthly meetings. The company felt that it would gain by these meetings, not least because it felt its position was steadily improving and that the IRC would recognise this if it was kept fully informed. These meetings would also consider any significant disposal of assets, because these required IRC approval under the terms of the five-year debenture.

More regular meetings were held and in most ways the IRC–DA relationship worked well. Between October 1969 and February 1970, Buckley negotiated a series of sales of minor assets, raising a total of more than £4 million without any material reduction of the group's profit potential. The assets released had a book value of under £2 million and, in aggregate, had recently earned no profit at all. DA's cash position had been significantly improved without damage to its main business. The IRC had been kept fully informed and had, indeed, assisted DA with several of its negotiations. On 2 March 1970, Villiers congratulated DA on achieving this slimming down so effectively and so smoothly. One ironic feature was that the IRC had introduced a buyer for DA's plastics machinery business. When DA had come to the IRC in November 1968 to begin negotiations for a loan, the expansion of its plastics machinery business had been a major priority. The IRC had refused to consider finance for this at the time and now DA itself, in a more sombre mood, was concentrating its attention on its main business.

Differing views on the definitions of this central business were, however, to cause a brief but heated row between DA and the IRC at the end of March. The argument was over DA's proposal to sell its roll making businesses to the British Steel Corporation. Matters came to a head on 23 March when the IRC learned that DA had almost completed an agreement with the BSC, to sell its roll making business for £3.5 million. Despite the regular meetings, this was the first the IRC had heard of the deal. It at once reminded DA of the need, under the terms of its debenture, to obtain consent for any disposal of assets and indicated that, in this case, consent would be by no means automatic. The executive met Bell and Buckley on 21 March and on 1 April Sir Frank Schon, an IRC Board member, lunched with Bell. The IRC executive put forward no less than ten detailed reservations to the proposed deal and these were explained to the IRC Board at its meeting on 10 April.

The reservations can be classified under two main headings. First, the IRC questioned the financial wisdom of the sale. Roll making was earning almost £600 000 per annum. So the price offered was low. Indeed, if the proceeds from the sale were used to reduce the group's borrowing or put on deposit they would raise little more than half the profit that would be foregone. If the proceeds were to be reinvested, the IRC wanted to know where. It also pointed out that every major US rolling mill contractor had its own roll business, because this steady replacement activity softened the effects of the investment cycle in steelworks plant.

The second, and main, issue was 'industrial logic'. The IRC had supported DA's acquisition of Brightside Engineering and Armstrong Whitworth. Indeed, its original commitment to the company had been for loans to finance the rationalisation of these roll making facilities. It had also supported the British Rollmakers (BR) acquisition of Johnson's roll business, from the receivers, in 1968. Both BR's and DA's businesses were now successful and they were the only major UK suppliers of cast rolls. (There were also two suppliers of the more specialist forged rolls.) Neither BR nor the IRC wished to see DA's business taken over by its major customer. The IRC had further reservations because it felt that BSC was an unenthusiastic purchaser and might not continue with DA's export business, which amounted to 25–30 per cent of roll sales. Moreover BSC had substantial under-used foundry capacity and might have been forced, for political and/or industrial relations reasons, to undo much of the work undertaken in rationalising DA's facilities. Finally, the IRC executives had discussed the deal with Molyneaux, BSC's Managing Director of Finance, and had learnt that the offer had been made largely to ease the working capital problems of a valued supplier. Given its other disposals, DA simply should not be so desperate for cash.

At the Board meeting on 10 April, the executive reviewed the background of the IRC's relations with DA, set out the arguments against the deal and recommended that consent, necessary under the debenture deed, should be withheld, at least until DA had explained how it intended to use the £3.5 million that would be raised. In the event, the IRC Board did not need to take any action because DA decided to call the deal off. Bell later apologised to the IRC for the failure to follow the strict terms of the debenture.

THE CONOCO SETTLEMENT AND DA'S RECOVERY

In their accounts for 1968/9, DA had allowed for a gross loss of £12 million on the Conoco contract and a net loss, after recoveries from claims, of £6 million. An amount of £0.6 million had been provided for in the 1967/8 accounts giving a net provision of £5.4 million for 1968/9. When agreement was finally reached with Conoco in August 1970, the gross loss amounted to £10.25 million, but DA had achieved only £4.25 million in recoveries. So the total provision of £6 million proved to be sufficient. There was some difference of opinion over the appropriateness of the form in which Conoco had advanced the £4.25 million, the IRC feeling that DA had settled for an unattractive scheme, by which cash would be made available over a period of about five years. But the contract, which had proved so disastrous, was now completed and DA's relationship with Conoco had recovered significantly.

With this settlement behind it and with the emergency loan of £4 million now repaid out of the cash raised by asset disposals, DA was in a much better condition. Buckley had firmly established himself as chief executive and was rationalising effectively the activities of the whole group. Despite the disagreement over the BSC deal, the IRC and DA agreed that DA should concentrate on engineering and contracting rather than manufacturing and that any further cash released from selling peripheral activities should be used to acquire design businesses in Europe and the USA.

For the year ending 31 March 1970, DA's pre-tax profits were £800 000 compared to the loss of £3.7 million in 1968/9 and a profit of £2.1 million in 1967/8. The company was, however, in a stronger position than the results implied. Despite the disposals of assets during the year, turnover was up from £53 million in 1968/9 to £72 million in 1969/70 with virtually no increase in numbers employed.

Several more deals were completed in late 1970 and early 1971. The IRC had been helping with negotiations to sell DA's steel foundry at Billingham to Head Wrightson and this sale was eventually completed for £650 000. The IRC also gave formal approval for the acquisition of two West German design companies. Bamay Verfahrenstechnik GmbH was bought from the receiver in July 1970 and Vickers Zimmers, a process contractor specialising in chemical plant, from Vickers in 1971.

DA's profits show steady and impressive improvement through the 1970s. The company earned £1.4 million in 1970/1, £2.3 million in 1971/2, over £4 million in 1972/3 and 1973/4, £6 million in 1974/5 and £10 million in 1975/6. In 1976/7 pre-tax profits almost doubled again to over £18 million and a peak of over £26 million was achieved in 1978/9. Over the period from 1970/1 to 1978/9 turnover increased eightfold to over £600 million while the number of employees in the UK increased from about 7000 to just over 11 000. So, despite more difficult times at the end of the 1970s, much was achieved from the opportunity provided by the financial arrangements made in the summer of 1969.

COMMENTS

The story of the IRC's involvement with DA spans Chapters 9, 10 and 11. The IRC had hoped to bring about significant rationalisation in both the steelworks plant and process plant industries. DA was central not only to these ambitions, but also to their failure. Five companies figured prominently in the IRC plans but of these Simon and Head Wrightson were unwilling to take on the suggested rationalisation, while Wellman's plans failed to gain the backing of the IRC. This left Whessoe and DA. Whessoe was ruled out partly by its purchase of DA's Stockton works, and DA was ruled out by its problems with the Conoco contract. With hindsight it could be argued that the IRC should have anticipated these problems, but with hindsight anticipation is never a problem. If the IRC had foreseen the extent of the loss on the Conoco project it would no doubt have approached the situation differently and also would have had more time to try to devise a solution. But the final result might not have been very different. Even with more time for consideration, it is unlikely that Simon would have been sufficiently enthusiastic about a merger with DA, and unlikely that DA would have agreed more readily to a takeover. DA's success since the crisis of 1969 shows the IRC's value. It both felt a responsibility and had the ability to support DA through a serious crisis.

These three chapters illustrate the context in which the IRC generally had to operate. The situation described in Chapter 6 on ball-bearings was unique; only once (in the case of Brown Bayley) did the IRC itself buy a company. The situations covered by Chapters 4 and 7 on the electrical industry and on British Leyland were also unusual. The IRC was not normally involved with huge merger bids. Its everyday work was very much concerned with attempting to improve the position of companies in fragmented industries, where effective rationalisation was hard to achieve. Its weapons were ideas and persuasion first, and cash only where ideas and persuasion had produced some results.

We can end this chapter with a slightly ironic footnote. A merger that the IRC, despite all its persuasion, failed to bring about has since occurred. On 23 November 1976 it was announced that DA was to take over Head Wrightson in an unopposed bid of over £7 million, achieving what the IRC would no doubt have called substantial rationalisation of the steelworks plant industry.

12

Rolls-Royce

The crash of Rolls-Royce (RR) was one of the most sensational in the history of British industry. It provided a rare occasion when a business story hit the front page of newspapers and stayed there for days if not weeks. Certainly the discovery in September 1970 that RR was on the verge of bankruptcy came as a bombshell to the newly elected Conservative Government, despite the fact that the City had been taking a very jaundiced view of the company for some time, and that its share price had fallen steadily over the previous year.

The Tory ministers learned of the impending RR disaster at the same time that the fate of the IRC was being decided and the two things became linked in many minds, although the IRC was already doomed. Two completely erroneous stories went around the City. The first was that after the election Edward Heath had phoned Villiers to ask about RR and had received the reply, 'The IRC has lent them £10 million and everything is all right'. The second was that the IRC investigation of RR had consisted only of sending one of its young executives to Derby for a day, after which they lent the company £20 million. As we shall see, the facts are very different. The IRC had produced a long, detailed and very critical report on RR based on three months' investigation and had set onerous conditions on the advance of any money to the company. Nevertheless, it is true that the IRC had lent RR £10 million only months before the company's collapse and had clearly underestimated the precariousness of RR's position.

In this chapter we shall examine the IRC's involvement with RR and try to answer some key questions. For example, why did the IRC become involved in an investigation of RR's financial position? There was, after all, no real suggestion of a merger. How was this investigation undertaken and what were its results? Were key problems missed or misunderstood? What remedies were suggested and to what extent were they accepted and implemented? The answers to these questions will give us further evidence on the value of the IRC in rescue situations.

THE BACKGROUND TO THE IRC INVESTIGATION

The IRC investigation of RR, under terms of reference agreed by the company and Mintech, began officially on 1 October 1969, but the IRC's first contact with RR had come more than a year earlier in the spring of 1968. RR had approached the IRC to discuss the possibility of a loan of up to £10 million to increase its working capital, but the Corporation had sent RR on to normal City sources. That was the end of the matter until March 1969, when RR again came to the IRC to discuss cash flow problems.

At that time the IRC executive was talking to Reyrolle-Parsons (R-P) and other companies in the heavy electrical generating field. RR indicated an interest in a merger with R-P as one way of easing its financial problems. R-P had relatively low borrowings: a bid offering RR equity for R-P would allow RR to reduce its debt ratio significantly and would provide scope for increased borrowings. Like most outsiders, the IRC then viewed RR as a technically brilliant company with severe financial problems but a cushion of continuing government support. There was some 'industrial logic' in a merger. In the USA, GE were producing both heavy and aero turbines, and a merger would provide RR with a means of reducing its reliance on the extremely risky aero-engine business and on government finance. However, neither the IRC executive, nor its Board, was willing to give any commitment without further consideration and RR itself then seemed to lose interest. Certainly, at that time, RR gave no indication of any impending crisis.

The IRC's interest in RR's financial position had, however, been firmly aroused. So when it heard, during the summer, that the company's short-term profit forecasts had been revised downwards, the executive tried to arrange a meeting to discuss this. The company, however, now seemed to have decided that it was preferable to deal directly with the government. Villiers tried to make personal contact with RR's Chairman and Chief Executive, Sir Denning Pearson, but he proved elusive. Then, one day in July, Villiers learned that Pearson was travelling from London to a lunch in Nottingham and joined the train at St Pancras in Pearson's compartment. This meeting provided the basis for a more open relationship between RR and the IRC. It was therefore no real surprise to Pearson when, in August, the Ministry of Technology deferred discussions on further 'launching aid' for RR's RB211 engine until a thorough investigation had been undertaken of its financial position and asked the IRC to carry out this investigation.

MINTECH'S REQUEST

'Launching aid' was the means by which the government 'invested' in the highly risky activity of developing new aero-engines. Launching aid was provided as follows. The applicant would estimate the cost of the total development work on a new engine. The company and the government would then agree on how this cost would be shared and on how the investment of both parties would be recovered from profits on the eventual sales of the engine. The formula allowed both parties to recover their costs and to make a return on their investment, provided of course that enough engines were produced and sold at a profit. In the case of RR, the basic questions for the government were therefore as follows: Were the estimated cost and sales figures reasonable? Was RR likely to be able to provide its share of the development costs and to produce the engine at a profit?

The arrangements for launching aid for the RB211 engine were exceptional, since this was a make or break project for RR. The RB211 was designed for the new generation of 'wide-bodied' civil aircraft and RR had to succeed in developing and selling an engine of this type to at least one US airframe manufacturer if it was to remain in the 'first division' of aero-engine producers. The alternative was an overall contraction of the company, but the costs and the risks were enormous. The original estimate, made in 1968, for the development of the engine was £65.5 million. The government had agreed to put up an unprecedented 70 per cent of this cost as launching aid, and RR had won the order to supply Lockheed's Tri-Star jet with the engine. However, by the summer of 1969 the costs of the work on the RB211 were rising rapidly, as were RR's overall cash requirements. RR turned to the government for more launching aid to help to ease the position.

Mintech was unwilling to commit itself further without an investigation of RR's financial position and prospects, but this raised problems because the government was RR's largest customer. An investigation by civil servants, or by accountants or consultants reporting to Mintech, was therefore unlikely to be welcomed. The IRC, as a quasi-governmental but independent organisation, provided the answer. RR could open its books to the IRC which would report back on the substance, but not the detail, of its investigation. (This point was not fully appreciated by those who later criticised the IRC for not providing the government with the complete report it wrote on the company.) In addition, the IRC had sources of cash which could be used to supplement launching aid.

The IRC Board had to decide whether or not it wished to comply with Mintech's request, but the arguments for doing so were very strong. For some time the IRC had been extending its role from the promotion and support of mergers and had been making use of Section 2(1)(b) of the IRC Act under which it could, at the request of the Secretary of State, give a wide range of assistance to individual companies. The executive put forward five reasons why the IRC should involve itself with RR:

(a) The IRC was enjoined by statute to intervene where doing so might help the balance of payments and RR was one of the country's most important exporters. In the year before the investigation (1968) its direct exports alone were worth £103 million.
(b) The government was deeply involved with RR. As a customer for engines for military aircraft and for Concorde, government purchases accounted for around half of RR's sales. The government had already put enormous sums of money into RR engines, and whether it would recover this money depended on how successful RR was in selling them.
(c) RR was engaged in the kind of highly technological activity in which it was felt that Britain had to excel in order to survive as a prosperous, industrial nation. With products of this kind, value added was often near 100 per cent. (Value added is the amount by which the price of a product exceeds the cost of the materials going into it.) Value added is important for the British economy, in that it represents payments to British labour, while some at least of the payments for materials go to non-Britons. RR was also spending some 10 per cent of its turnover on research and development, several times the industrial average, though of course it is the quality rather than the quantity of research that matters.
(d) RR was one of the UK's largest purchasers of machine tools, many of them advanced ones. The IRC was, at the time, deeply involved in its plans to rationalise the machine tool industry's capacity to make the more complex tools (see Ch. 8).
(e) The IRC executive took the view that RR was the only aero-engine maker in Europe that could compete with the giant US companies, GEC and Pratt and Witney. If RR was now weakened, both the UK and Europe would become even more dependent on the US aircraft industry.

The IRC Board decided to accept Mintech's request and to undertake the investigation. From agreement in principle, it took six weeks for terms of reference to be settled between the three parties and this was done in October. They proposed two basic aims:

> 1 To assess RR's capital shortfall and to make recommendations on how this could be met to ensure the long term stability of the company.
> 2 To make comments on the level and form of existing Government support to the aero-engine industry, with particular reference to launching aid.
>
> (Cmnd 4860, 1971, Annex B, p. 22).

THE IRC INVESTIGATION

The IRC was given from 1 October until 31 December to prepare its report and a three-man investigating team from the executive was established under a Board member, Michael Clapham. The first stage of this work was an intensive series of meetings with officials in Mintech responsible for negotiating aero-engine contracts, for market research, for investigating accounts and for technical development. This gave the IRC team valuable background information both on Mintech's views of RR and the aero-engine market, and on the importance of government orders and aid to RR's survival.

The next stage was a series of trips to Derby, RR's group headquarters, and to its six divisions. The largest of these was the aero-engine division, also based at Derby, which made the Dart, Spey and RB211 engines. Second, there was the Bristol engine division. This was the main unit which came from the merger with Bristol Siddeley Engines in 1966; it was producing the Olympus engine for Concorde and the Pegasus engine for the vertical take-off Harrier. Third, came the small-engine division which had substantial business in helicopter engines. Fourth, was the oil-engine division. Fifth, the motor-car division made the famous cars for the luxury market. Sixth, the industrial and marine division which modified aero-engines for these applications.

The IRC had meetings with the group's chief executive, with main Board directors and with key managers in each of the operating divisions. The team also studied the internal accounts and looked at the forecasts in RR's five-year plans, comparing forecasts with past results and earlier plans with later ones.

As it became clear that the key areas for investigation were financial control and forward planning, the IRC team also visited the finance directors of ICI, Courtaulds, Ford, British Leyland and GEC to find how their systems compared with that of RR.

As a result of its investigations, the IRC produced a detailed analysis of RR. Even the summary of this report, which was published in the Rolls-Royce White paper (Cmnd 4860, 1971, Annex B), could have left no-one in doubt of the seriousness of the company's situation. The diagnosis was that there was a fundamental weakness in RR's central financial control system and in its machinery for forward planning, and that this weakness was a direct result of the company's management structure.

The central management of RR was dominated by the aero-engine division (AED). Because it was located at Derby, close to RR's headquarters the AED had, until 1968, actually kept the headquarter's books. From 1945 until the Bristol merger, the aero-engine division had made up virtually the whole of the company, providing almost all its profits. It was still the dominant influence. Pearson, the group's Chairman and Chief Executive, was a former boss of the aero-engine division. Its head in 1969, Sir David Huddie, had spent six months in America negotiating the RB211 contract, and was regarded as Pearson's successor. The division was dominated by engineers: it had only one finance man on its Board, as against 21 engineers.

In mid November, on their fourth trip to Derby, the IRC team had individual meetings with eight AED Board members over a period of two days. These meetings confirmed that while the level of engineering expertise in the company was very high, there were question marks over some key areas of both engineering and commercial judgment.

It also became clear that the divisions ran themselves to a very large extent. The IRC had already discovered that central financial control was limited, and from these meetings the executive came to the following conclusions:

(a) To the extent that a central financial function existed in RR it was a service, rather than a control, function.
(b) There had been little detailed comparison made between the performance of the various divisions, and between the AED and the Bristol Engine Division (BED) in particular. They were very much separate units.
(c) Any decisions within the AED were essentially taken informally, below divisional board level.

In effect, many of the decisions, the keys to the success not only of the AED but of the whole RR group, appeared to be taken by an inner circle of the division's engineering management. The IRC team gave two examples which they felt illustrated how this dominance could mean that too little weight was given to vital financial and commercial constraints. The first arose out of discussions on over-spending on the Phantom Spey engine. This was justified on the ground that the volume of engineering work was on target but that the increase in wages had been greater than expected. The IRC team were disturbed by an apparent reluctance to accept that, if wage rates were rising, economies had to be made in other directions. This concern was increased when it was indicated that, in the preparation of budgets, etc., there was often pressure to put in a figure for wage rate escalation that could be 'afforded' rather than a forecast of the increase most likely to be experienced.

The second example related to the criteria for judging the merits of a new engine. The IRC team were told that the ratio between the total development cost and the expected selling price of an engine was used. Thus, if the selling price was £250 000 and the development cost £50 million, the ratio was 200. On this basis a ratio of 100–200 was considered good and one of 400–500 bad. Again, the IRC team felt that this might be a reasonable measure of the engineering work in an engine but that as a commercial criterion it was meaningless, unless the number of engines likely to be sold was also taken into account. A ratio of 150 was clearly disastrous if only 100 engines were sold, whereas a ratio of 400–500 with sales of 5000 engines might imply great success. It was the fact that this way of looking at success or failure appeared to be insufficiently challenged in the AED that really worried the IRC.

The reason that this was seen as a crucial weakness was because the chance of decisions of the AED being reversed by the central staff was small. The strength of the central financial team can be guessed from its size – nine, including supporting staff. Until 1966 the former Chairman, Lord Kindersley, had supplemented RR's financial team, but he spent only part of his time there, being also a partner of its merchant bankers. Moreover, his expertise was more in raising outside finance than in internal financial control.

The IRC team felt that the power of the group's Finance Director, Mr W.E. Trevan Hawke, was severely limited. He had taken over the full job only in 1967. Even in 1969, there appeared to be insufficient vetting by the centre of the five-year plans which were prepared in the divisions. New standing rules had been drawn up to help the central finance staff, requiring plans to be sent in at least one month before their submission to the Board. But even while the IRC team was there, plans were being delivered late, leaving no time for the centre to do anything except consolidate them.

There was a finance sub-committee of the Board, which included one of the non-executive main Board directors, Whitney Straight, as well as the chief executive and the main financial executives. But this sub-committee had started operating only in early 1969 and met only six times a year, as did the main Board. In short, the IRC felt that there was too little central financial control and planning and that this was a serious deficiency because financial control and planning were given only secondary concern in the AED and the other divisions.

RR'S FINANCIAL POSITION

The shortage of information, plus the uncertainty inherent in the forecasts of costs and sales, made it very difficult for the IRC to make a precise assessment of RR's financial position and prospects. The main reason for the IRC investigation was the downward revision of RR's own profit forecasts, but there could be no guarantee that the latest figures were accurate. Given the view it had formed of the weakness of financial control and planning, the IRC executive felt that it could not accept RR's own figures without question, but with very limited time in which to complete its investigations and report, the IRC could not undertake a detailed audit. The RR five-year forecast (FYF) simply had to be taken as a starting point.

In 1968, RR had made a pre-tax profit of almost £16 million (a 10 per cent return on stockholders' funds) and a significant improvement was forecast for every year covered by the 1969 FYF, which was completed in February 1969. By October 1969, the profit forecast for that year had been revised downwards twice and the provisional figures for the 1970 FYF were available. These showed that the projected pre-tax profits for 1970 and 1971 had been cut by half, compared with the previous plan.

Even so, the 1970 FYF forecast was that profits after 1971 would increase and would be very substantial by 1974. The IRC felt that this forecast was totally speculative and focused its attention on the measures required to help the group to survive the next two years. The profit figures disguised the cash flow problems of the group, partly because of a build-up of conventional capital spending, but also because of RR's practice of capitalising research and development expenditure. Expenditure on the development of a new engine, which was largely wages and salaries, was treated as an asset and added to the company's balance sheet, rather than being deducted from the current year's profits. The theory was that this expenditure would be written off against the profits earned from the eventual sales of an engine that was being developed. Whatever the theory, this practice had two basic flaws. First, it begged the question of whether or not the subsequent sales of the engine would generate sufficient profit to pay off the R&D expenditure. Second, it required sufficient cash to be raised to finance this theoretical asset until it could be written off. Several IRC executives and Board members viewed the practice (prophetically) as a road to bankruptcy. It was risky enough when development costs were under control and were being shared with the government, but when they exceeded the estimate it made RR very vulnerable. If R&D expenditure had not been capitalised, the FYF would have shown a loss in both 1970 and 1971.

This, plus the increase in other capital requirements, meant that RR's short-term borrowings were forecast to increase from about £45 million in 1969 to £70 million in 1970 and £90 million in 1971. The IRC executive checked through each divisional FYF in turn. They found nothing significant to object to in five divisions, excluding the AED, although they felt that a large amount of capital and management time was tied up in earning rather small returns. Most of the problems and risks were, however, associated with the AED and, in particular, with the RB211 contract.

The IRC recognised that some overspending on the development of the basic RB211 engine was inevitable but thought (as it turned out incorrectly) that the major technical problems had been overcome. Projected overspending of about £10 million was included in the 1970 FYF. The IRC was also concerned about the likely costs, and hence profitability, of producing the engine for Lockheed. The concern was increased by what the IRC was told about negotiations on the Lockheed contract. The was that during the six months of detailed discussions the required 'thrust' or power of the engine had been increased by over 50 per cent. This inevitably meant higher development and production costs, but the price was scarcely increased at all.

Doubts on the production costs of the basic RB211 engine, together with doubts about the development costs and sales potential of a 'stretched' RB211, meant that IRC saw RR's problems as much more fundamental than a short-term cash flow crisis. Continuing improvements in financial and management control were seen as essential to the survival of the group. But the IRC executive did accept its estimate of the short-term borrowing requirements as the best available, though inevitably subject to great uncertainty.

THE IRC REPORT

The IRC report was therefore directed towards the problem of meeting RR's short-term cash requirements in such a way that its future prospects were strengthened. A crucial requirement was a management structure committed to improving financial discipline. New appointments, from outside the industry, to both the Board and the finance sub-committee seemed essential.

In addition, the report contained a series of specific proposals for action by RR. The summary of the conclusions and recommendations of the report was subsequently published in the White Paper Rolls-Royce Ltd. and the RB211 Aero-Engine (Cmnd 4860, 1971). (This is reproduced as Appendix 12.1) The IRC recognised that RR was already taking steps to reduce its manpower (two phased 5 per cent cuts in the AED's labour force were proposed); cutting its capital spending programme; and raising a small amount of cash by selling some properties and subsidiary manufacturing interests. But the IRC team argued that much more radical action was necessary. Its first recommendation was that the AED and the BED should be integrated. The report held that, while the two divisions should be kept as separate profit centres, integration could produce significant economies. It would reduce two large engineering establishments; rationalise component manufacture to reduce stocks and improve plant utilisation; and co-ordinate forward investment and purchasing policies.

Second, the report recommended a significant increase in sub-contracting. Comparisons showed that, in the USA, the two aero-engine makers General Electric and Pratt and Whitney sub-contracted about half of their work, whereas RR sub-contracted only about one-third. Yet RR complained vigorously of the absence of a strong sub-contracting industry in Britain. The report contended that RR itself could take steps to improve this. Its purchasing policies could be more geared to guaranteeing on-going support to key suppliers. RR could then perhaps reduce its capital outlay on building new plant itself, and instead encourage suppliers to spend money on plant designed principally to satisfy RR's requirements.

Third, the IRC felt that RR should raise capital by selling off at least one of its non-aero-engine divisions. It argued that the cash needs of the RR's main business were such that it could not justify tying up capital earning relatively low returns in peripheral activities. The IRC considered recommending that at least the car division and the oil-engine division should be sold but, despite its reputation for arrogance, could not in the end bring itself to insist on the disposal of the famous Rolls-Royce car interests. The report referred only to the oil-engine division.

The sale of this division and other measures to release internal resources were expected to raise about £10 million. This still left a gap of £15 million between RR's resources and its cash requirements for 1970. The IRC felt it unreasonable to expect much of this to be provided by RR's clearing banks and, given the forecast drop in profits, a rights issue was out of the question. The gearing of the company was already twice the average for industrial companies, so that raising further long-term loans from the market was both unlikely and undesirable. The only answer appeared to be a loan which was convertible, at some stage, into RR equity. The report recommended to the IRC Board that it should discuss advancing £10 million to RR in this form, provided that a series of conditions was met.

The first set of conditions related to Mintech. To advance money where no merger was involved the IRC required a 'request' from the Secretary of State but it also asked, in this case, for an assurance of continuing support by Mintech for the aero-engine industry. The IRC went on to ask that the terms and timing of future launching aid should be discussed with it before they were agreed, and that the £10 million for RR should be provided outside the IRC's agreed budget for 1969/70.

The second set of conditions related to RR itself. In addition to the proposals set out above, RR was to agree with the IRC 'steps for strengthening the top management structure and forward planning and financial control systems' (Cmnd 4860, 1971, p. 25). The report went on to say: 'The managing director will wish to refer to this point at the Board Meeting'. It was felt that it was better to explain the IRC executive's views orally to the Board than for the executive to be too critical in writing of such an eminent and respected company.

Finally, the IRC report recommended that the provision of a further convertible loan of £10 million should be considered if development of the 'stretched' version of the RB211 went ahead, probably in 1971. But it added the proviso that sufficient progress must by then have been made in meeting all the conditions attached to the first tranche of the loan.

The IRC Board met to consider the report on 19 December 1969 and, subject to a few detailed amendments, its conclusions and recommendations were accepted. In addition, it was decided that RR should be asked to accept an IRC director on its Board. Discussions were therefore started immediately with Mintech and with the RR management.

We now know that the IRC team underestimated the seriousness of RR's position. The crucial issue, however, is not whether the IRC got its financial estimates right in such an uncertain situation, but whether the measures it proposed to deal with the problems it had identified were the right ones. Given the government's determination that there must continue to be a British aero-engine industry, the provision of £10 million, £20 million, or even £60 million, the amount the Conservative government later tried to raise, was seen as an acceptable price to pay if it could ensure the future of RR. The important test is whether the action taken was likely to lead to a real and lasting improvement in the performance of the company. This question is probably best answered by considering the events between the presentation of the IRC's report and the final collapse of RR at the end of 1970.

IMPLEMENTATING THE IRC RECOMMENDATIONS

Problems arose as soon as efforts were made to implement the IRC report. Early in January, Mintech and RR both received copies of the summary and recommendations of the IRC investigation. Neither saw the full report, because there were things in it which each side did not want the other to see. Delivery of the report was backed up by detailed talks between the IRC, the Ministry and RR. Mintech was in broad agreement with the IRC proposals but RR, after initially appearing to agree with much of the report, soon started to display a good deal of scepticism. In particular, RR did not agree that the financial situation was as bad as the IRC made out, an opinion which was shared by some of the company's financial advisors. Indeed, the financial advisors initially suggested that they could themselves give RR the help needed to solve its temporary liquidity problem.

Nor did RR like the idea of selling the oil-engine division. Instead, it suggested that it should explore the possibility of forming a joint company with British Leyland, to operate in this field. There were further disagreements about the management changes. The IRC had suggested that RR should appoint a full-time financial and commercial executive, preferably as a deputy chairman, and certainly as a Board member responsible only to the Chief Executive. The IRC had in mind someone of sufficient calibre to introduce a sound financial and commercial influence as a counter to the predominance of the engineers in RR. The company agreed to this in principle, but a further proposal for an IRC-appointed director caused far more problems. RR at first accepted it but then made the counter-suggestion that the IRC Board member should instead be someone who knew his way round Whitehall and could therefore help the firm in its relations with government. This was, at least in part, because RR felt badly treated. The company claimed that the British government both provided less support to aviation than the American government, and, moreover, delayed paying its bills. In fact, the IRC executive had found no evidence to suggest that RR had been treated less generously than its counterparts in the USA. The IRC stood firm in demanding that its representative on the Board should be a financial expert who would support the new full-time appointee, and in saying that this was incompatible with a lobbying function.

At the end of January, RR asked for a month in which to decide on the IRC recommendations and to explore other sources of finance. They insisted that the IRC money would not be necessary at all, unless and until RR went ahead with the 'stretched' version of the RB211. They therefore wanted a definite commitment that the government would support this engine before agreeing to the IRC proposals.

At the beginning of March, RR were still delaying a decision, arguing that the new five-year forecast, which the company hoped to produce within two weeks, might change the situation by refuting the IRC's case. When that time came, however, RR reported that it needed a further month to prepare the forecast. The company also continued to resist the IRC's proposals for the sale of the oil-engine division and the expansion of sub-contracting. Although there had been a large and an ominous worsening in the projected performance of the all-important aero-engine division, the company prepared a riposte to the IRC.

This riposte argued that RR's progress over the last decade hardly suggested there was anything wrong with their forward product planning. It had never been thought worthwhile to build up an extensive organisation for forward financial planning, since the situation on which the calculations would have to be based was always so uncertain. The RR Board was still of the opinion that this was correct. What they felt they needed was more 'horse power' at the top to make use of the systems which, in general, already existed.

During March, with RR management still stone-walling, the IRC's own intelligence showed that the position had worsened very considerably since its investigation. In particular, the Corporation learned that trouble with the fan blades on the RB211 might mean a very expensive redesign, with titanium replacing carbon fibre. (This was to prove correct, and very expensive for RR.) From another source, it emerged that Lockheed was experiencing severe financial problems. IRC executives prepared to fly to America in order to obtain first-hand knowledge about the latest position of Lockheed, both from the company itself and from the American government.

By the end of March everything had been arranged for the IRC loan, except for the agreement of the RR Board. The terms had been settled with RR's financial advisors, who now agreed that the money was needed, and with RR's finance section. The government had agreed that the money which the IRC would lend to RR would be an addition to the IRC budget, being classed as a 'special project of national interest'. All that was needed was the RR five-year plan. Then, at about the time the plan was expected, the government and the IRC were told that it would take yet another month to prepare.

As the next month began, both the IRC and the government began to lose patience. For one thing, it was discovered that the RR Board had still not been told of the proposal made three months earlier to appoint an IRC director.

April was the crucial month. As the five-year forecast figures were collected and analysed, the RR management finally acknowledged that there was a basis for the concern of the IRC and the government. A loss was now forecast for the aero-engine division, and the company's expected cash requirement rose from £90 million to £102 million for 1971 and to £115 million for 1972. Further overspending, this time of £20 million, had been discovered on the RB211 engine. RR's management finally realised that they would need the IRC loan, even if they did nothing about the 'stretched' RB211, work on which they now postponed for at least three years. This was the moment of truth. While worse was to come, from this moment the RR Board could no longer frame their approach as a request for support from government for taking breath before profitable new advances. It was now a company requesting finance from the government as banker of last resort.

Even so, negotiations were still protracted and it was not until its Annual General Meeting, held on 21 July 1970, that RR announced acceptance of the IRC loan and the appointment of two new Board members. The first was Lord Beeching who was to be a part-time member and the IRC's representative. The second appointment was of a new deputy chairman to be in charge of RR's financial affairs: this IRC recommendation, made several months earlier, was at last implemented. The man chosen was Ian Morrow, a veteran 'company doctor'.

Morrow is an accountant who, very early in his carreer, made the change-over to industrial management, but who always carefully recognised the crucial importance of basic accounting principles. In his first major industrial post, with the Brush electrical engineering group, he was faced with a well-known old engineering company whose products were renowned throughout the world, but which was less good at making profits. When Morrow joined it, Brush was in debt to the bank for a huge amount. He staved off liquidation in that case, and after two or three years arranged the sale of the company at a respectable price to Hawker-Siddeley. Morrow was perhaps best known for his role in rescuing Associated Fire Alarms and turning it into a reasonably profitable company. Although it was not evident at the time, the biggest difference between his task at RR and in his earlier assignments was that the scale of the losses was much larger. RR was going bankrupt in style. Indeed, the IRC contacted the new Conservative Minister of Technology, Geoffrey Rippon, on 20 July informing him both of the new Board appointments and of the continued deterioration of RR's financial position.

Throughout the summer, Morrow carefully sifted the facts from the fantasies and in September was ready with new figures. He estimated that if RR carried out the original Lockheed fixed price contract and made RB211 engines for about 180 aircraft, there would be a production loss of around £40 million. This was in addition to research and development costs, which by then totalled about £135 million. Furthermore, he estimated that to stay in business RR would need not just the anticipated £10 million from the IRC but £60 million of long-term capital, although part of this would be to replace overdraft facilities. RR had no choice but to turn to the government again. The Conservatives, having decided to wind up the IRC, took the line that the private sector should put up the money to save RR, not the taxpayers. The Governor of the Bank of England went round the City to help raise money for RR, a most unusual procedure, and not well received there. Normally, the Governor acts as the government's main spokesman in the City and as its main channel of communication with the government. He does not become involved in the finance of individual companies, so this action on behalf of RR was interpreted as unusually strong arm-twisting by the government. Banks, insurance companies and pension funds thought that they were being asked to put up money for non-commercial purposes. As a result, they resisted the government's appeal. Of the £60 million aid for RR announced in the House of Commons on 11 November, £42 million was to be extra launching aid and the rest was to come from RR's existing clearing banks. Also on 11 November, RR announced further management changes. Lord Cole was appointed as Chairman, and took over immediately. Sir Denning Pearson resigned as Chief Executive as well as Chairman and David Huddie, the head of the AED, who had been ill, retired from the Board and the company.

The £60 million was to be made available only after a detailed check on RR's financial estimates by independent accountants. While this investigation was still proceeding the estimated loss on the RB211 project rose again and, even more serious, RR had to admit that it could not meet the programme of development and production contracted with Lockheed. Cole and Morrow, together with Sir Henry Benson of Cooper Brothers, who had suggested Morrow's appointment, reported this to the government on 22 January 1971, and a series of meetings then took place culminating in the decision on 4 February to appoint a receiver. The story of these events is set out in more detail in the White Paper (Cmnd 4860, 1971).

COMMENT

It is worth looking back now and summarising just what the IRC did. First, it was prepared to aid RR only so long as the government wished to go on supporting a privately owned British aero-engine industry. This the government decided to do, both for balance of payments reasons and to encourage a high technology industry.

Second, the fact that the IRC provided only a summary of its report both to Mintech and to RR raises interesting questions about the relationship between a quasi-governmental body and the government. But that is not the main issue here. The important point is that even the summary of the IRC report, which went to the government and civil servants at Mintech, could have left no-one in doubt as to the true situation. The summary included the following points:

> In the past, RR's profit forecasts have been significantly over-optimistic. It cannot, therefore, be plausibly argued that RR's problem is only the short-term liquidity difficulty which will be solved when good profits are seen in 1974. . . . Measures required are: a strengthening of the management charged with the responsibility for financial control and forward planning systems; integration of the two aero-engine divisions at Derby and Bristol; more sub-contracting and the sale of at least one division. . . . The problem, therefore, is . . . to see the money is provided in a form and on conditions that will get at the basic management weakness in financial control and forward planning and put pressure on RR to meet its forecasts (Cmnd 4860, 1971, p. 23).

It is possible to argue that the IRC's medicine was not powerful enough. Moreover, its effect was reduced by the delay in its application. It took from early January until July before the key Board appointments at RR could be made. Even then, so far as any outside observer could tell, the existing management was left in control and some of the IRC's objectives, such as the sale of the oil-engine division, were not achieved at all. The transition from the Labour to the Conservative government in June 1970 could have affected later developments. Being under threat of disbandment, the IRC's position was clearly weakened.

Before that, however, the IRC chose to operate in the traditional City way, in a very English manner. There was no sense of RR's management being forced to accept specific recommendations, rather the IRC worked patiently to get the company to agree to its proposals. In retrospect, it might have been better if more decisive action had been taken more quickly, but this would have required explicit government intervention. The reason for not doing so was that this would have laid the IRC and the government open to the charge of interference in the running of a private business. It would also have dented the public image of RR, although much less severely than the final debacle in late 1970 did. And perhaps, even in the summer of 1970, it was already too late to prevent that debacle.

The underlying problem with this kind of situation is how the management of the company involved can be persuaded to accept changes. Shareholders, who have the power to change management, are usually ineffective in doing so. The IRC did as good a job, and in a similar way, as a bank which has discovered that one of its biggest clients is in grave financial trouble, or as an insurance company which has become worried about one of its major investments. The action of such institutions in these circumstances usually takes the form of quiet steps behind the scenes to secure the appointment of new management. But significantly, in the case of RR, the IRC acted when the banks and big institutional shareholders did not.

It will always be arguable whether the action that the IRC actually took could have been as successful as driving RR into liquidation, if Morrow had been given more powerful and continuing support early enough, from both the IRC and the government. The IRC and Lord Beeching made a last plea for this directly to the Prime Minister, two days before the receiver was appointed.

This question can never be answered. The IRC could not have been expected to make management changes unless its brief had been considerably enlarged. Moreover, it may well have been too late to avert disaster even before the IRC investigation began. All one *can* say is that the IRC did appear to recognise RR's financial problems earlier and more clearly than either the company's own management or its financial advisors, and that it did at least try to take action to put this right.

APPENDIX 12.1

This appendix comprises Annex B to the White Paper *Rolls-Royce Limited and the RB211 Engine* (Cmnd 4860, 1971, pp. 22–26).

ROLLS-ROYCE LTD
SUMMARY REPORT OF THE INDUSTRIAL REORGANISATION CORPORATION COMMUNICATED TO THE MINISTRY OF TECHNOLOGY ON 22ND DECEMBER 1969

Summary of conclusions and recommendations

1 The IRC investigation into Rolls-Royce commenced on 1st October and the deadline agreed with Mintech for the year end has been kept. Mr Michael Clapham has been the Board member with special responsibility and Mr Gardiner, Mr Ewart and Mr Wilkinson the executive staff assigned to the project.

2 The system of investigation followed IRC's usual pattern of intensive discussions with the company and financial and industrial appraisals. The executive wishes to record its appreciation of the fullest co-operation extended by Rolls-Royce and the Ministry of Technology, which made a special contribution as the sponsoring Ministry.

3 The terms of reference posed two basic questions:

1 To assess Rolls-Royce's capital shortfall and to make recommendations as to how this could be met to ensure the long-term stability of the company.
2 To make comments on the level and form of existing Government support to the aero-engine industry, with particular reference to launching aid.

The implications of Rolls-Royce's capital shortfall were found to be so pressing that the main body of the report has concerned itself with 1 above.

4 The main elements in the financial crisis facing Rolls-Royce are the following:

(i) Profits are forecast to fall from £13.3 million in 1969 to £8.8 million in 1970 and reach only £14.9 million in 1971.
(ii) However, these profit figures are struck after R and D capitalisation in 1970 and 1971 of £33.1 million (before tax).

(iii) Without this capitalisation of R and D there would be a loss of £5.1 million in 1970 and of £4.3 million in 1971; the turnround does not come until 1974 when profits are over £34 million after charging R and D costs incurred of £5.3 million.

(iv) Short-term borrowings are forecast to increase from £45 million to £90 million by the end of 1971, thereafter they rise slightly from this level until 1974.

(v) If the shortfall is met through bank borrowings, Rolls-Royce's gearing, at 44 per cent already over twice the national average, will rise to 53 per cent by 1971.

5 The calculations above have been extracted from Rolls-Royce's Five-Year Plan. They are considered a broadly accurate estimate of the short-term crisis though, as has happened in the recent past, there will be further revisions which are likely to increase the sums involved. One of the basic assumptions that has been made in forecasting the sharp rise in borrowings to 1971 and the high level at which they remain through to 1974, is that development work on the RB211 stretched will start up in 1970–71. Uncertainty still surrounds the future of the stretched version and the level and timing of IRC support has therefore been kept flexible in the recommendations to take this into account. Strict conditions must also be attached to any IRC finance for the reasons below.

6 In the past Rolls-Royce's profit forecasts have been significantly over-optimistic. It cannot, therefore, plausibly be argued that Rolls-Royce's problem is only the short-term liquidity difficulty which will be solved when good profits are seen in 1974 (when they are forecast to move to £39.4 million) and a rights issue can be mounted. The argument of jam tomorrow will not wash.

7 The steps being taken by Rolls-Royce to reduce manpower and to sell assets will help marginally to ease the cash crisis. But they are not comprehensive or far-reaching enough and the cuts in capital spending could be mortgaging the future. Further action will be necessary if Rolls-Royce is to achieve its profit forecasts in 1974 and to secure stability in the longer term.

8 Measures required are: a strengthening of the management charged with the responsibility for financial control and forward planning systems; integration of the two Aero Engine Divisions at Derby and Bristol; more sub-contracting and the sale of at least one division.

9 The problem, therefore, is not simply to make funds available to Rolls-Royce to enable it to ride the immediate liquidity strain but to see that money is provided in a form and on conditions that will get at the basic management weakness in financial control and forward planning.

10 Even if the banks could be prevailed upon to agree the massive increase in Rolls-Royce's short-term borrowings and thus alleviate the short-term cash crisis, it would only worsen the problem of excessive

gearing and would do nothing by way of financial incentive or pressure.

11 More Government subventions would also not tackle the basic weakness and, indeed, it is difficult for the Government to use its money as a lever to secure changes that will help the company's long-term viability. It is clear that the size of the problem is such that only strong measures with substantial financial backing will produce results. The financial proposals detailed below could involve IRC in its biggest single commitment of funds apart from British Leyland. It is considered that on grounds of balance of payments and technology Rolls-Royce is a sufficiently important national asset as to require IRC action on the proposed scale. The following considerations are relevant, though none can be taken to imply that Rolls-Royce must be supported irrespective of the costs involved.

12 Rolls-Royce makes a very substantial contribution to the balance of payments. Mintech does detailed calculations on this for projects for which launching aid is requested. In the past these have shown that the implied subsidy to Rolls-Royce is less, as a proportion of the foreign exchange earned, than the EEC countries allow on average for all their exports through the rebate of the value added tax. For aero-engines the criteria applied in judging the cost to Her Majesty's Government of generating foreign currency have been more stringent than with the computer industry or the aluminium smelters.

13 Rolls-Royce also makes important contributions to technology. It is in a high value added industry where raw materials are only between 5–15 per cent of production cost. The average value per ton of jet and gas turbine engines exported this year up to October was over £50 000 – this compares with an average for the mechanical engineering sector exports of £1000 per ton. Rolls-Royce has pioneered important developments in new processes, materials and equipment. These include advances in the use of titanium and in the development and use of carbon fibres and numerically controlled machine tools. In metal working techniques Rolls-Royce has evolved applications for electron beam welding, electro-chemical forming and electro-discharge machining.

14 A longer term consideration is the prospect of the United Kingdom's industrial role in Europe and the need to establish a European force in key areas of advanced technology. The aircraft industry has led the way in multi-national projects and it is important that the United Kingdom continues to make a full contribution. Rolls-Royce occupies a unique position in this respect.

15 In terms of IRC's criteria, quite apart from the strategic considerations of its substantial military work, Rolls-Royce must rank as a high priority. This is not to say that Rolls-Royce must be supported for ever and a day irrespective of the cost. To date it has earned its keep and the recommendations are designed to enable it to continue to do this.

Recommendations

16 Any proposals for the involvement of IRC finance with Rolls-Royce can only be implemented at the request of the Minister of Technology as provided for under section 2(1)(b) of the IRC Act. The three points on which satisfactory agreement must be reached with Government are:

(i) Mintech's support for the future of the aero-engine industry and for IRC's proposals;
(ii) Mintech's agreement that the terms and timing of launching aid will be discussed with IRC;
(iii) an understanding with the Government that IRC would have access to funds additional to the agreed budget for 1969–71 to do the Rolls-Royce project.

*Recommendation I**

17 It is recommended that, subject to satisfactory assurances on the above, IRC finance for Rolls-Royce be made available as part of a phased package of proposals as follows:

(i) IRC would agree to make available a convertible loan of £10 million on terms to encourage Rolls-Royce to meet its profit targets provided Rolls-Royce agrees with (ii), (iii), (iv) and (v) below;
(ii) Rolls-Royce would agree with IRC steps for strengthening the top management structure and forward planning and financial control systems. The Managing Director will wish to refer to this point at the Board Meeting;
(iii) Rolls-Royce would sell the Oil Engine Division and set a target for release of other internal resources to reach a total £10 million;
(iv) Rolls-Royce would agree to discuss with IRC proposals for integrating the Aero Engine Division and the Bristol Engine Division and extending its sub-contracting; and to provide IRC with quarterly financial information on each division;
(v) to accept an IRC director on Rolls-Royce Board.

18 This initial £10 million together with the £10 million released from internal resources, should be sufficient to meet Rolls-Royce's liquidity squeeze up to the decision of going ahead with the stretched version of RB211. This decision will have to be taken within a year. If the stretched version is developed it is likely that a further injection of capital will be required.

* The recommendation that the Oil Engine Division should be disposed of was subsequently set aside, following discussion between the Company and the Industrial Reorganisation Corporation.

Recommendation II

19 To meet this it is recommended that on evidence of Rolls-Royce's progress in achieving (ii), (iii), (iv) and (v) above and on condition that Mintech proceeds with launching aid in agreement with IRC, IRC should consider providing up to a further £10 million on terms to be decided in the light of the company's liquidity position at that time and of the arrangements for launching aid. This further loan could be convertible into Rolls-Royce's equity or into Rolls-Royce's shareholding in British Aircraft Corporation. The financial effects of this package are discussed in the report.

20 The IRC loan to Rolls-Royce comes at a critical period in the company's development. The escalation in the development costs in the sixties characteristic of the aerospace industries has been phenomenal. For example, the development costs incurred 10 years ago on the civil Spey were approximately £20 million, the equivalent sum being spent for the development of the basic RB211 was £80 million. Between these two periods there was no commensurate increase in Rolls-Royce's profits or cash flow and the gap has been bridged by capitalisation of R and D, higher borrowings and Government finance. In short, future profits have been heavily anticipated, and a further act of faith will be necessary if the stretched RB211 proceeds. In this situation there is little chance that a merger with Rolls-Royce would be acceptable to another United Kingdom company. A takeover from overseas would undoubtedly be resisted by Her Majesty's Government. Without additional finance to allow the basic RB211 programme to proceed Rolls-Royce would be forced to clip its wings and opt out of the big league.

21 This would be the wrong moment to take such action with so much already committed and the prospects insufficiently clear. Both Pratt and Whitney and General Electric have been severely hit by the escalation of development costs and there are signs that Rolls-Royce has a technical lead. The basic RB211 contract has given Rolls-Royce for the first time access to the high value United States market and it is possible that this position could be consolidated and built on. Rolls-Royce's engineering excellence has so far enabled it, despite the disadvantages of the relatively small United Kingdom market and the contracting military programme, to stay in the top flight of companies in one of the most advanced and costly technologies.

22 The purpose of the first part of the proposed package is to relieve the immediate cash crisis so that Rolls-Royce can proceed with its current work load under much tighter financial control; the purpose of the second part of the package is to create a situation in which discussions affecting the future programme of work of Rolls-Royce can be taken on a considered basis between Rolls-Royce, Mintech and IRC.

13

Cammell Laird

In the 1960s Cammell Laird (CL) passed its 100th anniversary and appeared to be thriving. It had recovered from a difficult period, when pre-tax profits dropped from £1.6 million in 1963 to around £500000 in 1964 and 1965. Profitability then rose steadily from £1.3 million in 1966 to £2.2 million in 1967 and £3.0 million in 1968. Moreover, the group appeared to be diversifying successfully away from the declining activity of British naval work into merchant shipbuilding at its famous Birkenhead shipyard and into a wide range of other industrial activities in the group as a whole. Scottish Aviation, a company based at Prestwick airport and manufacturing aircraft fuselage panels as well as refurbishing aero-engines, had been acquired in 1965. This was followed by the acquisition of a company building military equipment in Anglesey and by the purchase of British Federal Welder, a specialist engineering company, in 1968. In 1969, CL acquired Solar Industries, a group making a large range of manufactured products, including rubber seals for the car industry in the UK, France and West Germany, and long-range cable belts for the world's mining industry. The group also owned Metro Cammell which made both tube trains and bodies for commercial vehicles, and Patent Shaft Steel Works which was one of the largest steel companies to escape nationalisation in 1967. At the end of the 1960s, CL appeared to be a reasonably profitable company with a wide range of industrial activities. However, its dependence on, and its vulnerability to, the fortunes of its shipbuilding subsidiary was about to be dramatically illustrated. The publication of CL's 106th annual report and accounts for 1969 was delayed, but when they did appear, in July 1970, they showed total losses and provisions amounting to over £6.5 million. This chapter tells the story of how these losses were incurred and how the IRC was involved in devising and implementing a scheme to enable the group to survive them.

THE EMERGING LOSSES

For much of 1969, CL's management was exercised by the fate of another company, Handley Page (HP). Indeed, early in 1969, CL and HP came jointly to ask the IRC if a scheme to support HP could be arranged. HP was a small airframe manufacturer with a promising product, a light jet aeroplane called Jetstream, but it had overstretched itself financially. HP saw an excellent future for the Jetstream, with sales of up to 1000 aircraft, but HP had severe cash flow problems. Overall, HP estimated that it needed about £3 million of new finance to keep it in operation. CL was vitally concerned, because Scottish Aviation was supplying wing panels to HP for the Jetstream. This meant that it was owed £1.5 million, as well as standing to lose on existing work in progress and future orders. The IRC decided not to become involved with HP, but its executive did take the opportunity to look at the CL group. This meant that when the IRC was asked to help with CL's more fundamental problems in April 1970, it already had some knowledge of the group's activities.

CL's problems in the mid-1960s had been caused partly by the disastrous 'who drills the hole' labour dispute in its Birkenhead shipyard. This led to management changes and the yard seemed to be profitable again in 1967. A further problem emerged in 1968 when CL was told that the yard's substantial work on nuclear submarines was coming to an end. The government announced that from 1968 onwards there would be no new orders for nuclear submarines and that the only naval work the yard could take would be to build conventional submarines or ships for foreign navies. The management of the yard then set about building up a replacement business in merchant ships. It decided to seek orders for advanced vessels requiring a large amount of development work but, in fact, took a substantial amount of work on 'fixed price' contracts with only modest escalation clauses. Its success in winning orders was to prove its downfall when it could not fulfil them.

Even in March 1969, however, a profit of about £1.5 million was forecast for the shipyard for 1969 as a whole and in May, when CL went ahead with its acquisition of Solar Industries, its offer document included a profit forecast for the year of £3.2 million, a small increase on 1968. Solar Industries was expected to earn £1 million in the year to March 1970. CL's profit forecast was, of course, the responsibility of its directors, but the offer document included the normal supporting letters from its financial advisors and accountants. These contained the opinions that 'the forecast has been carefully and intelligently prepared . . .' on assumptions made after 'proper consideration' and 'the forecast, so far as the accounting basis and calculations are concerned, has been properly compiled on the footing of the assumptions mentioned [in the document] and are presented on a basis consistent with the accounting practices normally adopted by the company'.

The offer for Solar Industries was successful, but by the end of the year it was apparent that the whole group was deep in trouble. Although the ships actually delivered in 1969 had been produced at a profit, it was now clear that substantial losses would be incurred on the new merchant ship business. The Managing Director and the Chairman of the shipbuilding company both resigned. Performance in other parts of the group, including Solar Industries, was also below expectations. CL was likely to run into severe cash flow problems within a few months. The Board of the company decided to ask its auditors to make a full assessment of the position.

The report of the auditors made sobering reading. The orders for merchant ships had been taken at fixed prices and delays, together with higher than expected increases in material prices and labour costs, meant that losses were already certain, on work that had scarcely been started. On an order book of about £44 million, it was estimated that the shipyard would lose about £10 million even if it could achieve some savings in overheads. And if future rises in either material or wage costs were greater than forecast, or if there were any further delays, the losses would increase. Moreover, the facilities of the shipyard were both out of date and not really suitable for the work now being undertaken. The whole yard needed substantial capital expenditure on modernisation and re-equipment.

In February 1970, while the investigation was continuing, Handley Page finally went bankrupt and the loss incurred by Scottish Aviation was put at £2.2 million. So, when CL's auditors reported on 24 March 1970, they estimated that there would be a loss of £1 million in 1969, after providing for £3 million of losses on work undertaken in the shipyard, but before allowing for a further £7 million of losses there and for the £2.2 million loss in Scottish Aviation. The auditors also estimated that the CL group would need cash injections of £4 million in 1970, almost £5 million in 1971 and a further £1.5 million in 1972, before taking into account the capital expenditure necessary to modernise the shipyard. If nothing was done, the group would run out of cash and would be unable to pay its wage bill from May 1970.

THE PAYMASTER GENERAL CALLS IN THE IRC

CL's auditors considered a number of possible courses of action, including the liquidation of the shipyard. It was estimated that the deficiency on immediate liquidation would be as high as £20 million. The parent company had direct guarantees of £5 million and, even if it did no more than meet these, it was doubtful whether the group could continue in business. Moreover, there was a £3 million debenture which was charged against assets, including the shipyard. The appointment of a receiver to the shipbuilding company would give the trustees of the debenture holders an immediate right to appoint a receiver to the parent company and all the 'charging subsidiaries'. This effectively meant that CL could not let its shipbuilding company go into liquidation; nor could it continue in business without outside assistance. It decided to appeal to the government and to the Shipbuilding Industries Board (SIB).

The SIB was a statutory body set up in 1967 to 'stimulate the reorganisation, and to administer funds provided by the Government for the assistance of the [shipbuilding] industry' (HMSO, 1967). In origin and in objectives, it was not unlike the IRC, but it was far from keen to become involved with CL. The government, on the other hand, was very concerned. The jobs of 10 000 people were at risk on Merseyside, an area of high unemployment, and 20000 jobs in the group as a whole. Early in April the Paymaster General, Harold Lever, called in Villiers and asked the IRC to 'rescue' CL.

Villiers' immediate response was that the shipbuilding industry was the statutory concern of the SIB, so that the IRC would be extremely reluctant to become involved with a shipyard. However, anxious to take a positive line, he agreed that the IRC would try to produce a scheme that would meet the government's requirements, and perhaps allow the IRC to participate in rationalising CL's non-shipbuilding interests.

THE IRC'S CONDITIONS

The first formal meeting between CL and the IRC took place on 14 April. Mr P.B. Hunter, the CL Chairman, came to the IRC's Pall Mall offices with Sir Donald Perrott, his Deputy Chairman, and with representatives of the company's auditors. They met Leslie Cannon and the executives who would work on the case if the IRC became involved. Hunter outlined his company's position and problems. He confirmed the estimate of a loss of £10 million and said that CL required £2 million in cash in May, £2 million in August, about £5 million in 1971 and a further £1.5 million in 1972. Hunter requested an immediate £4 million loan from the IRC and a total facility of £6.5 million. The rest of the money could then be found. He outlined a plan for rationalising the activities of the shipyard to achieve a clearer separation of naval and civilian work. Once this was achieved, he hoped the SIB would reconsider the case for supporting the modernisation of the yard.

Hunter emphasized the urgency of the situation. He reported that the announcement of CL's results for 1969 had been postponed until 29 April, and that he would need an answer from the IRC before then. If he could not raise the initial £4 million he would have to put the shipyard, and almost certainly the whole group, into liquidation. What he was proposing was that the IRC should, in only two weeks, decide whether or not to put up £6.5 million for a company whose problems largely stemmed from the difficulties of an industry which was excluded from the IRC's remit.

Nevertheless, the IRC had told Lever that it would help if it could and the executive already had its earlier knowledge of CL, supplemented by informal discussions on the same day. CL had no chief executive and only a small central staff. Its Board was made up of the managing directors of its main subsidiaries, who were largely concerned with running their own companies, and by non-executive directors. The IRC therefore told Hunter that it was very unlikely that its Board would consider providing finance for CL without imposing clear conditions on its management and on its plans for securing the group's viability. Perrott suggested that such assurances were unnecessary because CL would repay the IRC fairly quickly with cash raised by disposal of assets, but the IRC executive said that this was not the way the IRC operated and reiterated that any support would depend on (a) the appointment of a group chief executive and perhaps other management changes; (b) a realistic and feasible scheme for the future, acceptable to both the IRC and the SIB; (c) assurances of consultations with the IRC on disposals of assets; (d) the involvement of the SIB, the government and CL's commercial customers in a scheme to support the shipyard; (e) full consultation with relevant trade unions.

On this basis, the IRC would seek to help CL and would aim, but could not guarantee, to meet the 29 April deadline. Hunter and Perrott, who were in a very difficult position, agreed to this and an IRC investigating team (the same group that had undertaken the Rolls-Royce investigation) was set up under Board member Leslie Cannon.

IRC PROPOSALS REJECTED

The IRC set about obtaining the maximum commitment, not only from the SIB and the government, but also from the CL shipyard's major commercial customers. The SIB's interest seemed clear. It had a statutory responsibility for shipyards and had the power to make loans to, or even to buy shares in, a shipbuilding company (under Section 6(b) of the Shipbuilding Act of 1967), although the last-mentioned was a power it had never used. The government seemed willing to support any action by the SIB or the IRC that would ensure CL's survival.

Fourteen ships were being built or were on order in the CL shipyard, but five of these were in a state at which they could be towed away and completed elsewhere. Of the remaining nine, three were for Canadian Pacific and six for P & O, with work barely started on the last four of them. In total, Canadian Pacific and P & O had paid more that £4 million in progress payments. If CL went into liquidation, the two companies would stand to lose this and to face delays, and almost certainly higher prices, if they had then to place the orders elsewhere. So, from the outset, the IRC determined that the shipowners could and should be persuaded to make some contribution to the rescue.

The IRC also decided, from the outset, that it could not put money into the group while CL remained responsible for the shipyard. This was partly because shipbuilding was the SIB's concern, but chiefly because the IRC felt that the potential losses on the outstanding orders were almost unlimited. Even if rescue arrangements could be made to meet the current crisis, the yard would remain vulnerable to any increase in inflation, to labour troubles, or to delays caused by its suppliers or its own performance. The IRC was simply not prepared to put its own money at risk in these circumstances.

A scheme was therefore devised that would make the CL group as a whole liable for the losses as currently estimated but would then deconsolidate the shipbuilding company from the accounts, leaving it alone responsible for any additional loss. If the losses turned out to be greater than expected, it would be for the government and/or the SIB to decide whether to continue to support the yard. The rest of the group, and the IRC's money, would be immune.

An outline of this scheme was rapidly worked out and was put to the Paymaster General on 21 April, only a week after the IRC's meeting with Hunter and Perrott. The key to the scheme was that the SIB should acquire a 50 per cent equity interest in the shipyard. This would effectively remove it from the rest of the CL group but, unlike liquidation, would not result in the 'call' of the £3 million debenture secured on the group's assets as a whole. It was also likely that the group's other financial arrangements, and in particular the overdraft facilities for both the parent and the shipbuilding company, could remain or be satisfactorily renegotiated. If the SIB agreed to take the 50 per cent equity stake, the other aspects of the scheme would be these:

(a) The IRC and CL would negotiate with the shipowners to reduce the estimated losses on the order book as far as possible.
(b) The remainder of the group, without the shipyard, would be responsible for the net losses.
(c) The IRC would make funds available to enable the group to meet this liability.
(d) These funds would be repaid by the group from its subsequent cash flow and from the proceeds of rationalising some of its activities. Its estimated profits were £3 million per year, and dividends would be restricted to a nominal sum until the IRC was repaid.
(e) The SIB and/or the government would give the IRC firm undertakings that the yard would be satisfactorily modernised under new management.
(f) The SIB and/or the government would undertake to make available grants to cover the disruption costs of modernisation.

The scheme had already been agreed in principle by CL and its financial advisors and Lever's reaction was wholly positive. He said it covered most of the points that Mintech would want to see in any rescue operation. He was impressed by the speed at which the IRC had worked and at the way in which a realistic commercial note had been injected into the proposal to save the CL group.

The crucial aspect of the scheme was, however, the 50 per cent SIB holding, and it soon became apparent that the SIB was unlikely to agree to this. Indeed, the SIB told the IRC that it would not be too disturbed if the CL shipyard did close down and that the Ministry of Defence had already said the same so far as naval work was concerned. The SIB's preferred solution was for the CL yard to be merged with those of another British shipbuilder, but the IRC pointed out that there was no hope that such an arrangement could be negotiated in time.

The SIB Board was not to meet to make a final decision until 27 April but it seemed certain that the IRC's first proposal would be turned down. The essential prerequisite for any financial commitment from the IRC was the separation of the shipyard from the rest of CL. The only alternative therefore seemed to be to find another candidate, or candidates, to take up the 50 per cent equity stake. Since there was no time to bring in any outside group, the IRC next turned to the shipowners.

NEGOTIATIONS WITH THE SHIPOWNERS

Talks had already started between Canadian Pacific, P & O and the IRC. Both companies were very disturbed by the events at CL, the more so because they felt that they should have been given more warning by the company of its problems. Indeed, the design and planning work on the orders had been good and, even on 17 March, Canadian Pacific had understood that their ships would be completed. When the full situation was explained to them, the reaction of the shipowners was co-operative but cautious. They said that there could be no question of renegotiating the price of the ships on order. This would set an undesirable precedent, and they pointed out that lower tenders for some of the ships had originally been received from both France and West Germany. They were, however, prepared to contribute financially in some other way if they could be given assurances that any settlement was a once and for all one, and that their ships would be completed. The scheme they would prefer would be for a bonus payment to CL on the completion of each ship.

This offer was seen merely as the beginning of a bargaining process, since completion bonuses would do nothing to alleviate CL's liquidity problems. Instead, CL asked P & O to pay an extra £3.25 million and Canadian Pacific an extra £1.2 million for its ships and to phase this *pro rata* to existing progress payments. CL argued that this part of its losses had arisen solely from unforeseeable increases in costs whereas the remainder had arisen, at least in part, from its own performance. The IRC argued that a contribution in one form or another of about £4 million seemed to be right. It would then put up a matching amount, and the remainder of the losses could be met by the CL group.

At the first meeting at the IRC, the shipowners agreed to consider alternatives to completion bonuses. They argued, however, that the ceiling on their total contribution should be what they would lose if they cancelled all the orders and placed them elsewhere. This, they claimed, was less than £4 million.

The parties then considered their positions. One of the Canadian Pacific representatives was a young lawyer, Graham Day. He stood out as extremely able and very constructive, and was to make a lasting impression on the IRC executives and Board members involved in the negotiations.

Various discussions took place during the week and the IRC asked whether each shipowner would take a minority stake in the CL shipyard. But no real progress was made and the IRC met the shipowners again on Sunday 26 April. At this meeting precise proposals did emerge. P & O offered to cancel the last four ships on CL's order book, which accounted for £2 million of the estimated losses. The shipowners collectively were prepared to put up £1.5 million, half as loans and half as 'gifts' in the form of increased prices. This left the total offer £500 000 short of the £4 million which the IRC had suggested. The shipowners did, however, also suggest that the progress payments, amounting to £1.6 million, already paid on the four cancelled ships, could be retained by the CL yard as a short-term loan. This would be repayable when all the other orders were completed. And only very small damages would be claimed on the cancelled orders.

This represented considerable progress, but the whole scheme would still be in jeopardy unless a way could be found to separate the shipyard from the remainder of CL. The shipowners were reluctant to take an equity interest in the yard themselves and, at the Sunday meeting, it was agreed that their proposals should be 'left on the table'.

On the next day, 27 April, the SIB formally rejected the IRC's proposals. When he heard the news, Day took the initiative in divising an alternative solution with the IRC. He proposed that Canadian Pacific should take 20 per cent of the shares in the shipbuilding company if P & O would do the same, and if the SIB would both take a 10 per cent stake and agree to go ahead with the modernisation scheme. Canadian Pacific would also do what it could to find stronger management for the yard.

Lockwood, the IRC Chairman, and Villiers immediately arranged to see the Paymaster General to put these proposals to him and to ask him to involve himself personally in persuading P &O and the SIB to accept them. Lever agreed and arranged to see all the parties on 29 April, the day when the CL deadline expired. Once more, however, despite the support of Mintech and the personal intervention of Lever, the SIB turned down the proposals. P & O also refused to consider taking a shareholding in the yard.

At 15.00 on 29 April, CL had to announce its results without being able to give a clear indication of what was to be done to overcome its problems. Its press release is reproduced as Appendix 13.1. As well as announcing the current and future losses of the shipyard,

CL had to reveal the £2.2 million loss resulting from the Handley Page collapse and the disappointing results from its latest acquisition, Solar Industries. The announcement said that presentation of the full accounts would be postponed but, on the discussions that had taken place with the government and the IRC could only report as follows: 'With the knowledge of the Ministry of Technology discussions are taking place with interested parties with a view to providing the necessary financial support for the shipyard to ensure its viability'.

THE FINAL SCHEME

The IRC had insisted that if agreement was not reached by 29 April its offer of support would lapse, but it would have been uncharacteristic of the Corporation to turn away from an unresolved problem. The IRC Board considered the situation at its regular meeting on 1 May. Those members who had not been personally involved had been kept informed of the situation by telephone and a detailed account of the background to the crisis, and of the events to date, was given at the meeting. The Board endorsed the action taken and confirmed that it would make no funds available to CL unless the shipbuilding company could be separated from the group. Board members asked the executive to continue to look for a way of achieving this, despite the rejection of its initial proposals by the SIB.

A number of possibilities were rapidly explored. They included the suggestion that Canadian Pacific should take up 50 per cent of the equity of the yard, but this was rejected by Day's superiors. Another possibility was that a City consortium should subscribe for the shares as a temporary measure. The idea would be to gain time to arrange a merger, probably with another shipyard. The consortium would have a 'put' option on the shares with the SIB or the IRC, if no buyer had been found after a fixed period. Other ways of involving the SIB were also suggested but none of these schemes was acceptable.

By 5 May, it seemed to the IRC that only one real possibility remained, namely for the 50 per cent holding to be taken up directly by the Government. This would give the appearance of a more direct government 'rescue' but would at least allow the rest of the IRC scheme to go ahead. Lockwood and the executive team therefore went to see Lever again on 6 May and put this proposal to him. The other aspects of the arrangement would be exactly as in the proposal involving the SIB. Lever had simultaneously decided that this was the only way forward and he and the IRC worked over lunch on 'heads of agreement' between themselves, CL and the shipowners. Lever saw CL and the shipowners on the same afternoon and obtained their agreement to this solution. The next morning, 7 May, Lever put the proposal to the Cabinet, where it was approved. In the afternoon he made a statement, included as Appendix 13.2, in the House of Commons.

This statement was relatively simple. Lever announced that the future of CL, and the jobs of 20 000 employees, had been in jeopardy and that the SIB had, for various reasons, been unable to help the company. Instead, the IRC had agreed to make up to £6 million available to the group, while the government was to take a 50 per cent stake in the shipbuilding subsidiary. In contrast, the detailed arrangements were extremely complex. No fewer than 33 separate documents had to be drawn up, approved and signed. Moreover, before this could be done, major issues had to be settled, including the problem of how to give suitable guarantees to the shipowners; the form in which the IRC money should be provided; the valuation of the shipbuilding company; and, most important, the future management of both the shipyard and the CL group.

FINANCE, GUARANTEES AND MANAGEMENT

Negotiating the financial arrangements took time. The position of the government, the IRC and the shipowners had been agreed in principle, but not in detail. As well as the trustees of the debenture holders, four clearing banks had substantial amounts committed to the CL group and all initially wanted either to improve their security or to reduce their commitments. Although it was clear that the position of both the debenture holders and the clearing banks would be vastly improved if the IRC rescue scheme was successful, the arrangements proposed gave most of them grounds for arguing that their security had, in theory, been reduced. In particular, the debenture had been secured in part on the assets of the shipbuilding company and, as this was to be deconsolidated from the accounts, the trustees said that they must ask for additional security on other assets remaining in the group. If this was accepted, it would trigger off complaints from some of the clearing banks that their position had worsened and would also reduce the amount of security against the money the IRC was to provide. It was decided to call all the interested parties together and, at a meeting on 14 May, the rescue scheme was explained to them. It was emphasised that the scheme would work only if the debenture holders accepted the reduced security and if all the banks (who in total were providing facilities of over £11 million) remained as they were.

The trustees of the debenture holders, however, indicated that they would want extra security and asked for a charge on Metro Cammell. Metro Cammell's clearing banker immediately retorted that if this was granted then his bank must either be given a similar security or it would call in its £2 million overdraft. Scottish Aviation's clearing bank also asked for extra security in view of the Handley Page losses. Villiers thanked the bankers for stating their position. However, he also pointed out that if everyone continued to ask for increased security the IRC scheme would collapse, and that the Paymaster General would then have to explain the reason for the collapse to the House of Commons. It was then agreed that all parties would reconsider their positions and that the matter would have to be resolved within a week.

Meanwhile a problem arose on the position of the shipowners. Before the cancellations, loans and 'gifts' they had agreed to were made, they wanted some guarantee that the remaining ships would be completed. The government had offered an arrangement whereby, if the yard were closed before the completion of the current order book, then the government would indemnify the shipowners for whatever payments they had made to the yard and also pay interest. The shipowners had agreed to this but it had become clear that such guarantees from the government would be impossible without legislation. The shipowners would not go ahead without the guarantees and, with no progress payments coming into the yard and stalemate with the bankers, the CL group was only days away from running out of cash completely.

The IRC was again asked to help out. The Treasury suggested that the IRC should give the necessary guarantees to the shipowners and that the government should arrange to repay the IRC if these guarantees were ever called. Villiers agreed to put this proposal to his Board.

The third strand of the hectic negotiations during May related to the management of both the shipyard and the group. Only the latter was to be the direct concern of the IRC, but Lever had asked the Corporation to keep a watching brief on the yard and to advise on its management until the formal transfer was completed. On 6 May Hunter, the CL Chairman, offered his resignation and was told that this would be accepted. On the following day the IRC contacted the Deputy Chairman, Perrott, asking him if he would continue in his post for six months. Four executive directors were also asked to stay on, but Perrott was asked to secure the resignation of all the remaining non-executive directors. (Details of the changes are given in Appendix 13.3) At the same time, the IRC decided that it would take a significant equity stake in the group. The original intention had been for the whole of the £6 million to be provided as convertible loan stock, but the Corporation felt that taking an immediate equity stake would give it a stronger position in relation to the company's reconstituted Board. Moreover, it was a prudent safeguard against the takeover bid that might well come once the immediate problems had been solved.

So, with most of the old Board gone, the IRC, which had almost complete discretion until the rescue documents were signed, and a substantial equity stake thereafter, was in a strong position to impose its will. An appropriate chairman, chief executive and Board members had, however, still to be found. Various successful industrialists were approached by the IRC to take the job of Chairman of CL (minus the shipyard) but all displayed a distinct lack of enthusiasm. Lockwood then decided that the key position was not that of the chairman, but that of the chief executive of the group. If a good chief executive could be appointed, it would be much easier to find a part-time chairman. Moreover, he felt that John Gardiner, one of the IRC executives working on the scheme, was an ideal candidate.

This was one of the proposals put to the IRC Board meeting on 15 May. The report given at this meeting also brought members up to date with the events of the previous two weeks. The meeting endorsed the action taken by the executive and agreed that, since the government's decision to take up 50 per cent of the shipbuilding company effectively deconsolidated it, the IRC could lend £6 million to the remainder of CL. A sum of £1.2 million would be used to take an equity stake of about 13 per cent; the remainder would be a loan for a maximum of five years, with a coupon of 10 per cent per annum. The Board also approved the action the executive had taken with Perrott. It then went into private session (i.e. without any of the IRC executives present) to consider the recommendation from Lockwood that John Gardiner should be appointed as CL's chief executive.

Superficially, it was an extraordinary proposal. Gardiner was barely in his thirties. He had a degree in economics from LSE and had then spent two years as an economist with Prudential Assurance. From there he had gone into financial journalism and by 1968, when he joined the IRC, he had worked his way up to become joint author of the Lex column of the *Financial Times*. He was also in joint charge of the paper's company pages. But he had no direct industrial experience and, unlike most of the other IRC executives, no experience in corporate banking or in accountancy. Other than the impression he had made on Lockwood and the IRC Board members, he had no obvious qualifications for the job. Nonetheless, the IRC Board accepted the proposal and Gardiner has been outstandingly successful as CL's chief executive.

The management problem in the shipyard, however, was not so easily solved. Following the resignations earlier in the year, a new Chairman, Mr West, had been appointed. However, West's resignation was already with Perrott and a possible replacement favoured by CL and the shipowners, a senior executive of Swan Hunter, had flatly rejected the job. The IRC continued to consult the shipowners, the SIB and others but felt that every support should meanwhile be given to the existing team in order to hold the yard together and to continue work on the existing orders. The IRC also insisted that no new orders should be taken until the rescue scheme had been completed.

The IRC Board met again on 29 May, by which time almost all the arrangements had been completed. Allowing for the four cancelled ships and for the contributions from the shipowners, losses were now estimated at £7.2 million. The arrangements made to enable the CL group, minus the shipyard, to pay off the losses but to remain eligible for tax relief were extremely complicated, but the ingenuity of the lawyers and financial advisors had allowed them to achieve what was required to the satisfaction of the Inland Revenue. The debenture trustees and the clearing banks had eventually agreed to the scheme, while both the Stock Exchange and the shareholders had consented to the issue of shares to the IRC. Formal resignations had been received from all the former CL Board members and Gardiner had accepted the position of CL Chief Executive.

At the Board meeting, the IRC members considered the final draft of the loan agreement and gave their formal consent both to this and to the guarantees to the shipowners, which had been requested by the government. They also agreed the text of the press announcement which was to be released when all the documents were signed. (This is Appendix 13.3 in this chapter.) Within about six weeks, the IRC had devised, negotiated and completed the arrangements for a scheme of daunting technical complexity and had succeeded both in rescuing Cammell Laird and in taking the first step towards restructuring its management.

CAMMELL LAIRD AND THE LAIRD GROUP

The IRC press announcement revealed that an independent assessor had put a value of £3 million on the CL shipbuilding company (after allowing for the fact that the estimated £7.2 million losses were to be met by the rest of the CL group). It confirmed that the government, through the public trustee, was paying £1.5 million for 50 per cent of the equity of the shipbuilding company and that the reconstruction would separate shipbuilding from the rest of the group. The remainder of CL continued to hold the other 50 per cent of equity of the shipbuilding company until the nationalisation of the shipbuilding industry in 1977, but the later fortunes of the two parts of the old CL group have been so different that it is best to consider them separately.

Any responsibility that the IRC had for the shipyard ceased when the agreements were signed. When, a few weeks later, the Tories took over, the new Minister asked Mr Caves, who was Managing Director of CL's ship repair company and who had been acting as joint Managing Director of the shipbuilding company, to take on the appointment formally. Caves also remained as Managing Director of the ship repair company which, for financial reasons (i.e. security for the various loans), had been left with the rest of the group. A major order was then gained by the ship repair company for the refit of the 'Ocean Monarch' and it was soon clear that a substantial loss would be made on this. Gardiner then asked Caves to leave the ship repair company and, from March 1971, Caves concentrated on shipbuilding. No progress was made on modernising the yard, but several new orders were taken, the progress payments on which meant that the company's liquidity position was initially good. Despite this reasonably healthy short-term cash position, it became clear during the summer of 1971 that losses were again mounting rapidly, not only on the 'IRC' ships but almost certainly on the new contracts as well. Gardiner decided that something had to be done. If nothing else, he strongly resented the fact that the £7.2 million which his company had been forced to put into shipbuilding was being dissipated, rather than buying time in which the yard could improve its performance. As a 50 per cent shareholder he could not control the running of the yard but, if he could get the government to agree, he could bring in a man of his own choice as Managing Director. Gardiner phoned Graham Day, the Canadian Pacific negotiator, who was then back in Toronto and persuaded him to take on the job of Managing Director of the shipyard. This was a gamble similar to that in Gardiner's own appointment, but the government accepted it and, in September 1971, Caves resigned and Day took over. He immediately began a complete investigation that revealed that in little over a year the losses of the yard had increased by about £5 million.

Day's assessment was that without substantial modernisation the yard had no future. If modernisation went ahead, and it was estimated that this would cost about £15 million, the yard might just be profitable. Moreover, up to £6 million was needed to cover the immediate financial position. This crisis, coming so soon after the previous one, at least confirmed the IRC's wisdom in separating off, and thus protecting, the rest of the group.

The government decided to go ahead with modernisation. The cost of this exceeded the estimates; moreover, the performance of the yard, like that of the rest of the British shipbuilding industry, was less than impressive. But the appointment of Day was a success. He handled a very difficult situation creditably and made a favourable impression both on the Tory government and on Labour Ministers when they returned to office in 1974. Indeed, Day became Chief Executive designate of British Shipbuilders under the nationalisation bill, although he eventually resigned in frustration over the difficulties and delay in putting the bill on the statute book.

In contrast to the disappointments of 1970 and 1971 in the shipyard, the rest of the group got off to a good start. An immediate stroke of good fortune was the finding of a new chairman. The IRC Board members were consulted on appropriate candidates and Lord Bridgeman suggested Maurice Banks, who had been one of his deputy chairmen at British Petroleum. Banks had recently retired from BP but was willing to take on the chairmanship, part-time. Two other part-time Board members were appointed. These were Lockwood, the IRC Chairman, who agreed to serve in a personal capacity and Phillip Shelbourne, a partner in Rothschilds and highly regarded in the City. Finally, Gardiner persuaded Nick Dow, who had for many years worked with Ian Morrow (see Chapter 12 on Rolls-Royce), to become the full-time executive finance director. This was a very strong Board for a medium-sized company and these appointments effectively silenced a small shareholders' pressure group, that had been asking for its own representation on the Board. Soon afterwards, the process of separation and reconstruction was recognised. The CL group, minus the shipyard, became The Laird Group.

The subsequent financial results of the company speak for themselves. In 1970, pre-tax profits, before any allowance for meeting the shipyard losses, were £2 million on a turnover of £56 million. By 1977, turnover had doubled but pre-tax profits had increased by four and a half times to just over £9 million. The results year by year have been as follows:

	Turnover (£ million)	*Pre-tax profits (£ million)*
1970	56	2.0
1971	61	2.8
1972	64	5.3
1973	70	6.3
1974	91	8.3
1975	89	6.8
1976	111	8.1
1977	119	9.1
1978	151	11.1
1979	207	10.7

The IRC loans were refinanced in 1971 and the IRC shareholding sold to institutions soon afterwards. Return on capital employed (albeit at historic book value) was raised to an impressive 25 per cent in 1972 and improved to 28 per cent in 1973 and 1974. In 1975, The Laird Group was hard hit by the steel recession which reduced, and later removed, the profits of its largest subsidiary, Patent Shaft. Profitability in other parts of the group improved and, despite the continuing steel recession and the eventual closure of Patent Shaft early in 1980, the overall return on capital was kept at about 20 per cent. But perhaps the single most striking feature of the company, which was only days away from failure in 1970, is the transformation of its financial position. In 1970 it had overdrafts of about £11 million and had to make provisions for the £7.2 million losses of the shipbuilding company. Its gearing ratio was above average at 40 per cent. (Gearing represents the proportion of capital employed accounted for by debt.) And gearing would have been higher, but for the injection of equity by the IRC. By 1977 The Laird Group's gearing had been reduced to under 20 per cent. Since then, the group has been able to withstand the closure of Patent Shaft and to continue its programme of diversification.

The Laird Group rapidly became established as a successful and financially sound company and has remained so despite the difficulties of recent years.

COMMENT

It can be argued that CL should have been allowed to go into liquidation in 1970. Its shipyard could have been closed down, because there was chronic over-capacity in the industry. In the year to March 1978, it accounted for £26 million of British Shipbuilders' total loss of £108 million. Most of CL's other subsidiaries would probably then have survived in one form or another. However, this was not for the IRC to decide. It was a course of action that had already been ruled out for political reasons. The IRC's job was to organise the rescue that had been decided on, in the most effective and constructive way.

Judged by this limited criterion, the IRC's action must be regarded as highly successful. It was right to divide the group into two, and right to accept the resignations of the old management of the CL group and to gamble on the appointment of one of the IRC's own executives. Not only has Gardiner been a successful chief executive of the Laird Group, he has been appointed to the boards of British Airways, British Leyland and the NEB, and is currently a member of the boards of Courtaulds, British Shipbuilders and ICL.

As will be seen later, it is sometimes argued that the development and encouragement of management potential was one of the most lasting of the IRC's contributions. This may, or may not, be too sweeping a claim. The Laird Group, however, clearly provides one example where the IRC's judgment on management ability was more than vindicated.

APPENDIX 13.1

The following represents the text of a press release issued by Charles Barker City Ltd on behalf of Cammell Laird and Co. Ltd on 29 April 1970.

CAMMELL LAIRD AND COMPANY LIMITED

Cammell Laird & Co. Ltd announce that the results for 1969 before tax for the various companies in the Group, other than the shipbuilding company, are as follows:

	1969 (£)	*1968* (£)
Patent Shaft Steel Works	1 110 000	765 000
Scottish Aviation Ltd	571 000	618 000
C. L. Anglesey Ltd	49 000	88 000
British Federal Welder Ltd	153 000	204 000 (15 months)
C. L. (Metro) Ltd	168 000)	became subsidiary com-
Solar Industries Ltd	295 000)	panies as from 1 January 1969

North Western Line (Mersey) Ltd	53 000	63 000
Ship repair	(165 000)	23 000
Holding Company	(334 000)*	(18 000)
	£ 1 900 000	1 743 000

* Increase reflects loan stock and bank interest charges.

Shipbuilding Company (1968 profit £1 354 000)

Although the operations of the Shipbuilding Company showed a small profit on contracts completed during 1969, substantial provisions will have to be made for losses on work done in 1969 on uncompleted contracts. After making these provisions, the net loss for the year of the Shipbuilding Company would be £2 227 000. In addition, however, cost escalations well in excess of the assumptions made in the estimates prepared for present uncompleted contracts, will give rise to further severe losses in 1970, 1971 and 1972, and it is the intention of the Board to make a provision in the accounts for 1969 against these.

With the knowledge of the Ministry of Technology discussions are taking place with interested parties with a view to providing the necessary financial support for the shipyard to ensure its viability.

Scottish Aviation

When Handley Page first got into difficulties, the choice for Scottish Aviation, which was manufacturing the wing sections for the Jetstream aircraft, lay between closing down the production line concerned, or continuing in the expectation that negotiations to ensure the future of Handley Page would be successful.

Following the sudden and unforseeable failure in February 1970 of the new company formed to continue manufacture of the Jetstream aircraft, the loss to Scottish Aviation amounts to £2 205 000 which the Board intends should be covered by a transfer from reserves. This loss is slightly lower than that of £2 250 000 anticipated – and announced – in September 1969, prior to the formation of the new company. The Scottish Aviation profits shown above are before charging these losses.

Solar Industries

The results of the Solar Group are disappointing. However, the working party which was set up to look into the integration of Solar with the rest of the Group has now completed its investigations, and its recommendations are being put into effect.

Accounts

Until the discussions on the future of the Shipbuilding Company are completed, the amount of the provisions to be made cannot be determined, and the audit of the Group accounts cannot be finalised. It has, therefore, been necessary to postpone the publication of the final audited figures.

In the meantime, the directors have decided that they cannot recommend a final dividend.

April 29th, 1970

APPENDIX 13.2

The following statement was made by the Paymaster General, Harold Lever, to the House of Commons on 7 May 1970.

STATEMENT BY THE PAYMASTER GENERAL ON CAMMELL LAIRD

With permission I would like to make a statement about Cammell Laird and Company Ltd.

This company announced last week that, with the knowledge of the Ministry of Technology, discussions were taking place with interested parties with a view to ensuring the viability of their shipyard. The shipbuilding subsidiary, which had made profits in earlier years, found itself faced with heavy losses and the parent company, although possessing valuable assets, was unable to make available the cash required for the normal operation of its shipbuilding business. Consequently the group faced a liquidity crisis which jeopardised the future of the 20 000 it employs in its various activities.

The Shipbuilding Industry Board's powers to assist the re-equipment and reorganisation of the yard were not appropriate to solve the wider problems of the group. But the Industrial Reorganisation Corporation has agreed to make secured loans available as required within a limit of approximately £6 000 000 to help the group meet the needs of its shipbuilding subsidiary.

The leading shipowner customers of the yard have for their part agreed to cancel certain orders and to assist the yard to complete other ships now on order by them, subject to reasonable refund provisions.

As part of these arrangements the Government have agreed to provide the finance for a 50% shareholding in the shipbuilding company at a price to be settled by independent valuation. Legislation and Supplementary Estimates as necessary will be submitted to the House in due course and any funds required immediately in connection with the purchase of shares will be provided from the Civil Contingencies Fund. The Group will apply the funds now being mobilised to relieve the shipbuilding company of all its expected losses.

The Government will expect the company to avoid further unprofitable orders. On the management side, there will be an early and extremely thorough management reconstruction.

As a result of these arrangements, not only will the liquidity crisis threatening the whole group be averted but the shipyard will be able to meet its obligations and get ahead with its shipbuilding business.

Putting it bluntly, we have rescued this company from total collapse, but this does not mean that the future of the company is guaranteed, still less guaranteed by the Government. The future of the company will depend on the efforts of management and workers in making it a viable competitive unit. In order to promote a realisation of this fact, and to give incentive to those most concerned, I am considering whether there are ways in which the shares in the shipyard might be so dealt with by, for example, placing them in a trust on behalf of the employees, or by some other similar means. I intend to discuss this with the trade unions and others concerned.

APPENDIX 13.3

The following press announcement was issued by the IRC following its Board meeting on 29 May 1970.

INDUSTRIAL REORGANISATION CORPORATION
and
CAMMELL LAIRD AND COMPANY LIMITED

The purpose of this announcement is to explain the involvement of Industrial Reorganisation Corporation ('IRC') in the affairs of the Cammell Laird Group and to give the shareholders of Cammell Laird full details of the scheme of financial assistance that has been worked out by IRC with the full support of the Company.

IRC's Role

IRC undertook its examination of the Cammell Laird situation at the invitation of the Paymaster General. The investigation established that the present crisis in the Group was almost entirely due to the heavy losses anticipated on the shipyard's current order book, and that there were important companies in the rest of the Group which could offer scope for IRC's restructuring role. IRC therefore insisted as a precondition of its involvement that the shipbuilding undertaking should become independent from the rest of the Group, leaving IRC free to promote the re-organisation and development of the Group's other activities. There will be full consultation with the Trade Unions on all matters affecting the interests of employees.

The Scheme in Outline

The shipbuilding undertaking has ceased to be a subsidiary of the Group by means of HMG providing finance for the acquisition of 50 per cent of its ordinary capital to be held by the Public Trustee. The remainder of the Group, which has reasonable prospects of operating profitably, will provide for the foreseeable losses on the shipyard's existing order book, with the assistance of loans from IRC and interested shipowners; thereafter the shipyard will operate as a separate concern. In the absence of these measures the almost certain result would have been the failure of the whole Group involving substantial unemployment and the dislocation of major contracts many of which were for export.

Financial Arrangements

The Public Trustee has acquired new shares representing 50 per cent of the ordinary share capital of Cammell Laird & Company (Shipbuilding and Engineering) Limited ('S & E') at a price of £1 500 000 which has been settled independently. The necessary consent has been obtained from the Trustees of Cammell Laird and Company Limited's ('CL') Debenture Stock to release S & E from the floating charge in their favour.

The net amount of the losses on S & E's current order book after various adjustments is estimted at £7 200 000. The scheme provides that CL will make good to S & E the actual amount of these losses up to but not beyond that figure. In order to help meet these obligations IRC has subscribed at par for 4 900 830 Ordinary Shares of 5*s* each (amounting to £1 225 207 10*s* 0*d* and representing 13.6 per cent of the enlarged capital) and IRC and certain shipowners have agreed to make loans to CL of up to £4 825 000 and £675 000 respectively, carrying interest at the rate of 10 per cent per annum and repayable between 1972 and 1975. There is no obligation on IRC to provide further finance to S & E and furthermore so long as IRC has an investment in CL, the Group will not have the right to invest in S & E beyond financing the current losses to the agreed limit.

The IRC and shipowners' loans will be repaid from retained profits and realisation of assets. Until the loans have been repaid dividend payments by CL will be subject to consultation with IRC except that dividends of not more than 1 per cent per annum may be paid for 1970 and 1971. The arrangements should enable the CL Group to obtain tax relief in 1970 and 1971 in respect of the major part of the S & E losses. CL will also be released from all material guarantees of liabilities of S & E other than in respect of two contracts under which no obligation is expected to arise.

Management

The Board of CL is being reconstituted. Mr Edward du Cann, Mr D. L. Donne and Mr P. J. D. Toosey have recently resigned. Mr P. B. Hunter, the Chairman, and the following non-executive Directors, namely Mr J. H. Bromfield, Mr R. W. Johnson, Mr H. West and Mr T. Draper Williams have resigned from the Board of CL as part of the arrangements. In addition Mr R. K. Calder and Mr J. MacNish have resigned from the Board of Solar Industries Limited, and its subsidiary and associated companies.

Mr M. A. L. Banks, formerly a deputy chairman of The British Petroleum Company Limited, has agreed to serve as non-executive Chairman of CL. The Board of CL has elected Mr John A. Gardiner to the Board of the Company as Managing Director and Chief Executive. Mr Gardiner will resign from IRC where he is now an executive.

Sir Donald Perrott, the present Deputy Chairman, has agreed to continue for the time being. Mr B. C. Bruce-Gardner, Mr T. D. M. Robertson, Mr W. Scott and Sir Thomas Padmore will remain on the Board.

General

Now that the above arrangements have been completed, the Report and Accounts of C.L. for the year ended 31st December 1969 can be finalised and will be sent to stockholders as soon as possible. The benefits of the reconstruction will take time to accrue and a forecast of future prospects would be inappropriate at this stage. A statement by the Board will be made at the AGM.

PART FOUR

THE IRC'S CONTRIBUTION

14

Review and Appraisal

Inevitably many of the questions that we would like to ask about the IRC's effectiveness, and about the results of its activities, cannot be answered. To do so would require a knowledge of what would have happened in the absence of IRC intervention, and this we can never know. Nor do we intend here to undertake any aggregate analysis of the IRC's work. It might be possible to devise some measure of corporate performance and then to compare the companies with which the IRC was involved with a 'control group' of other companies but, even if such an approach were valid, there would be numerous conceptual and data problems. We have not attempted it (the difficulties of such an exercise would be very considerable; see, for example, Newbould, 1971).

Instead, in this chapter, we undertake a qualitative assessment of the IRC's activities and importance. In particular, we attempt to evaluate the Corporation's work under four headings. The first is the appropriateness or otherwise of the IRC's original objective, which was to promote mergers. The second is the extent to which it was successful in meeting this objective. The third is how far the IRC's role, and its conception of that role, changed over its four-year life? Fourth, we shall consider what lessons can be learned from the IRC's experience. In examining these questions we draw heavily on the material in Chapters 4–13, but we shall also consider other IRC projects covered in Chapter 3 or in Appendix A.

THE IRC'S MERGER REMIT

In Chapter 1 we explained that the IRC was established as part of the Labour Government's policy of taking more direct and selective action to attempt to improve the performance of UK industry. We have seen that it was therefore given very wide but vaguely defined powers, especially under Section 2(1)(b) of its Act. It could do anything that might promote 'industrial efficiency and profitability' or assist 'the economy of the United Kingdom or any part of the United Kingdom'. We have also shown that, despite being given these more general powers, the overriding objective in setting up the IRC was the promotion of mergers and the 'improvement' of the UK's industrial structure. This was illustrated in Chapter 1, and especially in the extract from Ben Cant's original paper arguing the case for establishing the Corporation. Another Board member, Professor McClelland, writing after the IRC had been wound up, also argued that 'the case for the IRC stands or falls on the proposition that in many sectors British companies were not large enough, and that without intervention they would not become large enough, soon enough' (McClelland, 1972, p. 24).

Fashions change, not least in the conventional wisdom of economics, and many supporters of the IRC, including some of its own executives and Board members, would now argue that this predominant emphasis on size and mergers was misplaced. Small, it is now suggested, 'is beautiful'. It is, however, on its role as the government's merger broker, and in particular on its involvement in the creation by merger of the major firms in several important industries, that our attention in this chapter will initially be focused.

By far the largest mergers with which the IRC was concerned were those involving GEC, AEI and EE (Ch. 4) and British Motor Holdings and Leyland Motors (Ch. 7). Despite vociferous opposition at the time, few people would now claim that the GEC mergers have not been successful. On the other hand, British Leyland has had enormous problems and has survived only because of the injection of large amounts of public money. In both cases (as with many other IRC projects) it can be argued that the mergers would have gone ahead sooner or later anyway. This is particularly so in the case of British Leyland, where the merger was the final step in a chain of events which had gradually brought together virtually all of the British-owned motor industry. Moreover the government, and the Prime Minister personally, were pressing for the merger. The IRC's contribution, acknowledged publicly by Lord Stokes, was to help to facilitate the arrangements for, and bring forward the time of, the deal.

The GEC case is not quite so clear cut, although Weinstock has said that it was the IRC that put the idea of merging with AEI into his head. It is possible that without IRC support some other arrangement would have been made that could have prevented GEC's subsequent acquisition of English Electric.

So should we conclude that the IRC deserves a tick for its part in the GEC deal but a black mark for British Leyland? Of course it is not as simple as that. Indeed it is by no means clear, then or now, that BL's problems relate to its size. It is smaller than many of its American and European competitors and the recent takeover of Chrysler's European companies by Peugeot-Citroen is an illustration of the continuing concentration of motor vehicle manufacture in Europe.

For the IRC itself, the contrasting experiences with British Leyland and GEC seem to have reinforced its view that management was of crucial importance. Whatever the potential advantages of rationalisation, they are unlikely to be achieved without a really effective chief executive, supported by strong line managers. This was always a central tenet of the IRC's approach. (Indeed it has been argued that this was carried too far. There is a much quoted quip based on the 'Brookings Report' (Caves, 1968) that the IRC's aim was to find the best manager in the country and merge British industry into one big company under him.) Weinstock provides a positive illustration of this but Stokes and his management team were less willing and/or able to carry through the reorganisation required following the merger. It was British Leyland's lack of progress, and perhaps even more the experience with Kent described in Chapter 5, that taught the IRC that it was not enough to push through a merger but then leave the subsequent reorganisation to the management team it had backed. The IRC felt it necessary to stay closely in touch with the companies it supported and to monitor their progress. Moreover, the IRC concluded from the Kent case that if it had put itself in a position where it was a major shareholder, or was otherwise in control of events, then it could and should take the initiative in encouraging management changes in companies which were not achieving the results envisaged.

We pursue this point later. First, there is another issue, highlighted by the British Leyland and Kent cases, which is central to an understanding of the IRC's approach, at least until the last year or so of its life. Kearton and George Brown had persuaded a group of experienced and highly respected people to join the IRC Board. Grierson and Kearton had then recruited an executive team which was young, bright and highly motivated. Once the initial doubts about how aggressive the IRC should be and how far it should be prepared to make moves that would cause controversy had been resolved, as they were in the GEC—AEI case, the IRC became very clear that its major task was to promote mergers and that it should use all its talents and resources to this end. From this time on the balance of personalities and philosophies in the Corporation was heavily weighted in favour of 'accentuating the positive'. It would have been difficult for an IRC executive to have argued against the

BMH–Leyland merger unless he could have proposed a better deal. To have suggested to his Board, or to his colleagues, that doing nothing would have been better was not likely to have been popular. It would have been countered by the argument that there was no way in which doing nothing could improve the situation. Nor was the IRC likely to suggest that the best plan was to leave the two companies separate but to overhaul the management and organisation of BMH, even if it had possessed any leverage to achieve this. At that time, this was not seen as the IRC's role.

Similarly, although it recognised that the balance of the argument was only marginally in Kent's favour in its battle with Rank for Cambridge Instruments, the IRC threw all its weight behind the company it had decided to back. The justification for this approach, and it is a considerable justification, was that taking action which was likely to lead to improved industrial structure, and hence performance, even at the risk of making things worse, was better than doing nothing at all.

The danger in this is twofold. First, if the objective given to a very effective organisation is itself misconceived, then that organisation has been set on a course where it might do more harm than good. Second, the result of mergers cannot usually be seen for several years. The measure of the organisation's success therefore becomes the achievement of the merger, rather than being based on the effect of the merger in terms of industrial performance.

Judged on the subsequent performance of the three companies formed by these early IRC mergers, we may say this: GEC is undoubtedly a success, Kent–Cambridge a failure, whilst with British Leyland the IRC intervention, viewed ten years later, probably made little difference. The benefits of the GEC mergers, of course, far outweigh the losses incurred with Kent.

The fourth of the IRC's major mergers involved a series of complex deals that eventually led to the creation of the UK ball-bearing company Ransome Hoffmann Pollard (Ch. 6). This too must be counted as a considerable achievement for the IRC. It created, against all the odds, a major UK company in an industry dominated by multinationals, and also found a manager capable of carrying through the rationalisation required to put the company into a sound industrial and financial position.

While it is important to analyse the results of these major mergers, both for the firms concerned and for the IRC itself, this is too narrow a perspective on which to judge the activities of the Corporation. In the next section of this chapter we therefore turn to a more general consideration of the IRC's involvement in mergers. We shall then examine how the Corporation increasingly saw the limitations of this role and, with the encouragement of the government, began to perform a range of functions for which its unique position between Whitehall, the City and industry made it ideally suited.

MERGERS AND INDUSTRIAL PERFORMANCE

The IRC promoted, supported and/or financed over fifty completed mergers covering more than 150 companies. However, in the four years 1967–70 it is estimated that there were about 3400 mergers among industrial and commercial companies (see Ch. 1, p. 6). The deals in which the IRC was involved therefore amounted to less than 2 per cent of the total. Although they did represent a higher proportion in terms of assets transferred, the IRC's influence was still very partial and selective. This raises the question of how the IRC set about selecting the industries and firms with which it operated, as well as how it affected performance in these sectors.

McClelland argues that, for most of the IRC's life, 'the balance of payments situation demanded the highest priority'. This was why the Corporation 'paid little or no attention to industries, such as building, where there might have been scope for reorganisation but which were not direct importers or exporters on a significant scale' (McClelland, 1972, p. 28).

McClelland claims that 'the manufacturing sector was examined pretty thoroughly'. When the IRC began work it was provided with NEDC and DEA reports on industries like process plant, machine tools and electrical equipment. Later, it used 'an excellent internal document' which evaluated the different sectors of the economy in terms of indicators like export–import balance, the size distribution of firms, numbers of qualified scientists and engineers employed, etc.

But at least for the early stages of the IRC's activities, McClelland argued, and we accept the rationale, that

> a systematic strategy based on rational priorities was less appropriate than sitting at the receipt of custom and welcoming all comers, pushing the boat out, using one's "nose" to pick up a lead as to a possibly fluid situation. A degree of opportunism, in short, was the right answer to ignorance about the feasibility of IRC intervention.

Whether the contention that, later, 'it was possible to develop a sound sense of priorities and criteria' is quite so accurate is not clear (McClelland, 1972, p. 29).

It is convenient to classify the sources of IRC projects under three headings: government suggestions or requests; the IRC's own initiative; and reaction to events, including requests from companies. Government suggestions and requests for IRC action took a number of forms. We have seen that at its very first Board meeting the IRC was given a number of NEDC and other official industry reports. In addition, the DEA and Mintech had regular discussions with the IRC executive on problem areas in industries and on priorities for IRC action. The government also commissioned a number of reports by the IRC and asked for direct IRC assistance in particular situations. These suggestions and requests were not random, but arose out of the government's identification of priority areas for intervention, or from having to deal with specific industrial problems. References to the IRC therefore covered a wide range of industries, but the general point is that the government, not unnaturally, was directing the IRC's attention to what it saw as the *problem areas* of British industry.

The IRC's own planning work followed a similar pattern. It sought to identify industrial sectors where UK performance relative to that of overseas competitors was poor. So it looked at areas where imports were increasing faster than exports, where UK industry seemed to be lagging technologically, and where the productivity and profitability of UK companies was relatively poor.

We have, however, seen from our case studies that, despite the considerable planning work by the government, and to a lesser extent by the IRC itself, most of the Corporation's immediate involvements in merger negotiations came as a reaction to events. To say that is not to deny the importance of the background work. This gave the IRC extensive knowledge of, and contacts with, whole areas of British industry, and made industrialists more aware of what the Corporation was trying to achieve and what it could offer them. But it is clear that the IRC was, more often than not, thrust into a situation either as the result of a request from one of the companies concerned, or as a reaction to a takeover bid or the imminent possibility of one. This was true with the Plessey bid for English Electric and with the Rank bid for Cambridge Instruments. In the ball-bearing case, the IRC was also reacting to the likelihood of a Skefco takeover of Ransome and Marles and the chance that the whole UK ball-bearing industry would soon be in foreign hands.

Even in cases under this third heading, reaction to events, the IRC was most likely to become involved in situations where the performance of UK companies gave cause for concern. If two efficient UK companies decided to merge, or even if one made a takeover bid for another, this was likely to be either a matter for general approval or a case for the Monopolies Commission. It was much more likely that the IRC would become involved, as it did under our first two headings of government requests and the Corporation's own initiatives, where the performance of the industry or one or more of the companies concerned was poor relative to that of international competitors.

In this respect, therefore, the IRC's role was the promotion of industrial restructuring largely through mergers, in an attempt to improve industrial performance in areas where the UK was lagging behind its foreign competitors. It was hoped that in some circumstances performance would be improved through the benefits that restructuring would bring: the concentration of resources, in some cases in production, but more generally in R & D and marketing; the provision of a stronger financial base; etc. In other instances, the main benefits of mergers were seen as giving greater scope to proven and successful managements.

With hindsight, these objectives can be viewed as highly ambitious. It is by no means clear how far the UK's chronically bad industrial performance can be put down to firms being too small. Moreover, the IRC could certainly not have been expected to put right more than a relatively small proportion of the UK's management problems. We have doubts about the IRC's possible effectiveness in pursuing its original, narrow objective. Indeed, it is unlikely that a public corporation will ever again be formed in the UK with such a specific merger role. (The NEB, for example, had a far wider remit.) But when we judge the performance of the IRC itself, we must bear in mind that where it may appear to have failed, failure was already highly probable in the absence of IRC intervention. Where the IRC appears to have succeeded, success is to that extent more praiseworthy.

The ball-bearing industry almost certainly falls into this category. A strong British company was created, against all the odds, and an exceptional manager, Bill Barlow, was found to 'turn it round'. Ransome, Hoffmann, Pollard seems to have survived both Barlow's departure to the Post Office and intensive foreign competition, especially from the Japanese. Indeed in the late 1970s Skefco, the subsidiary of the giant Swedish company, appeared to be suffering in the UK to a greater extent than RHP.

The International Compressed Air Corporation, formed by the merger of Broom and Wade and Holman, also appears to be an example of a company that owes its existence, at least in part, to the IRC. It continued to operate successfully through the 1970s.

In the electrical and electronics industry, several useful deals were promoted by the IRC in addition to the GEC mergers. In the mining machinery sector, the efforts of the IRC were also quite successful. They resulted in a much stronger and more substantial grouping of companies in the face of reduced demand from the NCB and the increased need to compete in export markets.

In other industries, where the IRC tried long and hard to achieve reorganisaton – industries like textiles, numerical control, and mechanical engineering generally – performance has been mixed. In machine tools, for example, the IRC investment of £1 million in Herbert Ingersoll (discussed in Ch. 8) did nothing to prevent the failure of the company. The Alfred Herbert group as a whole, which the IRC tried to support, survived until 1980 only with the help of Department of Industry money and funds from the NEB. On the other hand, Staveley Industries, which resisted the IRC's attempts to reorganise its machine tool interests, has fared reasonably well.

Of the other areas covered by the case studies, that of the 'plant makers' (Chs. 9–11) is perhaps the most interesting. It is hard to say that the specific deals encouraged, and in one instance financed, by the IRC were particularly successful. Indeed, they may have contributed to the subsequent financial problems of the companies involved, especially those of Whessoe. Yet Whessoe did survive to enjoy better days, at least partly because of IRC help. The case of Davy Ashmore is more clear cut. Its problems stemmed directly from the disastrous Conoco contract (see Ch. 11), not from any of its acquisitions, and it is hard to see how it could have overcome its financial problems in 1969 without the substantial and skilful support of the IRC. It has now developed into a strong and successful group in both the UK and international markets. Davy Ashmore, now Davy International, also provides a case where the intervention produced a new chief executive, John Buckley, who steered the company to its current position.

As might always have been anticipated, the subsequent record of the companies involved in IRC-supported mergers is far from an unblemished story of improving performance. There are the substantial successes of GEC, RHP, International Compressed Air, Davy International and others. But in many chronic problem areas, in mechanical engineering and elsewhere, the IRC appears to have made little impact on performance. Certainly, on its own main criterion – the UK trade balance of manufactured goods – the position has continued to deteriorate.

So, despite considerable success, the IRC mergers have not reversed the relative decline in the performance of UK manufacturing industry. Nor could they have been expected to do so. Moreover, within its own relatively short life, the IRC was already looking at other and broader areas of intervention. This was partly because the stock market conditions which had acted to encourage mergers in the mid-1960s no longer prevailed but, more important, because the feeling grew that the particular brand of talent and expertise acquired by the IRC could be brought to bear on broader industrial problems. It is to this feature of the IRC that we now turn.

SECTION 2(1)(b) AND A 'DEVELOPMENT BANK' ROLE

It is ironic that despite all the emphasis on mergers, and despite the IRC Board's decision that its first project should be chosen very carefully, the IRC's first publicly announced deal came under Section 2(1)(b) of the Act which covered its non-merger role. The Secretary of State at the DEA, Michael Stewart, asked the IRC to 'assist in the future development of Rootes Motors Limited' and the IRC took up a shareholding of Rootes and put a nominee on to the company's Board. Whatever the mechanism of the IRC's involvement there was, however, at least a technical takeover situation because the Chrysler Corporation was increasing its shareholding in Rootes to give it a controlling interest.

The next 2(1)(b) projects were different in two respects. First, there was no question of a takeover and, second, the initiative for the deals came from the companies involved and from the IRC, rather than the government. In other words, the Corporation had to request a 'request' from the Secretary of State. The projects concerned were two 'de-inking' investments undertaken in January and June 1968 by the Reed Paper Group and by Peter Dixon & Son (Holdings). In both cases, the companies received loans from the IRC to enable them to build plants for de-inking waste paper to be used as a substitute for imported pulp. The use of a domestic waste product to replace an imported raw material had obvious environmental and balance of payments advantages and the IRC was keen to support the projects. However, they were isolated cases (no other 2(1)(b) projects were completed until January 1970) and they arose, at least indirectly, out of the IRC's 'paper and board industry survey' (see Appendix A, p. 256) which was concerned with the possibilities for reorganisation in the paper industry. Hence, these early cases of IRC support for investment schemes, rather than for mergers, should be seen as a by-product of its main merger role.

Moreover, apart from Rootes Motors, which was a border-line case, the government did not initially view the IRC as having a significant role outside the area of mergers. Indeed, it introduced the Industrial Expansion Act to provide powers for direct government involvement in the support of investment and of other industrial projects. The cases where the government commissioned IRC investigations and reports were chiefly in areas where it was thought that structural changes were required. This was true of the telecommunication industry survey (Appendix A, p. 252) in 1967 and of the nuclear and trawling industries investigations in 1968 (Appendix A, pp. 265 and 278). There were a few cases where the government asked the IRC to assist in an investigation of an individual firm. For example the IRC was asked, in 1967, to make an assessment of the financial position of The Cunard Steam-ship Company and of possible terms for government assistance to the company. There was also a case (Aluminium Smelters) where the government asked the IRC to appraise specific investment proposals, but during the first three years of its life the government clearly viewed the IRC as, first and foremost, a merger broker.

Even in mid-1969, when the IRC Report and Accounts for the year ending in March 1969 was published, the Corporation still saw itself as working predominantly to promote mergers:

> Over the last few years fundamental restructuring has taken place in several key industrial sectors in Britain but the Board of the IRC is convinced there remains a continuing need for an active policy to promote industrial reorganisation. IRC now has a heavier work load than at any time since it was established, and is systematically analysing manufacturing industry and other sectors of the economy to identify priority areas where structural fragmentation is inhibiting current performance or prejudicing future prospects (IRC, 1968/9, p. 19).

A change in the IRC's perception of its role clearly took place during 1969, however, and by the time the report and accounts for the year ending March 1970 were published, the emphasis had changed significantly.

> IRC's function is "promoting industrial efficiency and profitability and assisting the economy of the UK". The major influences upon these objectives are market forces and the Government's overall economic and industrial policies. IRC works at the micro level with individual companies and at the difficult interface between public and private sectors which is largely unexplored. IRC has identified three main fields of activity in this work (IRC, 1969/70, p. 5).

The first of these three fields was still 'reorganisation' but the IRC was, by mid-1970, reflecting much more on the difficulties involved.

> IRC does not pursue a policy of size for size's sake. Size has no absolute merit: indeed size has absolute disadvantages where it increases managerial problems and lengthens lines of communication. The spur of

> competition can also be blunted. Size must be gauged in each case in relation to the competing concerns at home and overseas, and in relation to the products and markets concerned (IRC, 1969/70, p.6).
>
> . . . Whilst reorganisation is difficult enough to achieve, it is still more difficult to get the benefits of reorganisation. Renewing outdated industrial structures is often an uphill struggle from behind to repair the results of years of divergent policies and neglect. The rationalisation and redeployment involved cause upheavals in labour relations. Above all, reorganisation imposes severe strains on management, which in Britain in particular is still in scarce supply. But reorganisation is useless unless new management energies are released or transferred (IRC, 1969/70, p. 7).

Two new objectives were identified in the annual report. They were 'stimulation' and 'selective investment'. Under the heading 'stimulation', a strong attack was launched on inadequate management:

> Whilst there is a continuing need for an active policy to promote reorganisation poor performance in many sectors is not necessarily the effect of fragmentation. Low productivity, late delivery, slow switch of markets, mediocre products and a lack of management control characterise many companies more than large enough to be viable units (IRC, 1969/70, p. 7).
>
> . . . It would be beneficial if bankers were more aware of the industrial and management problems of their clients. In a number of cases IRC has secured management changes which are having beneficial results. Often these changes have involved the introduction of men from outside the group concerned. Existing managements have no prescriptive rights and if they fail to deliver the goods they should make way for those who can. The problem is to shift the sub-standard top hamper before it is too late. (IRC, 1969/70, pp. 7–8).

These comments no doubt represented a general reflection on management problems. The IRC Board members and executives had been involved with discussions and negotiations with literally hundreds of senior managers of companies, across the whole spectrum of UK industry. But the comments were also a reflection of the IRC's more direct involvement in companies which it had encouraged and supported in rationalisation measures. In Chapter 5, for example, we saw that the IRC was initially reluctant to become involved in decisions on Kent's management. It thought that the group required a new chief executive to carry through the necessary reorganisation following the acquisition of Cambridge Instruments, but it decided that it was up to the company to find such a man. This was probably a mistake, because Kent's managers considered that the IRC was in such a powerful position relative to the company that it was bound to make its will felt. So valuable time was lost, with both the IRC and Kent's own management hesitating to take the vital decisions. The IRC learnt from this experience and acted much more firmly in the ball-bearings case (Ch. 6). Also, when Whessoe and Davy Ashmore ran into trouble (Chs 10 and 11) the IRC took the initiative in seeking top management appointments, which it could support, as it did in its later involvement with Rolls-Royce and Cammell Laird (Chs 12 and 13).

Responsibility for monitoring the performance of, and if necessary insisting on the appointment of new senior management of the companies in which it had a continuing financial interest, was perhaps an inevitable development of the IRC's role. Clearly it wanted to protect its investments whether they were shareholdings or, as often was the case, unsecured loans. The most effective way of doing this was to stimulate the performance of the companies concerned. To enable it to do this, the IRC adopted a formal 'follow-up' procedure. Where there was an IRC-nominated director on the board of a company (and in April 1970 there were eight) he was clearly responsible for keeping the Corporation informed of the company's progress both financially and in meeting the industrial objectives of the merger. In other cases, Ben Cant was given specific responsibility for conducting follow-up visits and the executive produced regular statistical and financial reports for the IRC Board.

If formal follow-up procedures, and involvement where necessary in finding new top management, were inevitable developments of IRC's role, its increasing activity in promoting 'selective investment' represented a more specific change of emphasis. The reasons for this were set out in the 1969/70 annual report, which included the following observation:

> Britain cannot make everything and must concentrate on doing more of what it does best. IRC has been privileged to see many of the installations of our competitors overseas and is of the view that to keep our place we shall have to renew and extend our industrial apparatus selectively, but on a scale larger than is now taking place. There is a need in Britain for a concerted effort by industry, finance and Government to catch up by massive but selective investment. Many countries have done this successfully; we have a chance to do this now and we should take it (IRC, 1969/70, p. 9).

There were also more specific reasons for the IRC's decision to devote a greater part of its efforts to stimulating investment rather than promoting mergers. By 1969, it had spent several years working intensively to promote reorganisation in some of its priority areas, but with very few tangible results. In addition to the machine tool and process plant industries, examples of this included the private sector steel makers and the wool and cotton textile industries. In these areas, either the IRC could not find a company that was sufficiently strong to become the nucleus for reorganisation or the companies themselves were just not interested. This, together with the problems following the mergers in the process plant sector, convinced the Corporation that it should consider alternative ways of meeting its objective of promoting industrial efficiency and profitability.

In addition, the government had by now come to see the IRC as a body which was very flexible, generally effective and reliable, and acceptable to the bulk of industrialists and to the City. It was therefore very useful for dealing with a number of situations where rapid action was required or where the government wished to support industry at 'arm's length'. So, in 1969 and 1970, the IRC took on several new activities. On its own initiative it promoted the ingenious but controversial scheme (described in Ch. 8) designed to help both British Leyland and UK machine tool producers. It also financed, with mixed success, specific investment schemes for Marwin, Herbert Ingersoll and Kearney and Trecker, all providing facilities for the production of advanced, specialist machine tools. In addition, in the special steels industry, it provided investment funds for Samuel-Osborn. In 1969 the government asked the IRC to investigate the pig processing industry and to comment on 'the future form and levels of financial support from public funds which the industry should receive' (IRC, 1969/70, p. 15). In its annual report, the IRC referred to this as follows: 'An important area of the IRC operations has been acting as the Government's merchant bank in a range of assignments dealing with industrial/financial problems where there is an interface with Government' (IRC, 1969/70, p. 15). This was an explicit reversal of the early conception of the IRC. Indeed, in his seminal speech to the *Financial Times* conference at Strathclyde University in March 1967 (see Ch. 3, p. 27), Grierson had said specifically; 'we are not a state or public merchant bank'.

An even more marked step in this new direction came in June 1970, when the government asked the IRC to administer a scheme to provide investment finance for cotton textile companies. The government had announced its intention to remove quotas on imports of cotton textile goods in 1972, and it saw the IRC as an ideal body to consider applications from companies in the industry for funds to replace or modernise their production facilities in advance of this.

We have also seen, in Chapters 12 and 13, how the government used the IRC for the financial investigation of Rolls-Royce and for the rescue of Cammell Laird.

The IRC's success in these wider activities was mixed, as it was in its merger role. Again this was to be expected, because the IRC was most likely to become involved where firms or industries were already experiencing severe difficulties. The point here is not that the IRC was entirely successful in this wider role, but that the major disadvantage of a predisposition to see the mergers as the only solution to industrial problems was removed. Indeed, of seventeen new projects listed in the IRC Report and Accounts for 1970/71 only three were full-scale mergers. Of the others, three involved the purchase of assets or the transfer of a subsidiary, two were concerned with joint ventures between companies, and nine with investment schemes in individual companies.

The IRC itself saw enormous potential in this 'development bank' role. If it had survived it would certainly have argued for access to far greater funds than the amount of between £30 million and £50 million per annum which it had received as a merger broker. This was a tiny proportion of the total support given by government to encourage industrial investment. But, of course, the IRC did not survive, so its ability to operate effectively as a development bank was never really tested. Nevertheless, in assessing the IRC its potential in this area should not be ignored. Nor should its role as a buffer between the government and particular industries or individual firms. The merits of the decision to rescue Cammell Laird, for example, may be debated, but the skill and speed with which the IRC operated, once the decision had been made, could hardly have been expected from a government department. Government officials have neither the expertise, nor the freedom of action, enjoyed by the IRC.

The intervention of governments in situations like that facing the cotton textile industry, Rolls-Royce and Cammell Laird is probably inevitable. Certainly, intervention has continued under both Conservative and Labour administrations since 1970. Given this, the abolition of the IRC left a gap in the government's apparatus for industrial intervention. It is an interesting question for the City why, even under a Conservative government, it has not proved entirely capable of filling this gap.

A FINAL COMMENT

We have attempted to describe the origins and workings of the IRC, and to trace the development of its role, from a behind-the-scenes agency cautiously encouraging willing industrialists, to an aggressive and self-confident arm of government-sponsored intervention in industry. In the case study chapters, we have given a detailed description of the IRC's role in some of its most significant projects. It has been our intention to provide sufficient material for the reader to gain an understanding of what the IRC did and how it worked. If we have achieved this, we have also provided a basis from which the reader can form his own judgment on the success or failure of the Corporation as well as an indication of the value, or otherwise, of this type of institution as one instrument of government industrial policy.

It is far from easy to summarise our conclusions. Even if the IRC were to be judged solely on its merger role, the task would be difficult. In terms of pure mechanics, the Corporation was surely an outstanding success. It worked quickly and effectively. The executive was a very small, efficient team which undertook an astonishingly large amount of work and did most of it very well. Grierson must take credit for establishing the Corporation's reputation as a sensible, impartial body, and for organising the recruitment of its initial staff. Kearton was, however, the real force behind the emergence of the IRC. It was his drive, vision and organisation that enabled the Corporation to adopt such an active and positive role from the GEC–AEI merger onwards. And it was his statesman-like approach that ensured wide acceptance of this active role for the IRC. Lockwood succeeded Kearton as Chairman but it was Villiers who, under Lockwood's sage direction, took up and developed Kearton's role. The second executive team was recruited, and proved as effective as the first. Villiers' talent for both motivating and controlling his staff was impressive. So too was his ability to identify the achievable and to 'handle' leading industrialists. With the support of Lockwood and the other IRC Board members, he personally oversaw many of the most difficult and delicate negotiations with considerable success. In general, once it entered a merger negotiation, the IRC achieved the deal it wanted.

All this is on the credit side. But, as we have said, it is not possible to be so enthusiastic about the initial concept that the promotion of mergers was a general solution to the UK's industrial problems, nor about the results of some of the deals that were achieved.

We can be more enthusiastic about a body like the IRC with a less specific objective. It might occasionally be used to devise merger schemes and sometimes be asked to seek all-British alternatives to foreign takeover bids. But the majority of its activities would not relate to mergers at all. It would operate more on the lines along which Villiers was guiding the IRC in its final years. It would act as the government's merchant bank and would organise and implement those parts of government policy that were aimed at the individual firm. And it would perhaps reproduce some of the IRC's less tangible benefits. Young and Lowe cite two of these:

> . . . those who dealt with the IRC found its executives to be sensible and helpful. In this connection the IRC fulfilled a further important and useful role. Because the Corporation was part of Whitehall, individuals working for it knew their way around very well. The IRC was thus in a good position to help a firm that wanted to find out the sort of reaction that the Government would make to some proposal by making discreet inquiries. This saved the firm time as it could avoid becoming enmeshed in bureaucratic tangles (Young and Lowe, 1974, p. 89)

and

> The most important intangible result of the IRC activity was probably its direct attempts to persuade institutional investors to be more aware of the responsibilities that came from having large shareholdings in big companies; and indirectly to pressurise them by trying to change the attitude of others like the CBI working in the same field (Young and Lowe, 1974, p. 89).

In these and other ways the IRC tried to help to improve management standards in UK industry, to remove some of the obstacles to good management, and to increase understanding between the government, the City and industry.

It is beyond the scope of this book to debate the extent to which the creation of the National Enterprise Board was an attempt to replace the IRC. One obvious difference was that the NEB was frequently seen as a much more political institution. It may well be that any government would find that it paid to separate the guardianship of public sector companies and public sector shareholdings from the kind of shorter-term intervention that the IRC was beginning to engage in, just before it was abolished.

More recent events imply that there is a clear role for a small, very flexible and, as far as possible, apolitical institution to act as a go-between and to develop an expertise in this difficult area linking government and industry. The IRC could have filled this role had it been allowed to continue in existence. Whether it should have been allowed to do so raises broader issues than we have been able to consider here. It may be that one question all governments should ask is how often institutions of this kind, inherited from their predecessors, should be put into cold storage, for possible reactivation, rather than removed totally from the statute book.

Postscript

The IRC's other Legacy

The IRC fulfilled one more valuable and unusual function. It is often argued that there is a need for a much greater exchange of senior people both between the public and the private sectors of industry and between industry, the City and government. Various attempts have been made to promote this exchange. There are schemes for the secondment of industrial managers to the Department of Industry and other ministries. Private industrialists and bankers are also appointed as non-executive members of the boards of public corporations. But there is still much less movement than many commentators feel is desirable. Moreover, it has often proved to be very difficult to fill senior full-time positions in state-owned corporations with suitable candidates from the private sector. This is no doubt partly due to the problems of working with the government as shareholder, but it is also partly due to the difficulty that managers in the middle of their careers perceive in returning from the public to the private sector.

The IRC provided, without deliberate intent, an ideal body for facilitating this private sector–public sector exchange. We have seen that IRC Board members were mostly senior industrialists from the private sector and also that there was little difficulty in finding people of sufficient calibre and experience to serve in this part-time role. Of more relevance here, though, is the experience with the full-time executive staff.

We have consciously avoided reference to the activities and views of individual IRC executives in the case study chapters in this book. This is because it was the decisions and actions of the IRC Board, or of the executive as a whole acting on behalf of the Board, that were important. In examining this particular contribution of the IRC, however, it is both necessary and interesting to look at the backgrounds of individual executives and at their subsequent careers.

They almost all came from the private sector and the exceptions,

Roger Brooke and David Waterstone, were unusual in that they were both previously career diplomats. There were two border-line cases, Alastair Morton who came from the World Bank and Geoffrey Robinson from Transport House, but there was no-one from the home civil service. Most of the executives had a financial, rather than an industrial, background. There were also two lawyers, Graham Hearne and Lawrence Ziman, and two journalists, Geoffrey Owen and John Gardiner, both from the *Financial Times*. Almost all executives were recruited in their early thirties, and the age range was from twenty-nine to thirty-six.

The executives did not have formal contracts, but it was understood that they would remain with the IRC for only two years. It was felt that this was long enough for them to become known and to achieve something in the sector of industry to which they were allocated. It was thought that after two years, most of their best ideas for rationalisation would have been used up and that it would be time for them to move on. This may or may not have been correct, but it did mean that there were three groups of executives during the life of the IRC. Even with some overlap, there were never more than ten at any one time and only twenty-two people in total were employed as IRC executives – including the two Managing Directors Grierson and Villiers. Moreover, six executives were recruited only in the spring and summer of 1970, when the IRC's effective life was almost over. So, virtually all the day-to-day work described in this book was undertaken by only fourteen people, supported, of course, by the two Managing Directors and the IRC Board, and very occasionally by consultants (and from 1968 to 1970 by three assistant executives).

Given this tiny number, it is of considerable interest that many of the executives have since risen rapidly to very senior positions. Perhaps the most striking is Christopher Hogg. He was a merchant banker with Hill Samuel before joining the IRC with the first group of executives in 1966. He had an MBA from Harvard, on a Harkness Fellowship, but when he joined the IRC he had no direct industrial experience. He specialised in the electrical engineering sector and worked on the two GEC mergers before leaving to join Courtaulds in 1968, as director of International Paint.

It was not surprising that Kearton, as Chairman of both the IRC and Courtaulds, should have recruited Hogg nor, despite his previous experience, that Hogg should have chosen to join a major company in a problem area of British industry. What has been remarkable is his spectacular rise through the company. He joined the main Courtauld's Board in 1973, was made one of three deputy chairmen in 1979 and in 1980 became Chairman and Chief

Executive, following the early retirement of Sir Arthur Knight who had succeeded Kearton. So, at 43, with little more than ten years of industrial experience, Hogg was one of the youngest men at the head of a major UK company.

John Gardiner's background and his achievements after being appointed by the IRC as Managing Director of The Laird Group are set out in Chapter 13. Like Christopher Hogg, he had no previous industrial experience but was successfully running a major company in his mid-thirties. Not only has The Laird Group out-performed most other UK companies in the major problem area of mechanical engineering, Gardiner has also found time to take on a string of public and private sector board appointments. They have included British Airways, British Leyland, the National Enterprise Board, British Shipbuilders, ICL and Courtaulds.

The other IRC financial journalist, Geoffrey Owen, was recruited by Stokes and had a spell with British Leyland's international division. He returned to the *Financial Times* in 1972 as Deputy Editor and in 1980, at the age of 46, was appointed as Editor of this most influential and successful newspaper.

Geoffrey Robinson was also recruited by Stokes and became financial controller of British Leyland in 1971. In 1972, he was made Managing Director of Leyland Innocenti in Milan and, in 1973, he came back to the UK to become chief executive of Jaguar. He was then aged 35. He left British Leyland in 1975 after disagreements arising from the Ryder Report and the subsequent reorganisation of the company. In 1976 he was elected as Labour MP for Coventry North West and his other activities have included guiding the formation and operation of the Meriden Motor Cycle Workers' Cooperative, where he became honorary chief executive.

Alastair Morton was another IRC executive recruited by Kearton, but in this case not until Kearton had left Courtaulds and joined BNOC. Morton himself left the IRC in 1970 and worked in the financial and investment field until 1976. He then became joint Managing Director of BNOC, with responsibility for financial and commercial affairs. He left BNOC in 1980 and in 1982 was appointed, amid much publicity, as Managing Director of Guinness Peat, with a remit to rationalise its activities and strengthen its financial base.

One of the two IRC executives who had had previous industrial experience was Christopher Zealley who came from ICI. Interestingly, he chose not to return to industry and when he left the IRC in 1970 he became Director of the Dartington Hall Trust. This is the progressive and substantial trust, set up in the 1920s, which as well as financing a major co-educational boarding school, runs a chain of companies and co-operative ventures. In 1976, he also became Chairman of the Consumers Association.

Of the two IRC executives with legal backgrounds, Lawrence Ziman decided to return to the law and set up his own firm of solicitors. Graham Hearne initially went into merchant banking. He was one of the first IRC executives, joining in 1966 and leaving for N.M. Rothschild & Sons in 1968. In the late 1970s, however, he decided to move into industry, joining Hogg at Courtaulds as Finance director in 1977. He was already a non-executive director of BNOC and the Dover Harbour Board. Then, in 1981, he moved to become chief executive of the medium-sized oil company Tricentrol.

Roger Brooke left the IRC in 1969 to become managing director of Scienta SA, an organisation set up by a group of European institutions to invest in small and medium-sized companies involved in advanced technology in Europe. In 1971 he moved on to join S. Pearson & Son as an executive director, serving on all the group's main divisional boards, including those of Lazard Brothers and the *Financial Times*. From 1976, he was Vice-Chairman of Pearson Longman Ltd and Chairman of the Longman Group publishing house and of Goldcrest Films. In 1979 he was appointed Group Managing Director of EMI but left in 1980 after the merger with Thorne. He then became the chief executive of Candover, which is an investment company specialising in the organisation and financing of 'management buy-outs'.

David Ewart, a chartered accountant, joined the IRC in 1968 and left in 1970 to work in Jim Slater's banking offshoot. He then moved on to become a director of the merchant bank Guinness Mahon. He had been appointed as a director of Ransome Hoffmann Pollard after the merger of the three UK ball-bearing companies (see Ch. 6). When he left the IRC the company asked him to stay on its Board. He remained with the ball-bearing group in a non-executive capacity, and in 1979 became Chairman of RHP.

The tally, then, is as follows. Among the fourteen IRC executives who served their full two-year term with the Corportaion, there are now two chairmen and three chief executives of major UK companies as well as an MP, the editor of the UK's leading financial newspaper, the chief executive of an investment company and the director of a major trust and Chairman of the Consumers Association.

The careers of some of these men might have been equally impressive without their IRC experience. So, the achievements of the IRC executives reflect in part the recruiting skill of the IRC Board and especially of Grierson and Villiers (who himself, of course, became Chairman of the British Steel Corporation). But it is undoubtedly true that the IRC was an ideal vehicle for giving 'bright young men' experience of both the government machine and of the workings of private industry at the highest level. It is difficult to think of a better bridge for, say, Hogg or Gardiner between their previous financial careers and their subsequent roles in industrial management.

Moreover, it is important that people in senior positions in the private sector should have had some personal experience of working for the government and vice versa. We seem to find this difficult to achieve in this country and any contribution to breaking down the barriers must be welcomed.

It has been suggested that the IRC proved to be not only a very effective means of providing cross-fertilisation between the public and private sectors but that it was a kind of elite state-owned business school. This was 'action learning' with a vengence! In fact few if any business schools, no matter how high the quality of their intakes, can claim such a high success rate for 'graduates' as has been achieved by the IRC executives.

It is possible that if the IRC had lived longer and moved into a development bank role, the high quality of its recruits would not have been maintained. Even so, it seems very likely that it would have continued to provide a unique and valuable training ground for British industrialists of the future.

Appendix A

Summary of Projects

The contents of this appendix has been abstracted from the annual reports of the IRC for the four years from 1967/8 to 1970/71.

PART 1: 1967/8

Publication date	*Payments made in 1967/8*	*Commitments at 31st March 1968*
5th January 1967		
Telecommunications Industry Survey	–	–

The announcement stated that the First Secretary of State, in consultation with the Postmaster General and the Minister of Technology, had invited the IRC to examine the structure of the telecommunications industry and its relations with the Post Office as the major home customer, with the object of seeing whether these could be improved in the national interest. It was also announced that the study would be confidential and that the results would not be published.

The IRC appointed Mr J. P. Berkin, a member of the Corporation, and Mr John Corbett, a partner in Peat Marwick Mitchell & Co., to undertake the study. Their report was

Publication date	*Payments made in 1967/8*	*Commitments at 31st March 1968*
submitted to the Government Departments concerned on 2nd October 1967		
17th January 1967		
Rootes Motors	£1 662 228	£1 350 000
The formal request from the First Secretary of State, which summarises the IRC's part in the arrangements for reconstituting the financial structure of Rootes, is set out [elsewhere]. The IRC acquired from Chrysler Corporation 7 561 140 new 7% Cumulative Preferred Ordinary shares of 4*s* each of Rootes at par. It also subscribed £150 000 for 8% Unsecured Loan Stock 1981 and is committed to subscribe, if requested, a further £1 350 000. The IRC has the right to call upon Chrysler to purchase all the above securities at par on 1st January 1972, together with any accrued but unpaid dividends or interest. It also has the right, while these securities are held, to nominate a director to the Board of Rootes. Mr B. Boxall, a member of the Corporation, was so nominated and joined the Board of Rootes on 7th March 1967.		
22nd June 1967		
The English Electric Company/ Elliott-Automation	£15 000 000	–
The formal offer document sent to the shareholders of Elliott-Automation on 17th July 1967, stated that the IRC recognised the importance to the		

Publication date	*Payments made in 1967/8*	*Commitments at 31st March 1968*
national economy of rapid acceleration of growth in the fields of industrial control and automation, computers and electronics and had agreed to support the merger by the provision of £15 million of new finance. The IRC's investment is in the form of Subordinated Unsecured Loan Stock 1975. The stock is free of interest up to 31st August 1969, and thereafter bears interest payable half-yearly at 8% per annum. The IRC has the right to convert the stock into ordinary shares of English Electric during the years 1973–75. The arrangements regarding payment of interest have approximately the same effect as if the stock were to carry interest at a flat rate of 5½% per annum while it is outstanding. The conversion terms are such that the IRC can, in certain circumstances, realise a capital profit on the disposal of its English Electric Ordinary shares sufficient to bring the total return on its investment up to the equivalent of approximately 7½% per annum over the whole life of the loan. The IRC has stated that it does not intend to hold any English Electric ordinary shares as a long-term investment.		
28th September 1967 **The General Electric Company/ Associated Electrical Industries**	–	–

Publication date	*Payments made in 1967/8*	*Commitments at 31st March 1968*
An exchange of letters between the IRC and the GEC was published in the formal offer document sent to AEI stockholders on 13th October 1967. The IRC's letter confirmed that the proposed combination of the businesses of the GEC and AEI had its full support but added that it was for the shareholders of AEI to decide what was in their own interest. The offer was resisted by the Board of AEI and an exchange of letters dealing with the resignation of Sir Charles Wheeler from the IRC Board and AEI's counter-proposals for rationalisation in the electrical industry was published on 27th October 1967. The GEC offer was successful and the GEC now owns the whole of the ordinary stock of AEI		
24th October 1967		
Dunford & Elliott (Sheffield)/ Hadfields	–	–
The formal offer document sent to the shareholders of Hadfields on 8th November 1967 stated: 'In view of its declared intention of helping constructive measures of rationalisation in the private sector of the steel industry, the Industrial Reorganisation Corporation was consulted at an early stage in the negotiations and gave full encouragement to the merger proposals. The IRC has also expressed its willingness to consider the provision of finan-		

Publication date	*Payments made in 1967/8*	*Commitments at 31st March 1968*
cial support at a future date should this be thought desirable'. The offer was successful.		
30th November 1967		
Paper and Board Industry Survey	–	–
As a consequence of a confidential report on 'structure and productivity' produced by the Paper and Board EDC in June 1967, the British Paper and Board Makers' Association invited the IRC to examine the industry's structure in the light of the EDC's report and to suggest ways in which the industry might proceed. The IRC's report has now been completed.		
6th December 1967		
Nuclear Enterprises	£ 500 000	£100 000
Nuclear Enterprises acquired from Electric & Musical Industries the nucleonic instrument activities carried on at Hayes and Wells, and, from Elliott-Automation, Isotope Developments and the nucleonic instrument activities of the Baldwin Instrument Company. The IRC made a loan of £500 000 to Nuclear Enterprises in connection with these acquisitions and has undertaken to subscribe £100 000 for new ordinary shares, to be paid shortly. The loan is repayable not later than 31st December 1977 and there are provisions for payment of interest in respect of the first two years of the		

Publication date	*Payments made in 1967/8*	*Commitments at 31st March 1968*
loan to be deferred. The IRC's target rate of return, taking both shares and loan together, and the make-up of this return as between fixed interest on the loan and capital gain on disposal of the shares, are broadly similar to those in the English Electric investment outlined above.		
10th January 1968		
Coats Patons/West Riding Worsted and Woollen Mills	–	–
The letter from the Chairman of West Riding which formed part of the formal offer document sent to West Riding shareholders on 29th January 1968 stated: 'Coats Patons and your Company have been willing parties to the proposed operation and the direct assistance of the Industrial Reorganisation Corporation has not been necessary. Both companies, however, wish to acknowledge the interest of the Industrial Reorganisation Corporation in securing an increased measure of rationalisation in the industry and of that organisation's separate approach to both companies on the subject.' The offer, which was for 40% of the issued ordinary capital of West Riding, was successful.		
13th January 1968		
The British Oxygen Company/Edwards High Vacuum International	–	–
The formal offer document sent to the shareholders of		

Publication date	*Payments made in 1967/8*	*Commitments at 31st March 1968*
Edwards on 2nd February 1968 stated that the IRC fully supported the proposed merger in the belief that it would strengthen considerably Britain's position in the high vacuum industry. The IRC indicated to BOC its willingness to make funds available at a later date if required. The offer for both preference and ordinary shares of Edwards was successful.		
17th January 1968		
The Leyland Motor Corporation/British Motor Holdings	–	£25 000 000
The formal offer document despatched on 6th March 1968 on behalf of British Leyland Motor Corporation, the new company formed to acquire the share capitals of Leyland and British Motor Holdings, stated: 'The Industrial Reorganisation Corporation has agreed to make £25 million available to the New Company on terms which are still under negotiation and will be announced later. The request to the Industrial Reorganistion Corporation for this loan has been based on the best estimate which can be made at this stage of the cash and capital requirements of British Motor and Leyland, but a combined capital programme has not yet been completed. It is, however, already clear that the Industrial Reorganisation Corporation loan is essential to enable the New Company to proceed with rat-		

Publication date	*Payments made in 1967/8*	*Commitments at 31st March 1968*
ionalisation and development as rapidly as both the national interest and the interest of the New Company demand.'		

The terms of the IRC loan were announced in an exchange of letters between the IRC and British Leyland published in the press on 26th March 1968. The letter from the IRC stated:

(a) The loan will be for a period of seven years and will be subordinated and unsecured. Interest, payment of which may, if required, be deferred for the first two years, will be equivalent to a rate of 5½% per annum while any part of the loan is outstanding.
(b) If the total ordinary dividend of British Leyland paid in respect of any financial year begun while any part of the loan is outstanding exceeds a rate equivalent to 10% on the initial ordinary share capital of British Leyland when the merger becomes effective, British Leyland will pay an additional amount by way of interest equivalent to 2% per annum on the loan over the whole seven years thus raising the return to IRC the equivalent of 7½% per annum.
(c) British Leyland may repay the loan in whole or in part at any time before the final repayment date at par

Publication date	*Payments made in 1967/8*	*Commitments at 31st March 1968*
plus accrued interest sufficient to bring IRC's return on the amount so repaid over the whole period from the date of advance to the date of repayment, up to the equivalent of 7½% per annum.		
It is expected that the merger will become effective on or about 14th May 1968, and that the loan will be made shortly thereafter.		
18th January 1968		
W. H. Allen Sons & Company/ Belliss & Morcom	–	–
The formal offer document sent to the shareholders of the two companies on 16th February 1968 on behalf of the new company, Amalgamated Power Engineering, stated: 'The Industrial Reorganisation Corporation has welcomed the merger which in its view should lead to improved efficiency in an important section of the engineering industry.' The merger has now become effective		
1st February 1968		
Reed Paper Group	–	£1 500 000
The IRC loan is being provided to help finance two plants to de-ink and reconstitute printed paper. The formal request required for this development loan under Section 2(1)(b) of the IRC Act is set out [elsewhere].		

Publication date	*Payments made in 1967/8*	*Commitments at 31st March 1968*
The loan is a medium-term unsecured loan. The timing of the repayments is based on the anticipated cash flow from the project. Provision is made for interest to be deferred in respect of an initial period. The return which the IRC is scheduled to receive over the life of the loan is equivalent to an annual return at a commercial rate.		
6th February 1968		
Davy–Ashmore Acquisitions	–	–
Davy-Ashmore announced on 21st December 1967 an agreement to acquire The Brightside Foundry and Engineering Company, a wholly owned subsidiary of Brightside Engineering Holdings. It subsequently announced in February 1968 an agreement to acquire from Tube Investments its subsidiary companies, Loewy Robertson Engineering Company and W. H. A. Robertson & Company. The circular sent by the Chairman of Davy-Ashmore on 5th April 1968 to his shareholders gave full information about these acquisitions and stated: 'These acquisitions, which were discussed with and have the full approval and support of the Industrial Reorganisation Corporation, mark an important stage in the rationalisation of the steel and non-ferrous works equipment industry in this country in which your Company is playing a leading part.' The circular went on to state:		

Publication date	*Payment made in 1967/8*	*Commitments at 31st March 1968*
'We shall meet the cost of the two acquisitions out of our own resources and from the facilities which our bankers have agreed to provide if we need them. Should we find at some future date that the process of rationalisation requires the use of longer term funds the IRC has indicated to us that it would be willing to discuss an offer of financial support. For the moment we do not require such support.'		
22nd March 1968		
Whessoe Acquisition	–	£3 500 000
The announcement of the acquisition by Whessoe of the fabrication business of Ashmore, Benson, Pease & Company, a wholly owned subsidiary of Davy-Ashmore, stated: 'The Industrial Reorganisation Corporation has participated in the negotiations and fully agrees that the acquisition will strengthen the British process plant industry and improve the export prospects. The IRC has agreed to lend £3 500 000 to Whessoe Limited for the development of their group and in particular to help finance this transaction'.		
The loan, which is unsecured, is repayable not later than five years from the date of advance. Provision is made for interest to be deferred in respect of an initial period. The return which the IRC is scheduled to receive over the life of the loan is		

Publication date	*Payments made in 1967/8*	*Commitments at 31st March 1968*
equivalent to an annual return at a commercial rate.		
Totals per accounts	£17 162 228	£31 450 000

PART 2: 1968/9

	Payments made in 1968/9	*Commitments at 31st March 1969*
April 1968		
Broom & Wade/Holman	–	–
On the 26th April 1968 Broom & Wade and Holman Bros announced that they proposed to merge their two companies to form The International Compressed Air Corporation. The announcement stated that IRC which had been actively concerned with the negotiations welcomed the merger as a significant strengthening of the British compressed air industry.		
May 1968		
The British Oxygen Company	£2 500 000	–
At the time of the British Oxygen Company's successful offer for Edwards High Vacuum International, the IRC indicated that it would make funds available to BOC at a later date if required to assist and accelerate the development of BOC's activities in the high vacuum industry. In May 1968 IRC made a loan of £2.5 million to BOC. The loan is for a period of eight years, is unsecured and subordinated, and bears interest at the rate of 7½% per annum. It may be repaid in whole or in part at any time at BOC's option.		

Publication date	*Payments made in 1968/9*	*Commitments at 31st March 1969*
June 1968		
George Kent/The Cambridge Instrument Company	£6 504 874	–
June 1968		
Army Kinema Corporation/ Royal Air Force Cinema Corporation	–	–

June 1968

George Kent/The Cambridge Instrument Company

In a contested bid for Cambridge Instrument, IRC announced its support for George Kent's revised offer of 5th June. On 14th June IRC stated that it had purchased a substantial number of Cambridge shares in the market and that it would participate in the underwriting of the Kent offer. The Kent offer was successful. As a result of these actions and subsequent purchases IRC now holds 3 017 577 ordinary shares and 1 244 180 deferred ordinary shares in Kent, representing 24.9% of the equity.

On 5th July the Directors of George Kent invited Mr C. R. E. Brooke as nominee of IRC to join the Board of Kent and agreed to make another seat available to IRC if required. In April, 1969 Mr Brooke left IRC and resigned from the Board of George Kent. Mr M. J. Knight was appointed in his place.

June 1968

Army Kinema Corporation/ Royal Air Force Cinema Corporation

At the invitation of the Ministry of Defence IRC carried out an examination of the Army Kinema Corporation and the Royal Air Force Cinema Corporation. The IRC report recommended in favour of an amal-

Publication date	Payments made in 1968/9	Commitments at 31st March 1969
gamation of the two corporations and detailed arrangements by which this could be accomplished. The merger proposals were carried through.		
July 1968		
Peter Dixon	£350 000	–
A loan of £350 000 has been made to help finance a plant to de-ink and reconstitute printed paper. The formal request required for this development loan under Section 2(1)(b) of the IRC Act is set out [elsewhere]. The loan was made in two tranches, the second being drawn on 1st October 1968. It is unsecured and is repayable in equal instalments from 31st September 1969 to 31st March 1971. The overall rate of interest is 7⅞% and the company has exercised its option to defer the interest payments due in the first year of the loan.		
July 1968		
Nuclear Reorganisation		
On 17th July the Minister of Technology invited IRC 'to assist the nuclear industry in the creation of two design and construction organisations to be established in place of the three commercial firms and the design teams working within the Atomic Energy Authority'.		
It was announced on 16th September that IRC would join with Babcock & Wilcox, English Electric, Taylor Woodrow Con-	£26	–

Publication date	*Payments made in 1968/9*	*Commitments at 31st March 1969*
struction and the AEA in establishing Babcock English Electric Nuclear (subsequently renamed British Nuclear Design & Construction). IRC took up 26% of the equity and nominated to the Board Mr R. A. Morton who has subsequently been succeeded by Mr L. D. Ziman as from 15th May 1969. IRC has since committed itself to subscribe £260 000. On 15th January 1969 an announcement was made that IRC would join with Reyrolle Parsons, Sir Robert McAlpine & Sons, Clarke Chapman, John Thompson, Head Wrightson, Strachan & Henshaw, Whessoe and the AEA in establishing The Nuclear Power Group. IRC took up 10% of the equity as from 1st April 1969 and nominated Mr J. P. Berkin to the Board. IRC has since committed itself to subscribe £150 000.		
August 1968		
Davy Ashmore/Armstrong Whitworth	–	–
On 13th August it was announced that Davy Ashmore was to make an agreed offer for the whole of the issued share capital of Armstrong Whitworth (Metal Industries). This received the full support of IRC as 'a further important step in the process of rationalisation in the steel and non-ferrous equipment industry in the United Kingdom'. On this occasion, as when Davy Ashmore earlier acquired		

Publication date	*Payments made in 1968/9*	*Commitments at 31st March 1969*
Loewy Robertson Engineering Co. and Brightside Foundry and Engineering Co., IRC expressed its willingness to discuss financial support for Davy Ashmore if this should become necessary. On 28th April 1969 IRC announced that it was joining with Finance Corporation for Industry in making up to £4 million available to Davy Ashmore on terms which provide for interest at 8% per annum and an option to convert one quarter of the loan into shares of Davy Ashmore at a price equivalent to 15/– per share.		
September 1968		
The General Electric Company/ The English Electric Company On 6th September GEC and English Electric announced their intention to merge, and on 13th September IRC gave its support to the merger having obtained certain assurances from the two companies. These assurances referred among other things to the proposed new company's intention (a) to confer with the appropriate trade unions and government departments about any matters arising from the merger which would significantly affect the workpeople, and with appropriate government departments about other action having an important bearing on the government's regional policies, and (b) to appoint one director on the Board of the new company in consultation with IRC and to		

Publication date	Payments made in 1968/9	Commitments at 31st March 1969
renegotiate the £15 million IRC loan to English Electric repayable in 1975 (made at the time of EE's acquisition of Elliot-Automation). Following this, £5 million was repaid on 31st March 1969, together with interest on the whole of the loan up to that date at 5½% per annum; the terms of the remaining £10 million have been renegotiated so as to provide for repayment by instalments and in full by 31st August 1971, at an effective rate of interest of slightly below 6% per annum.	(£5 000 000) (repayment)	–
September 1968		
National Film Finance Corporation Report	–	–
IRC undertook to advise the President of the Board of Trade on the capital structure of the National Film Finance Corporation and on the commercial and financial aspects of its operations. It was agreed that the report would be confidential and that the results would not be published. The IRC appointed Mr A. G. B. Burney, OBE, Partner, Binder, Hamlyn & Co., and Mr D. Berriman, Managing Director, Morgan Grenfell & Co., to carry out the study. Their report was submitted on 14th January 1969.		
November 1968		
The Weir Group/Harland Engineering Company	–	–
On 29th October The Weir Group made an offer for		

Publication date	*Payments made in 1968/9*	*Commitments at 31st March 1969*
Harland Engineering Company. Subsequently Mather & Platt announced a counter offer. IRC considered both proposals and concluded that it was not possible to state definitely that one was superior to the other from the point of view of the rationalisation and development of the pump industry. In IRC's view the merger of Harland Engineering with either Mather & Platt or Weir would be a useful first step in strengthening the industry. IRC did not, therefore, take sides The Weir offer was successful.		
November 1968		
Sigmund Pulsometer Pumps/ Plenty & Son The merger between Sigmund Pulsometer Pumps and Plenty & Son Ltd was announced on 29th November. The announcement stated 'IRC, which has been consulted during the negotiations, welcomes the proposed merger which it regards as another step forward in the rationalisation of the pump manufacturing industry'.	–	–
December 1968		
The British Rollmakers Corporation/Johnsons' Rolls On 31st December, The British Rollmakers Corporation announced that it had acquired the business and trading assets of Johnson's Rolls Ltd. IRC, which had already supported rationalisation in this industry, welcomed the acquisition.	–	–

Publication date	*Payments made in 1968/9*	*Commitments at 31st March 1969*
January 1969 **The Weir Group/Studebaker-Worthington Inc.**	–	–

The Weir Group and Studebaker-Worthington Inc. made it known on 3rd January that they were having discussions with IRC on the future development of the British pump industry. Both companies had previously made bids for Worthington-Simpson, a British company in which Studebaker-Worthington had a minority interest. The companies asked IRC to arbitrate as to which should proceed with a bid for Worthington-Simpson if their wider discussions broke down. By 21st February the two companies had reached agreement to establish a joint company to promote the sale of various products on an international basis and for Studebaker-Worthington to proceed with a bid for Worthington-Simpson. IRC was not, therefore, called upon to arbitrate. IRC welcomed the agreement as being of great benefit to the pump industry in the UK.

January 1969 **Racal Electronics/Controls & Communications**	–	–

Racal Electronics and Controls & Communications announced terms on 7th January for merging the two companies. The formal offer document sent to the shareholders of Controls & Communications stated the

Publication date	*Payments made in 1968/9*	*Commitments at 31st March 1969*
following: 'The IRC welcomes the proposed merger as an important step in the strengthening of the communications industry. The company has agreed to study in cooperation with the IRC further rationalisation proposals concerning the activities of the group'.		
January 1969		
British Leyland Motor Corporation	£15 000 000	£10 000 000 (Paid 1st April 1969)

At the time of the merger of the Leyland Motor Corporation and British Motor Holdings, IRC agreed to make available £25 million in the form of subordinated loan capital for a period of up to seven years. £15 million of this loan was taken up in August 1968, and the balance on 1st April 1969. For the period to 30th September 1968, British Leyland paid a total ordinary dividend of 11%. Under the loan agreement British Leyland will pay interest at 7½% per annum over the whole period of the loan.

In the British Leyland 1968 Annual Report and Accounts the Chairman stated: 'This report on the progress of the merger would be incomplete without a reference to the part which the Industrial Reorganisation Corporation played in the original discussions. They made a particularly valuable contribution to the negotiations preceding the merger'. With

Publication date	*Payments made in 1968/9*	*Commitments at 31st March 1969*
regard to the IRC loan, the purpose of which was to assist in the financing of the rationalisation and expansion programme, the report continued: 'Our net cash balance at 30th September 1968, after deducting bank overdrafts, short term loans and purchase tax, was just over £½ million. Over the next four years we expect to spend more than £200 million on modernisation and expansion of production facilities and on tooling for new models. In addition substantial amounts of cash will be required in winter months to assist in the financing of distributors' stocks. However, taking into account the balance of the loan from the Industrial Reorganisation Corporation which we plan to draw in April, other available borrowings, and our likely cash flow we do not foresee any major difficulty in financing these requirements'.		
January 1969		
IRC Offer for Brown Bayley	£5 370 000	£448 300
On 30th January 1969 IRC announced its intention of making an offer for the whole of the issued share capital of Brown Bayley Ltd, which had a controlling interest of 4 800 000 ordinary 5*s* shares in The Hoffmann Manufacturing Company and a controlling interest of 1 202 000 ordinary 10*s* shares in Brown Bayley Steels. The terms of the offer were:		

Publication date		*Payments made in 1968/9*	*Commitments at 31st March 1969*
For each Brown Bayley Ltd share	45*s* in cash plus one unit of partici- pation		

The unit of participation was designed so that, in the event of IRC disposing of Brown Bayley Ltd's investments in The Hoffmann Manufacturing Company and Brown Bayley Steels at an aggregate price which after deducting expenses exceeded the basic cash consideration, the surplus would be passed on to existing Brown Bayley Ltd shareholders.

The terms of the offer for Brown Bayley were increased on 13th February, to 48*s* in cash plus one unit of participation. This revision to the terms was accompanied by a recommendation from the Board of Brown Bayley, together with their financial advisers, Lazard Brothers & Co. Ltd, that the offer was fair and reasonable and should be accepted.

The IRC offer was successful.

On 11th March, Mr C. H. Villiers and Mr B. R. Cant were appointed to the Board of Brown Bayley Ltd, the former being elected Chairman. The following appointments were made to the Boards of the subsidiary companies on 8th April:

> Brown Bayley Steels: Mr B. R. Cant, Director; Mr R. Morton, Director; Mr J. H. Chaplin, Joint Secretary.

Publication date	*Payments made in 1968/9*	*Commitments at 31st March 1969*
The Hoffmann Manufacturing Company: Mr B. R. Cant, Joint Vice-Chairman; Mr D. J. Ewart, Director; Mr J. H. Chaplin, Joint Secretary.		
January 1969 **Donside Paper Mill**	£ 2 000 000	–
Agreement was reached on 31st January between The Inveresk Paper Company, Reed Paper Group and The Bowater Paper Corporation, for the joint acquisition by Bowater and Reed of the Donside Paper Mill, Aberdeen. The purchase was the result of an initiative by IRC which made a loan to Reed and Bowater of £1 million each. The loans are for eight years and are unsecured. The overall rate of interest is 8¼% and the companies have an option to defer interest payments for the first year, or the first two years of the loan. The announcement stated: 'The sale of Donside and the proposed joint marketing agreement will assist the rationalisation of coated paper production and marketing in the U.K. and it is in accord with regional policy and with the recommendations of the IRC Report on the Paper Industry'.		
February 1969		
Pegler Hattersley/Newman Hender	–	–
Serck made an offer for Newman Hender & Co. on 10th February. IRC considered this initiative as a possible first step		

Publication date	*Payments made in 1968/9*	*Commitments at 31st March 1969*
in restructuring the valve industry. However, the Serck bid was rejected by Newman Hender, who then agreed terms for a merger with Pegler Hattersley. In IRC's view, this merger was a viable alternative towards the rationalisation and strengthening of the industry. The merger proposals were carried through.		
February 1969		
Clarke Chapman Acquisitions	£2 000 000	–
On 21st February an agreement was announced for Clarke Chapman & Co. to make an offer for the entire ordinary and preference share capital of Sir William Arrol & Co. This was welcomed by IRC which was involved with the discussions throughout. IRC was also involved in the talks which led to the announcement on 4th March that Clarke Chapman had further agreed to acquire the crane-making interests of The Wellman Engineering Group, namely Wellman Machines, Wellman Structures and Wellman Boyd. An IRC loan of £2 million to Clarke Chapman was negotiated to assist the rationalisation of this part of the crane industry. The terms provided for payment of interest to be deferred until 31st December 1970, but so as to assure IRC a return of 9% per annum on repayment on or before 31st December 1975, Clarke Chapman have the option to		

Publication date	*Payments made in 1968/9*	*Commitments at 31st March 1969*
repay £1 million on 31st December 1970, subject to satisfaction of this interest requirement.		
March 1969		
Guest, Keen & Nettlefolds Acquisition	–	–
On 12th March, GKN announced their acquisition of R. H. Windsor, a subsidiary of General & Engineering Industries. This move was supported by IRC as an important step towards strengthening the plastics machinery industry.		
March 1969		
Dobson Hardwick/William Park & Co. (Forgemasters)	–	–
It was announced on 18th March that Dobson Hardwick and William Park had reached agreement on terms for merging the two companies. The formal offer document dispatched on 18th April on behalf of the new company Dobson Park Industries stated: 'The National Coal Board and the Industrial Reorganisation Corporation have given full support and encouragement to the proposed merger, which in their view should lead to improved efficiency in an important section of the mining equipment industry'.		
March 1969		
Reyrolle Parsons/Bruce Peebles	–	–
Reyrolle Parsons and Bruce Peebles agreed terms on 28th		

Publication date	*Payments made in 1968/9*	*Commitments at 31st March 1969*
March for a merger. The announcement stated: 'This merger will bring together two groups having major interests in the manufacture of transformers and electric motors and will further strengthen the outstanding position which Reyrolle Parsons has already achieved in the heavy electric manufacturing industry. The merger has been fully discussed with IRC, which has given its support to the proposals and has agreed to consider making finance available to the enlarged group to assist with its subsequent development'. Early in April IRC agreed to supply a standby credit of up to £4 million to be available at three months notice, up to the end of 1972. The loan would be for a maximum of five years at a rate to be agreed at the time the money is drawn if it is required. It would be unsecured and repayable without penalty at any time after two years.		
March 1969 **Bacon Curing Industry**	–	–
On 25th March it was announced that IRC had agreed, at the invitation of the Ministry of Agriculture, Fisheries & Food, to make an independent and confidential examination of the structure of the bacon industry, including a study of existing and alternative forms of government support. The statement went on: 'It is the policy of the government to encourage the		

Publication date	Payments made in 1968/9	Commitments at 31st March 1969
expansion of British bacon production based on the curing industry's efficient use of resources. The purpose of IRC's examination is to see whether further strengthening of the industry's organisation and competitive position is possible'.		
April 1969		
Ross Group/Associated Fisheries	–	–
On 2nd April 1969, Associated Fisheries and Ross Group agreed in principle the terms for forming a new jointly owned company on which their trawling interests will be combined under a single management. The announcement stated: 'IRC has been closely concerned in the negotiations leading to the formation of the company, and has been invited to nominate a Director to the Board'. It was also agreed that the Chairman would be appointed in consultation with IRC.		
In the period under review the following transactions not referred to elsewhere in this summary also took place in relation to IRC's investments and commitments, the full details of which were given in the first IRC Report and Accounts:		
Whessoe	£3 500 000	–
From April to June 1968, £3 500 000 was advanced to Whessoe pursuant to IRC's commitment.		

Publication date	*Payments made in 1969/70*	*Commitments at 31st March 1970*
Reed Paper Group In June 1968 and January 1969 £500 000 each were advanced to Reed Paper Group pursuant to IRC's commitment. The last tranche of £500 000 will be advanced in July 1969.	£1 000 000	£500 000
Nuclear Enterprises In June 1968, £100 000 was subscribed for 'B' ordinary shares in Nuclear Enterprises pursuant to IRC's commitment.	£100 000	–
Rootes Motors In March 1969, IRC was released from its commitment to Chrysler Corporation to subscribe £1 350 000 8% Unsecured Loan Stock 1981 of Rootes Motors.	–	–
Totals per accounts	£33 324 900	£10 948 300

Changes in Commitments during 1968/9

Of £31 450 000 commitments outstanding at 31st March 1968, £19 600 000 was paid during the year under review, and the Corporation was released from a commitment of £1 350 000, leaving £10 500 000 which, together with a commitment of £448 300 entered into but not paid during 1968/9, represents the total commitment of £10 948 300 outstanding at 31st March 1969.

Publication date	*Payments made in 1969/70*	*Commitments at 31st March 1970*
PART 3: 1969/70		
April 1969		
Rowntree/Mackintosh	–	–
The Directors of Rowntree and Company and John Mackintosh and Sons announced on 2nd April that they had agreed terms for a merger of their two companies. IRC had studied the industrial merits of the proposed merger and supported the conclusion of both companies that it represented an important step towards concentrating the resources of this sector of the UK food industry, and added strength to its overseas capability.		
April 1969		
Allied Textiles/H. F. Hartley	£1 000 000	–
On 18th April Allied Textile Companies and H. F. Hartley announced their intention of merging their two companies. The announcement stated that IRC had been consulted and welcomed the agreement as a valuable step forward in the rationalisation and integration of the woollen and worsted textile industry and indicated that IRC would be prepared to consider a case for providing finance for subsequent re-equipment and re-organisation. The merger proposals were carried through towards the end of May 1969. On 2nd June, 1969 IRC made a loan of £1.0 million to the company repayable on 30th May 1975 or earlier		

Publication date	*Payments made in 1969/70*	*Commitments at 31st March 1970*
at the company's option. Interest is payable at 9½% per annum and the loan is unsecured.		
April 1969		
Reyrolle Parsons/Bruce Peebles	–	–
At the time of the announcement of the Reyrolle Parsons/ Bruce Peebles merger IRC agreed to consider making finance available to the enlarged group to assist with its subsequent development. Early in April IRC agreed to supply a standby credit of up to £4 million in connection with expenditure on rationalisation and upon proof of need.		
April/May 1969		
Ransome & Marles/Hoffmann/ Pollard		
On 30th April Ransome & Marles Bearing Company announced its intention to make an offer for the ordinary share capital of Pollard Ball and Roller Bearing Company. The announcement stated, 'The present offer is the outcome of discussions which have taken place over several months between leading manufacturers in the UK and IRC with a view to strengthening the industry and forming a strong British-controlled bearing group capable of competing in world markets. For this purpose it is envisaged that the acquisition of Pollard by Ransome & Marles will be followed by the addition		

Publication date	*Payments made in 1969/70*	*Commitments at 31st March 1970*
of The Hoffmann Manufacturing Company'. Subsequently a revised offer was announced on 13th May. In order to assist Ransome & Marles in implementing the revised offer, IRC undertook to subscribe at par for up to £6.7 million Convertible Loan Stock 1984 in Ransome & Marles, to be offered as consideration for the ordinary share capital of Pollard, in so far as the stock was not taken up by Pollard shareholders. This resulted in IRC subscribing £6 211 004 for the stock. The Board of Pollard agreed to recommend the revised offer on 21st May and the offer was successful.	£6 211 000	–
On 13th May the Boards of Ransome & Marles and Hoffmann (controlled by IRC through its ownership of Brown Bayley Limited) announced agreed terms for a merger of their respective companies. These proposals were successfully implemented.		
In addition to the above IRC agreed to make a loan of £3 118 000 to Ransome & Marles to assist in effecting offers for Hoffmann and Pollard. Payment of interest may be deferred at the option of Ransome & Marles until 30th June 1973 and the minimum rate of interest of 5½% will be raised by reference to increases in the rate of dividend on the ordinary shares. The loan is unsecured and is repayable on 30th June 1976 or earlier at the company's option.	£3 118 000	–

Publication date	*Payments made in 1969/70*	*Commitments at 31st March 1970*
IRC also purchased a small number of ordinary shares of Ransome & Marles in the market. Mr B. R. Cant and Mr D. J. Ewart represent IRC on the Board of Ransome Hoffmann Pollard.	£132 000	–
July 1969		
British United Trawlers	–	–
On 1st July, British United Trawlers was formed, bringing under joint management the fleets of Ross Group and Associated Fisheries. IRC was closely involved in the negotiations with the companies and the government. Mr B. Boxall was invited to be Chairman of the company and Mr C. B. Zealley is a director representing IRC.		
May 1969		
Fletcher & Stewart/Sutcliffe/Wild	–	–
The merger of Fletcher & Stewart, Richard Sutcliffe and A. G. Wild and Company was anounced on 7th May. The statement included the following reference to IRC, 'The IRC initiated the negotiations and both it and the National Coal Board welcome the merger as a significant step forward in the rationalisation of the mining equipment industry'.		
June 1969		
Dowty Group/Bonser Engineering	–	–
On 2nd June Dowty Group and		

Publication date	*Payments made in 1969/70*	*Commitments at 31st March 1970*
Bonser Engineering announced their intention to merge the mining equipment business carried on by Dowty Mining Equipment and Bonser Engineering. The announcement stated, 'These proposals are made in order to take full advantage of the rationalisation of the mining equipment industry which is proceeding at the initiative of the National Coal Board and IRC, who are fully in support of this amalgamation'.		
July 1969		
BICC Acquisition	–	–
On 17th July, Insulated British Callenders Cables and Associated Electrical Industries announced that agreement had been reached for BICC to acquire the business of the Supertension Cable and Construction Division and the Transmission Line Division of AEI as from 1st August 1969. The IRC assisted in the nogotiations leading to this acquisition and agreed to offer a standby facility of up to £2.5 million available subject to proof of need up to 30th June 1970.		
July 1969		
Pirelli/Enfield-Standard	–	–
On 17th July Pirelli General Cable works and Enfield-Standard Power Cables announced their intention to rationalise their production of super-		

Publication date	*Payments made in 1969/70*	*Commitments at 31st March 1970*
tension cables by the creation of a new joint company. The anouncement stated, 'The negotiations have been conducted throughout with the closest possible co-operation with the IRC and the Board of Trade, both of whom have given all possible assistance'.		
July 1969		
Weir Group/Osborn-Hadfields	£1 250 000	–
On 24th July the Weir Group announced that it had agreed to acquire Osborn-Hadfields Steel Founders Limited owned by Samuel-Osborn & Co. and Dunford & Elliot (Sheffield). The IRC had been in close touch with all the parties concerned and with other steel founders. It welcomed the proposed move as an important first step in the restructuring of the steel castings industry. In order to assist Weir in its rationalisation programme IRC agreed to provide finance of up to £1.25 million. This was taken up on 30th October 1969, repayable on 30th September 1976 or earlier at the company's discretion. The loan is interest free for two years and later payments are calculated to give a return to IRC equivalent to 10¼% per annum over the whole life of the loan.		
July, 1969		
Davy-Ashmore		
On 30th July, following the announcement of a serious		

Publication date	*Payments made in 1969/70*	*Commitments at 31st March 1970*
overrun on a major contract, it was announced that IRC, Finance Corporation for Industry and the company's bankers were joining to make £5 million available to Davy-Ashmore. £1.2 million of this was provided by IRC; £600 000 by a short-term unsecured loan, guaranteed by the institutions standing surety for completion of the contract, and at a rate of interest linked to bank rate, and	£600 000	–
£600 000 in the form of a secured loan, advanced on 11th August, repayable on 30th September 1974, and at 10½% interest.	£600 000	–
On 1st August IRC announced that Davy-Ashmore and Simon Engineering had accepted its invitation to start talks on the possibility of the two groups forming a closer association. On 9th October it was announced that, 'detailed and constructive discussions have revealed that the industrial, financial and managerial positions of the two groups do not fit sufficiently well to justify a close association'.		
September 1969		
Steel Group/Priestman	£1 000 000	£500 000
The Steel Group and Priestman Brothers announced on 8th September that they had agreed a basis for a merger of their two companies. The formal offer document contained the following reference. 'The IRC welcomes the proposed merger as a means of strengthening an		

Publication date	*Payments made in 1969/70*	*Commitments at 31st March 1970*
important sector of the crane and construction equipment industry in the UK. The IRC will make available £1 million to assist the rationalisation and development of the crane and construction equipment business of the group'. In addition a further £500 000 standby is available up to 30th June 1970 for the purpose of further rationalisation and development and subject to proof of need. Interest is payable on the loan at 10¾% and on the standby on terms to be agreed. Both are unsecured and repayable on 31st March 1973 or earlier at the company's option.		
September 1969		
BTR/Leyland & Birmingham	–	–
BTR Industries and Leyland and Birmingham Rubber Company announced on 17th September that they had agreed terms for a merger of the two companies. The announcement stated, 'The proposed merger has been fully discussed with IRC and in their view represents a constructive move towards the rationalisation of the rubber manufacturing industry'.		
October 1969		
Airmec/Plessey	–	–
Following detailed discussions with IRC and the Ministry of Technology, the first major step in the rationalisation and reorganisation of the numerical control sector of the machine tool		

Publication date	*Payments made in 1969/70*	*Commitments at 31st March 1970*
industry was announced on 1st October, when Racal Electronics announced that it had agreed to sell the numerical control business of its subsidiary Airmec-AEI to The Plessey Company.		
October 1969		
Bacon Curing Industry	–	–
In October IRC submitted its report on the bacon curing industry to the Ministry of Agriculture, Fisheries and Food. The report contained a confidential assessment of the structure and efficiency of the industry and specific recommendations for a revision of the Bacon Curing Stabilisation Scheme. The short-term adjustments recommended in the report were implemented by the government from the beginning of January, 1970.		
November 1969		
Lucas Acquisition	£3 000 000	–
On 18th November Joseph Lucas (Industries) announced that its aircraft equipment subsidiary, Rotax, had acquired from The General Electric and English Electric Companies the business of English Electric Company's Special Products Group. The statement contained the following paragraph, 'The IRC fully supports the merger of the two businesses as a significant contribution to the rationalisation of the UK effort in the aircraft equipment field. The IRC carried out a det-		

Publication date	*Payments made in 1969/70*	*Commitments at 31st March 1970*
ailed investigation of the industry and concluded that the combined businesses of Rotax and SPG will open new opportunities abroad as well as ensuring the full usage of the considerable R & D effort in this field made by the two businesses. In order to achieve these benefits the IRC has made a loan of £3 million to Lucas repayable on 14th November, 1973'. the loan is unsecured and carries interest at a rate of 10¾% per annum.		
November 1969		
Aeroquip/Super Oil Seals	–	–
It was announced on 27th November that Aeroquip Corporation of the US was proposing to make an offer for Super Oil Seals and Gaskets. The formal offer document released on 18th December stated that, 'IRC has been informed of the offer and has discussed with Aeroquip Corporation their objectives for the accelerated rate of production and investment at Super Oil and notes in particular the intended increase in exports from the UK. The IRC supports these objectives as making a valuable contribution to the economy of the UK'.		
December 1969		
Plessey/Ferranti	£3 000 000	–
On 11th December The Plessey Company and Ferranti announced their agreement to merge their numerical control activities through a sale of		

Publication date	*Payments made in 1969/70*	*Commitments at 31st March 1970*
Ferranti's interests to Plessey. Following the earlier acquisition of Airmec by Plessey, IRC fully supported this as achieving a strong UK presence in this important field. The IRC subsequently agreed on 26th March 1970 to make £3 million available for the purpose of accelerating the development of Plessey Numerical Controls repayable on 31st March 1976. The rate of interest rises over the life of the loan and a levy is payable on redemption geared to the growth of the business. Sir Steuart Mitchell has agreed to act as IRC's nominee on the Board of the new company.		
December 1969 **ICAC/Reavell**	–	–
On 17th December it was announced that International Compressed Air Corporation had agreed terms for the purchase of Reavell & Company, manufacturers of air compressors and exhausters, from James Howden & Godfrey. The IRC welcomed this step as a logical extension of the original Broom & Wade/Holman merger which had created ICAC.		
December 1969 **Dowty Group/Anderson Mavor**	–	–
The Dowty Group announced on 31st December that they proposed to merge their mining equipment interests with those of Anderson Mavor. On		

Publication date	Payments made in 1969/70	Commitments at 31st March 1970
account of subsequent downward revision in NCB requirements for some of Anderson Mavor's products, Dowty stated that it could not proceed with the merger in its present form. Negotiations are continuing between the parties concerned.		
January 1970		
Hawker Siddeley/Brook	–	–
On 21st January Hawker Siddeley Group and Brook Motors announced that they had agreed terms for a merger. On 11th March Hawker Siddeley announced that the offer had been successful and IRC stated, 'In recent months IRC have had discussions with the major electric motor manufacturers and as a result formed the view that greater concentration was desirable particularly in standard motors. IRC therefore encouraged Hawker Siddeley and Brook to reach agreement to merge and welcomes the news that the offer has been successful. The merger should lead, through increased investment, to substantial economies of scale in production, and is an important step towards rationalising the electric motor industry'.		
January 1970		
Klinger/Qualitex	£2 000 000	–
The Klinger Manufacturing Company and Qualitex Yarns announced their intention to merge early in January. In the		

Publication date	*Payments made in 1969/70*	*Commitments at 31st March 1970*
formal offer document dispatched on 5th February it was stated, 'Both ICI and IRC have been kept informed of the progress of the merger negotiations since their commencement. The proposed merger has received their full support and they are making facilities available to the new group with a view to ensuring that the benefits of the merger can be achieved'. On 24th March it was announced that IRC had made a loan of £2 million to Klinger, bearing interest at 9%, with provisions for deferment of interest. The loan is repayable at IRC's option between 31st July 1973 and 30th April 1975. IRC has the right to have £1.75 million of the loan converted into up to 2.5 million of the ordinary shares of Ernest Scragg & Sons (Holdings) held by Klinger. The name of Klinger has subsequently been changed to Qualitex.		
February 1970		
Samuel-Osborn	–	£1 750 000
On 11th February it was announced that Samuel-Osborn & Co. had concluded arrangements under which IRC would make available up to £1.75 million under Section 2(1)(b) of the IRC Act to enable the company to proceed with the rationalisation and re-equipment of its special steelmaking and processing facilities. An initial £1 million will be drawn by mid-1971 and the		

Publication date	*Payments made in 1969/70*	*Commitments at 31st March 1970*
balance may be drawn by end-1972. The sums will be repaid within 4 years of drawing and will bear interest at rates in line with the market rate at the time each loan is made. IRC anticipates that this project will materially strengthen the special steels industry in the UK. The loans are secured and repayable at the company's option.		
March 1970		
Marwin	£750 000	£750 000
On 25th March IRC announced that it had agreed to make available up to £1.5 million to Marwin (Holdings) to enable the company to continue its expansion in the production of numerically controlled machine tools. £750 000 was taken up immediately in the form of a convertible loan at 8% interest with an initial life of 5 years. The conversion rights, which are exercisable at IRC's option, would, if fully exercised, give IRC 10% of the enlarged equity. The further £750 000 is available at the company's option between 1st January 1971 and 1st January 1974 on proof of need. The loan will bear interest in line with market rates at the time of drawing, and will last for a period of five years, repayable earlier at the company's option.		
In the period under review the following transactions not referred to elsewhere in this sum-		

Publication date	*Payments made in 1969/70*	*Commitments at 31st March 1970*
mary also took place in relation to IRC's investments and commitments:		
British Leyland Motor Corporation		
On 1st April 1969 IRC advanced £10 million to BLMC pursuant to its commitment.	£10 000 000	–
Reed Paper Group		
In July 1969 the final tranche of £500 000 was advanced to Reed pursuant to IRC's commitment.	£500 000	–
Peter Dixon & Sons		
Instalments of £175 000 in repayment of the loan under the terms of the agreement were received from Peter Dixon	(£175 000)	–
English Electric Company	(£2 500 000)	–
During the year under review a further £2.5 million was repaid by English Electric Company in accordance with the revised arrangements made, following the merger of that company with The General Electric Company, for the early repayment by instalments of the original loan of £15 million of which £5 million was repaid on 31st March 1969.		
The terms of the original loan provided an interest free period until 31st August 1969. Under the terms of the revised arrangements interest at 5½% on £15 million was paid on 31st March 1969 in respect of the preceding nineteen month per-		

Publication date	*Payments made in 1969/70*	*Commitments at 31st March 1970*
iod, but no further interest was was payable on the balance of £10 million in respect of the remaining five months of the interest free period to 31st August 1969; thereafter interest accrues at 8% per annum payable half-yearly on the outstanding balances. (The effective rate of interest accruing on that part of the loan outstanding from 1st April 1969 to the final repayment date of 31st August 1971 is slightly under 6% per annum.)		
Davy-Ashmore		
£300 000 of the short-term loan to Davy-Ashmore was repaid on 31st March 1970.	(£300 000)	–
British Nuclear Design & Construction	£260 000	£2 340 000
In June 1969, £259 974 was subscribed for 259 974 ordinary £1 shares (at par) in British Nuclear Design and Construction. IRC's investment represents 26% of the equity. The shareholders have also agreed to lend or guarantee up to £9 million if required of which IRC's share is £2 340 000.		
The Nuclear Power Group	£150 000	£850 000
Between April and July 1969, IRC subscribed £150 000 for 150 000 ordinary shares (at par), representing 10% of the equity of The Nuclear Power Group. The shareholders have also agreed to subscribe up to £8.5 million loan capital if required of which IRC's share is £850 000.		

Publication date	*Payments made in 1969/70*	*Commitments at 31st March 1970*
The Hoffmann Manufacturing Company	(£840 000)	–
As part of the consideration for the sale of the 4 800 000 shares in Hoffmann to Ransome & Marles Bearing Company, Brown Bayley received £840 000 in cash, thus reducing IRC's cost of investment in Brown Bayley by that amount.		
Totals per accounts	£29 756 000	£6 190 000

PART 4: 1970/71

Publication date	*Payments made in 1970/71*	*Commitments at 30th April 1971*
April 1970		
Portals/Permutit		
In April it was announced that Portals Holdings Limited had made an offer for the Permutit Company Limited. The IRC was consulted in detail about the proposals for consolidation in the water treatment and allied fields. It welcomed the proposed link 'as a step which should lead to increasingly effective UK effort in international markets'.	–	–
May 1970		
Booker McConnell		
In May, it was announced that Booker McConnell had sold the Gateshead Division of SPP Group to Ingersoll-Rand Pumps. The sale of the Gateshead Division was in line with the policy	–	–

Publication date	*Payments made in 1970/71*	*Commitments at 30th April 1971*
of consolidating SPP's leading position in the fluid-handling field. The acquisition of the Gateshead Division by Ingersoll-Rand Pumps would enable the range of Gateshead products to be extended. The IRC welcomed these developments for the contribution they would make to the planned increase in the activity and exports of both companies.		
May 1970 **Miles Roman** In May, IRC announced that it had undertaken to provide assistance to Miles Roman Limited should this prove necessary in connection with the company's acquisition and development of General Precision Systems from Singer Corporation. This represented the IRC's first direct financial stake in the software industry. Miles Roman was given an option, exercisable between 1971 and 1973, to require IRC to subscribe £211 000 for a small stake in the Miles Roman equity. If the option is not exercised, the IRC has the right in 1973 to take up shares to the same total value, but at a higher price per share, geared to earnings.	–	£211 000
May 1970 **Rolls-Royce** The Minister of Technology invited the IRC in August 1969 to examine and report on the overall viability of Rolls-Royce's fut-	£10 000 000	–

Publication date	*Payments made in 1970/71*	*Commitments at 30th April 1971*
ure plans in the light of its forecasts of cash requirements and profitability. Investigations were completed and conclusions and recommendations sent to the Ministry of Technology in December 1969. These made it clear that Rolls-Royce would require substantial further capital to finance its forward programmes for new engines. IRC's proposals for providing additional finance were agreed by Rolls-Royce and the Minister and announced on 19th May 1970. They involved the advance, under Section 2(1)(b) of the IRC Act, of £10 million in August 1970 and up to a further £10 million in the course of 1971. In announcing the government's decision on the provision of further support for the RB211 project on 11th November 1970, the Minister of Aviation Supply also announced that the Corporation would be providing no further assistance beyond the £10 million already committed.		
May 1970		
Herbert-Ingersoll		
On 20th May, IRC announced that it had agreed to make available to Herbert-Ingersoll Ltd (HIL) a total of £2.5 million under Section 2(1)(b) of the IRC Act to finance the expansion of the Company's Daventry factory. An initial £1 million was taken up on 3rd June, £525 000 as equity and £475 000 in the	£1 000 000	£1 500 000

Publication date	*Payments made in 1970/71*	*Commitments at 30th April 1971*
form of a loan. The loan bears interest at a rate of 9¼% per annum and is repayable in May 1977. The further £1.5 million is available to HIL in the form of a standby credit which can be called upon as the expansion scheme progresses.		
June 1970		
British Leyland Motor Corporation		
On 1st June, IRC announced that it had approached the British Leyland Motor Corporation as a major user of machine tools in the United Kingdom with a scheme aimed at stimulating investment in the machine tool industry. Under the scheme, the Corporation agreed to make available to British Leyland a revolving facility of £10 million which British Leyland will use, together with its own finances, for the purchase of machine tools to modernise and expand its production facilities. The facility is to be drawn in four equal instalments each repayable after three years. Interest is calculated separately on each advance at a rate per annum equivalent to ½% above the rate at which IRC can borrow at the time of the particular advance. An initial £2.5 million was drawn on 1st June. Further advances of £2.5 million were made on 15th July 1970 and 3rd February 1971.	£7 500 000	£2 500 000

Publication date	*Payments made in 1970/71*	*Commitments at 30th April 1971*
June 1970		
Cammell Laird		
The government invited IRC to undertake an investigation of the Cammell Laird Group. This established that a liquidity crisis had arisen from heavy losses in the shipbuilding subsidiary. IRC has no remit for the shipbuilding industry and the Corporation insisted as a precondition of its involvement that the shipbuilding undertaking should become independent from the rest of the group, leaving IRC free to promote the reorganisation and development of the Group's other activities. The shipbuilding undertaking, Cammell Laird (Shipbuilding and Engineering) Ltd (S & E) ceased to be a subsidiary of the group. A scheme of financial assistance was announced on 4th June which provided that The Laird Group (formerly the Cammell Laird group) would make good to S & E the actual amount of the losses on the current order book up to £7 200 000. In order to help meet these obligations, IRC subscribed at par for 4 900 830 ordinary shares of 5/– each (amounting to about £1 225 000 and representing 13.6% of the enlarged capital) in The Laird Group. In addition, IRC and certain shipowners agreed to make loans to The Laird Group of up to £4 825 000 and £675 000 respectively carrying interest at the rate of 10% per	£3 820 000	£2 230 000

Publication date	*Payments made in 1970/71*	*Commitments at 30th April 1971*
annum and repayable between 1972 and 1975.		
June 1970		
Spirella		
In June, it was announced that an agreement had been reached between the IRC, N. M. Rothschild & Sons and Spirella whereby the Corporation and Rothschilds would make available to Spirella up to £1 250 000 to assist in restructuring a section of the household textile industry. As part of these proposals, Spirella announced that it had reached agreement with the Board of Stott & Smith on terms for the acquisition of that company. As part of a wider restructuring, the Corporation undertook to make a total sum not exceeding £1 300 000 available to Spirella. £900 000 was advanced as a loan at a rate of 10% per annum repayable by 30th June 1977. £400 000 was subscribed in cash at par for 10% Convertible Unsecured Loan Stock 1977.	£1 300 000	–
June 1970		
Clarke Chapman/John Thompson		
A proposal in September 1968 for a merger between Clarke Chapman, International Combustion and John Thompson was not implemented. In June 1970, a merger between Clarke Chapman and John Thompson was strongly supported by the Corporation as creating one of	£5 000 000	–

Publication date	*Payments made in 1970/71*	*Commitments at 30th April 1971*
Europe's premier heavy engineering groups. IRC had already made available in 1969 a loan of £2 million to Clarke Chapman to support acquisitions now forming its crane division. The Corporation expressed willingness to consider any necessary financial support for the rationalisation and development programme following the Clarke Chapman/John Thompson merger. A loan of £5 million was made to the company on 14th January 1971 bearing a rate of interest of $9\frac{5}{8}$% per annum and repayable on 31st December 1975.		
June 1970		
Reyrolle Parsons		
In June it was announced that Reyrolle Parsons had reached an agreement with North American Rockwell to set up a joint venture in the USA. The IRC had already agreed in April 1969 to supply a standby credit to the company in connection with the merger with Bruce Peebles. It welcomed the agreement with North American Rockwell as enhancing the group's position internationally.	–	–
July 1970		
Laporte		
In July, details were announced of the terms of an association between Laporte Industries (Holdings) Limited and Solvay & Cie, SA of Brussels, Belgium. The IRC was kept fully informed	–	–

Publication date	*Payments made in 1970/71*	*Commitments at 30th April 1971*
of the progress of the discussions leading up to this arrangement and endorsed the industrial reasons for it.		
August 1970 **Power Gas Corporation** In August, it was announced that Power Gas Corporation, the process plant contracting subsidiary of the Davy-Ashmore group, had acquired the German design and contracting organisation Bamag Verfahrenstechnik GmbH. The IRC had remained in close touch with Davy-Ashmore since sponsoring financial support arrangements in July 1969. The Corporation welcomed this new step 'to strengthen a major British contracting organisation by the establishment of a significant presence in the EEC'.	–	–
October 1970 **Harwood Cash** The government invited the IRC to consider applications for finance for re-equipment by the medium-sized and smaller companies in the cotton and allied textile industry. In October, IRC announced that they had agreed, subject to contract, to make a secured loan of £1.2 million to Harwood Cash and Co. Limited under the re-equipment scheme. The loan bears interest at a rate of 10% per annum and is repayable over seven years.	–	£1 200 000

Publication date	*Payments made in 1970/71*	*Commitments at 30th April 1971*
November 1970 **Perseverance Mill** This was the second project under the re-equipment scheme. In November, IRC announced that they had agreed, subject to contract, to make a secured loan of £500 000 to Perseverance Mill Limited, a wholly-owned subsidiary of the RFD Group. The loan bears interest at a rate of 10% per annum and is repayable over seven years.	£250 000	£250 000
November 1970 **Highams** This was the third project under the re-equipment scheme. In November, IRC announced that they had agreed, subject to contract, to make a secured loan of £325 000 to Highams Ltd. As in the previous cases, the loan bears interest at a rate of 10% per annum and is repayable over seven years.	–	£325 000
December 1970 **Kearney & Trecker** On 18th December, IRC announced that agreement had been reached whereby the Corporation and the Midland Bank Finance Corporation would subscribe at par in equal amounts and on the same terms for an issue of 600 000 £1 Redeemable Convertible Third Preference Shares in Kearney & Trecker Limited. The investment was to provide funds for the expansion of the company under Section 2(1)(b) of the IRC Act. The conversion rights re-	£300 000	–

Publication date	*Payments made in 1970/71*	*Commitments at 30th April 1971*
present approximately 31% of the equity.		
April 1971		
Vantona/Hartley		
In April 1971, IRC agreed, subject to contract, to make a secured loan of £275 000 to Vantona Ltd to be used at Albert Hartley Ltd and Ainsworth Mills. This would be the fourth project under the re-equipment scheme.	–	£275 000
The following information is given in relation to IRC's investments and commitments not referred to elsewhere in this summary:		
British Nuclear Design & Construction		
No call has yet been made on the shareholders to lend or guarantee up to £9 million if required of which IRC's share is £2 340 000.	–	£2 340 000
Steel Group/Priestman		
The further standby credit of £500 000 available to 30th June 1970 was not required.	–	–
Davy-Ashmore		
The remaining £300 000 of the short-term loan to Davy-Ashmore was repaid on 31st July 1970.	(£300 000)	
Reed Paper Group		
In September 1970, the first tranche of £300 000 was repaid	(£300 000)	–

Publication date	*Payments made in 1970/71*	*Commitments at 30th April 1971*
in accordance with the agreement on the de-inking project.		
Samuel-Osborn		
On the 1st October 1970, IRC advanced £1 000 000 to Samuel-Osborn pursuant to its commitment.	£1 000 000	£750 000
Ransome Hoffmann Pollard		
On 17th November 1970, a standby credit was made available to the group.	–	£1 000 000
Marwin		
On 15th January 1971, IRC advanced the further £750 000 pursuant to its commitment.	£750 000	–
English Electric Company		
During the period under review two further tranches of £2 500 000 were repaid in accordance with the revised arrangements made following the merger with The General Electric Company for early repayment by instalments.	(£5 000 000)	–
The Nuclear Power Group		
On 2nd March 1971, IRC sold its shareholding representing 10% of the equity of The Nuclear Power Group in equal parts to Sir Robert McAlpine & Sons Ltd and Head Wrightson & Co Ltd.	(£171 953)	–
Peter Dixon & Sons		
Under the terms of the agreement, instalments of £175 000 were received in repayment of the loan.	(£175 000)	–
Totals per accounts	£24 973 047	£12 581 000

List of works cited

Bailey, R. (1968). *Managing the British Economy* (London: Hutchinson).

Brittan, S. (1971). *Steering the Economy*, 3rd edn (Harmondsworth: Penguin).

Caves, R. E. (and associates) (1968). *Britain's Economic Prospects* (London: George Allen and Unwin).

Cmnd 2764 (1965). *The National Plan* (London: HMSO).

Cmnd 2889 (1966). *Industrial Reorganisation Corporation* (London: HMSO).

Cmnd 4860 (1971). *Rolls-Royce Limited and the RB211 Engine* (London: HMSO).

Cmnd 7198 (1978). *A Review of Monopolies and Mergers Policy* (London: HMSO).

Duffy, H. (1979). The ballbearings industry. *Financial Times*, 23 January.

Evans, H. (1978). *Vickers: Against the Odds* (London: Hodder and Stoughton).

Industrial Reorganisation Corporation Act (1966) (London: HMSO).

Industrial Reorganisation Corporation (1967–71). *Report and Accounts* (London: HMSO), published annually.

Lejeune, (1967). IRC: friend or foe. *The Director*, October.

McClelland, W. G. (1972). The Industrial Reorganisation Corporation – an experimental prod. *Three Banks Review*, no. 94, June.

Morley, C., and Jones, R. (1968). Lessons of the Cambridge fight. *The Times,* 21 June.

Newbould, G. D. (1971). *Management and Merger Activity* (Liverpool: Guthstead).

Posner, M., and Pryke, R. (1965). *New Public Enterprise* (London: Fabian Society).

Prais, S. J. (1976). *The Evolution of Giant Firms in Britain* (Cambridge: Cambridge University Press).

Rowley, A. (1975). An unhappy example of intervention by the government. *The Times*, 14 October.

Shipbuilding Industry Act (1967) (London: HMSO).

Skuse, A. (1972). *Government Intervention and Industrial Policy*, 2nd edn (London: Heinemann).

Turner, G. (1971). *The Leyland Papers* (London: Eyre and Spottiswoode).

Wilsher, P. (1968). IRC: sharp claws for the paper tiger. *Sunday Times,* 23 June.

Young, S., and Lowe, A. V. (1974). *Intervention in the Mixed Economy* (London: Croom Helm).

Index